Illustrated VP-Info®

UPDATED TO INCLUDE VERSION 1.4

Mick McAllister

Wordware Publishing, Inc.

Library of Congress Cataloging-in-Publication Data

McAllister, Mick.
Illustrated VP-Info.

Includes index.
1. Relational data bases. VP-Info (Computer program) I. Title.
QA76.9.D3M3935 1989 005.75'65 88-20543
ISBN 0-55622-070-7

1506 Capital Ave.
Plano, Texas 75074

Printed in the United States of America

ISBN 1-55622-070-7

10 9 8 7 6 5 4 3 2 1
8806

All inquiries for volume purchases of this book should be addressed to Wordware Publishing, Inc., at the above address. Telephone inquiries may be made by calling:

(214) 423-0090

Trademarks

dBASE II, dBASE III, and dBASE III Plus are registered trademarks of Ashton-Tate.
IBM is a registered trademark of International Business Machines Corporation.
MS is a registered trademark of Microsoft Corporation.
SideKick is a registered trademark of Borland International.
VP-Info is a registered trademark of Paperback Software.

Contents

Contents (Continued)

Recommended Learning Sequence

Recommended Learning Sequence (Cont.)

Preface

About VP-Info Paperback Software's VP programs — VP-Planner, VP-Info, and VP-Expert — occupy a special place in the software industry. Each sells for about one hundred dollars and offers the power of similar programs costing hundreds more.

Although not as easily learned as dBASE III Plus, VP-Info offers commands not available in any dBASE product thus far, and it offers its power in the form of a compiler. This combination of price and value makes VP-Info the same sort of revolutionary product that Turbo PASCAL was when it revolutionized the value for dollar of compiled programming languages. With a compiler you can write clear, well-documented programs without worrying that their size will slow them down; the compiler makes copies of your programs as compact and highly efficient machine code. With a compiler you can also protect your programs from tinkering and destructive modification by the curious user. Speed, size, and security — all three are benefits of using VP-Info for your database applications, and the low price is icing on the cake.

The computer novice can create a filing system and then write procedures to store, retrieve, edit, and display on-screen menus and user-help information in a matter of a few hours. This places the ability to develop custom software in the hands of accountants, marketing and sales people, bankers, and many others.

The VP-Info Documentation While the VP-Info reference manual is big, heavy, and intimidating, it is comprehensive. However, the paper, at least in early editions, is thin and can make paging through for information frustrating. The index is small, and the reference information sometimes a little sketchy. *Illustrated VP-Info* organizes VP-Info information into easy-to-locate modules. It contains descriptions of each command and function and hundreds of working VP-Info examples that are designed to clarify. You can use these examples as models from which to design your own applications.

About Illustrated Books As a classroom instructor, I find myself constantly searching for books that can help me learn; books that are ready-made to help me teach others. With computer books, especially, I want to get at the "heart" of the information fast. I want to learn principles through practice. And I want to feel that the author is more interested in teaching me than in impressing me with the complexity of the subject or with his grasp of it.

The *Illustrated* series is designed to provide quick, easy-to-understand, well-illustrated information about what are often complicated applications; to present things simply, but thoroughly and accurately. With *Illustrated* books on dBASE, MS-DOS, and other applications, I have been able to familiarize myself quickly with a new program and get to work in it almost immediately while referring to the alphabetical listings for more information as I needed it.

The *Illustrated* format lets you find an area of interest quickly. A description, applications, and a step-by-step illustration are provided. This combination gets results. It provides quick answers, and it provides models that help solve real problems. You will find that the *Illustrated* approach goes beyond standard documentation and books that treat software theoretically or in broad, and sometimes vague, terms. The series is used by a diverse group that includes classroom teachers, professional users, students, and computer "buffs." I hope readers enjoy using this book as much as I have enjoyed writing it.

Very few books are the product of one mind, although often only one name appears on the title page. This book is no exception. Russull A. Stultz, as anyone familiar with his three *Illustrated* books on dBASE products would quickly perceive, provided a model for the organization and presentation of the material. He and his staff at Wordware have been patient, helpful, and understanding through the long process of producing a book about a computer product that was released only six months before this manuscript had to be finished.

Producing an accurate and complete manuscript so quickly would have been impossible without the help of Cynthia Towle, Janet Walden, and Brad Bechtel of Paperback Software. Paperback Software's Technical Support is a model of usefulness, and their customer relations should be a model for any company hoping to create and maintain the sort of customer loyalty that ensures repeat purchases and discourages unethical and illegal copying of software.

Finally, I must thank my son, Jeof, who "playtested" troublesome modules, and my personal editor (and wife), Trudy McMurrin, who helped with development but primarily contributed by maintaining her calm while electronic beeps and toots popped out of my office, accompanied by shouts of rage, dismay, and triumph, punctuating her own work. This is the first piece of my writing in five years that she has not had the opportunity to copy edit. Any errors in it are, of course, mine and not accountable to the helpful people here acknowledged; Trudy will be gracious enough, if such errors reach print and are pointed out, not to say "See?"

Mick McAllister

Module 1

ABOUT THIS BOOK

INTRODUCTION

This book describes Paperback Software's VP-Info, a relational database management software program, Release 1.4. It describes how you can use VP-Info in the office and home, and it presents detailed information about the many VP-Info commands. Each command is accompanied by examples.

The book is designed for a broad range of users. It is for beginning users who wish to learn the VP-Info program from scratch. It is for intermediate and advanced users as a quick reference that contains working command examples. And finally, it is for the classroom instructor as an instructionally designed VP-Info textbook.

There is one other class of reader for which this book is intended — the experienced dBASE II or dBASE III user looking for a less costly, alternative compiled relational database. If you are an old hand at using dBASE II or III, you will find VP-Info to be syntactically similar (though not enough so to allow dBASE applications to run without some modification). If you are a consultant writing database applications for your customers, VP-Info, for around one hundred dollars, can offer them a compiled system, including not a merely runtime package, but a fully operational database program. Paperback Software also offers licensing for a runtime package, for when that approach is preferred.

The VP-Info program is a sophisticated piece of software and often appears to be overwhelming to inexperienced computer users. But it is not as hard as it looks. In fact, if you are a beginning user who is not afraid to "mess around" with commands, you will discover in a matter of minutes that VP-Info is really easy to use. You can do useful things by learning only a half-dozen or so commands. The more you use VP-Info, the richer it becomes. After a week or so, you will begin to feel like a veteran computer user. One of VP-Info's strengths is that it can be as simple or as powerful as you want to make it.

To prove to yourself how easy VP-Info can be, you might want to jump over to Module 2 and go through the sample session with your computer. There, you will actually have VP-Info doing useful things. You will find out how you can have the program working for you in a matter of a few hours. The only limitation is imagination, and if you have enough imagination to be using a computer, then you are exactly the right person to be using VP-Info.

Beginning in Module 2, you are going to encounter many VP-Info commands. At first, they may not be crystal clear, but their usefulness quickly becomes apparent with a little use and practice. They were unclear to me for the first hour or so, but as I continued to experiment with VP-Info, things began to make sense. So don't worry, things will clear up for you too, just by using VP-Info.

ORGANIZATION

To fit the broad range of users that this book addresses, the book is organized into small, easy-to-read *modules*. These modules provide descriptions, applications, and illustrations that provide insight to how VP-Info can be used to solve practical, everyday problems. Literally hundreds of examples are presented in the Description, Applications, and Typical Operation sections of the modules.

These examples can be used to design applications of your own. Working examples that let you experiment with VP-Info commands take the mystery out of what might otherwise be a technical obscurity. In addition to conducting "hands-on" experimentation, you will probably find yourself having a lot of fun, because VP-Info is a delightful program to operate.

With the exception of Modules 1 through 3, most of the modules in this book contain information that pertains to specific VP-Info commands, functions, or families of commands or functions.

This first module provides information about the book and briefly describes the equipment required to operate VP-Info.

Module 2 introduces you to VP-Info. It describes the term *database*, lists some of VP-Info's capabilities and limitations, and walks you through a sample VP-Info session. If you are the kind of person that likes to "dive in," you will enjoy the sample programming session in Module 2. You will quickly discover how VP-Info commands are used, and you discover it by actually using your computer.

In addition to using some of the basic VP-Info commands, you will prepare a sample program, called a *command file*, and run it. By the time you complete Module 2, the power of VP-Info will be apparent because you will have demonstrated how databases and corresponding command files are prepared and used to solve common, everyday problems.

Module 2 also contains information about VP-Info's full-screen editor, which is used to create and save command files. A brief discussion of how word processors and desktop utility programs are used to create command files is also provided.

Module 3 contains a recommended sequence for learning VP-Info commands. As you work your way through this book, you can check off the modules you complete. They are arranged in a simple-to-complex sequence, which can be modified to fit any classroom curriculum. If you are a teacher, you may wish to use Module 3 as an aid to curriculum design.

Modules 4 through 72 describe and illustrate the many VP-Info commands and functions. The commands are arranged in alphabetical order for easy reference.

Appendixes A through E contain reference information about VP-Info file types, operators, functions, networking, and a list of terms and definitions.

Appendix F is provided for both classroom and self-teaching situations. It contains VP-Info exercises. If you are a classroom instructor, you may wish to include these exercises in student assignments. If you are learning VP-Info on your own, the exercises are a good way to check your understanding of what you have learned about a command. If you can answer the questions, you are ready to move on to the next module in the learning sequence.

HARDWARE AND SOFTWARE REQUIREMENTS

The VP-Info program operates with the PC- and MS-DOS operating systems. Its minimum hardware requirement is an IBM PC, PC/XT, or PC-compatible microcomputer equipped with two or more floppy disk drives or one floppy disk drive and a fixed disk. The VP-Info program requires 256K of random access memory (RAM). However, that amount is quickly used up, and more may be required for your own applications, especially if you are using DOS above 3.1 or running memory resident programs. Also, using two floppy disk drives necessitates some disk swapping, because the A drive must always contain the VPI.EXE file and related programs. So for full use of the program, you should have 384+ K of RAM and a hard disk rather than a second floppy drive. You will need a printer if you want paper copies of your database reports. Optionally, VP-Info also allows you to add color to your programs, if you have a color monitor.

Your DOS startup disk should have a CONFIG.SYS file that includes these lines:

```
FILES = 20
BUFFERS = 20
```

This sets up your computer for operation with VP-Info. Module 2 describes preparation of this file.

WHAT YOU SHOULD KNOW TO BEGIN

You should be familiar with your computer, its keyboard, and the commands available on your operating system which allow you to list a directory of your diskettes (or hard disk), format a disk, and copy, rename, and delete files. If you can do these things, you are ready to begin using VP-Info. If you are not familiar with common DOS commands, you may wish to obtain a copy of *Illustrated MS/PC-DOS* from Wordware Publishing, Inc.

Module 2

VP-Info OVERVIEW

INTRODUCTION

This module describes the term database, and presents information about how VP-Info is used to create and apply files of information, or *databases*, to the solution of everyday problems. A description of how the VP-Info program is used to create and manipulate the information within databases is presented as a basis for understanding the many VP-Info commands described in this book.

This module also describes the use of the VP-Info full-screen text editor, which is used to prepare VP-Info procedure (or command) files. Although the VP-Info editor is good for creating and editing procedure files, many VP-Info users use word processing programs or "pop-up" editors like Homebase or Sidekick to create and modify their files.

WHAT IS A DATABASE?

A database is a collection of information that is organized in a predictable, structured way. The structure of a database is graphically represented in Figure 2-1. This database could be an address book database because each record contains information about a different person. For example, record number 1 contains the name, address, city, and state information for John Smith.

Figure 2-1 Database Structure

DATABASE			
RECORD NUMBER	FIELD 1 (NAME)	FIELD 2 (ADDRESS)	FIELD 3 (CITY_STATE)
1	JOHN SMITH	12 MAIN ST	TAMPA, FL
2	PAUL JONES	32 SOL AVE	CAIRO, IL
3	J.T. HOOD	99 N. FIRST	SLC, UT
4	MARY MAXIM	20 CLUB DR	RENO, NV
5	LOIS JAKS	92 OAK ST	TRUCHAS, NM

RECORDS AND FIELDS A database may contain from 1 to 65,535 records; each record can contain from 1 to 256 fields. The figure shows five records, numbered 1 through 5. Each record in the figure contains three fields.

FIELD TYPES The field types used in the example are called character fields, because they contain text strings consisting of characters. VP-Info has three different types of fields. They are:

Field Type	Maximum Bytes (or Characters)
Character	254
Logical	1
Numeric	20

Character fields contain text and numbers and are commonly used for things like names, addresses, and part numbers.

Logical fields contain either a "true" or "false" (or "yes" or "no") value. Logical fields are often used to show the status of a record. For example, in an accounting database, you might want to know if a sales transaction record is paid. A true or false value can be used to show whether or not a customer has paid a particular bill.

Numeric fields contain numbers, which are often used in conjunction with other numeric fields to perform calculations.

The following list summarizes the types of fields used in VP-Info.

Character	Text strings made up of letters, letters and numbers, or letters, numbers, spaces, and punctuation marks.
Logical	T for true; F for false (or Y for yes; N for no).
Numeric	Numbers (numeric values), which may include decimals. Letters and internal spaces are not permitted.

VP-Info CAPABILITIES AND LIMITATIONS

VP-Info is quite versatile, as you will quickly see when examining Table 2-1. This table describes system capabilities and limitations.

The specifications are not the whole story. VP-Info's compiled command files and matrix variables make VP-Info uniquely powerful. The sample procedure in this module is only a light brush with VP-Info commands. You will learn many more by working your way through this book. You will see that nearly any kind of application can be developed using VP-Info. The major limitation is user imagination, and it can be expanded as you explore the power of new commands.

Table 2-1 Capabilities and Limitations

Description	*Capability/Limitation*
Maximum fields per record	256
Maximum characters per record	8,000
Maximum records per database	64K
Maximum characters per database	2 billion
Maximum characters per character field	254
Accuracy of numeric fields	15.9 digits
Largest number	1 × 10 to the +308
Smallest positive number	1 × 10 to the −307
Maximum memory variables available	128
Maximum files open at one time	20
Maximum database files open at one time	6
Maximum index files per open database file	7
Maximum characters in a command line	254

Note: Some values vary with computer hardware and disk capacity.

USING VP-Info

How do you get started with the VP-Info program? And how is a database created? How is it used?

The VP-Info program allows database creation, updating, displaying, and printing. It also lets you write command files, which are VP-Info programs (or procedures) prepared to control input, editing, mathematical computations, and screen or paper output. To familiarize yourself with how these functions are accomplished, perform the following sample session with your computer. If you are an impatient user, this activity should satisfy your eager spirit.

GETTING STARTED WITH VP-Info Your purchased copy of VP-Info is provided on two disks which you should register with Paperback Software. Your non-copy-protected disk allows you to copy the entire VP-Info program onto a hard disk and then set the originals aside permanently. It also can be used to install VP-Info on a boot disk (created from a blank disk formatted with the DOS command FORMAT B:/S). A boot or startup disk contains the COMMAND.COM file needed for using DOS while working inside VP-Info.

Your non-copy-protected disk allows you to copy the entire VP-Info program onto a hard disk and then set the originals aside permanently. It also can be used to install VP-Info on a boot disk (created from a blank disk formatted with the DOS command FORMAT B:/S). A boot or startup disk contains the COMMAND.COM file needed for using DOS while working inside VP-Info.

Your two disks include a disk labeled VP-Info, which is the program disk, and another labeled Sample Files, which includes files Paperback Software has provided to demonstrate parts of the VP-Info database. The procedures for installing VP-Info on a two-floppy system or a hard disk system differ slightly, so they are going to be described separately. The rest of the modules are generally oriented toward the user with a two-floppy disk system.

INSTALLING VP-Info ON A TWO-FLOPPY DISK SYSTEM To use the original VP-Info disk on a two-floppy drive system, you should format a system disk for a working copy of the program and a blank data disk for use in drive B. To prepare your data disk, perform the following steps:

1. Format a system disk by placing your DOS disk in drive A and a blank disk in drive B. Type **FORMAT B:/S** and press **Return.**
2. Place original program disk in your A drive and type **COPY A:*.* B:** to make a copy of the program files.
3. Insert the newly formatted disk in drive B.
4. Type **COPY A:*.HLP B:** and press **Return** to copy the Help file onto the disk.
5. Remove the Sample Files disk from drive A.

You can set up your system to use drive B automatically for all new database and program files. This is accomplished by modifying a file on your VP-Info program disk named VPI.CNF. Make this modification to your working copy. Never modify an original disk.

VP-Info "looks" at the VPI.CNF file when it starts. To make your system work like the one used to write this book and create the examples, you need to replace the existing VPI.CNF file with one that includes these statements:

```
SET MEMORY TO 64
FILES
*.DBF,B:\
*.NDX,B:\
*.PRG,B:\
*.TXT,B:\
*.LIB,B:\
*.CPL,B:\
*.FRM,B:\
VPI.HLP,B:\
ENDFILES
```

You can do this with any editor that can produce a DOS file, including EDLIN on your DOS disk. The instructions under the section on installing the program on a hard disk suggest a quick method for creating this file. This new VPI.CNF file sets the extra memory limit to 64 so you have room to use the RUN command, and it notifies VP-Info to look for all program files on the B drive. If you have a hard disk, and you plan to keep the VP-Info program files and the data files all together on the hard disk, then your VPI.CNF file only needs the one line:

```
SET MEMORY TO 64
```

Then you can copy all the files from both VP-Info disks onto the hard disk. However, a database program does a lot of reading and writing of disks, and, at least during the learning process, it is safer to have this happening on a floppy disk. So you might consider substituting "A:\" for "B:\" wherever it occurs in the floppy version of the VPI.CNF file and using the data disk you created with VPI.HLP on it as your work disk in your A drive.

In order to use VP-Info, you must have configured your system to allow 20 files and 20 buffers in use at a time. This is done by including on your startup disk a file called CONFIG.SYS. Creating this file is also described in the section on installing the program on a hard disk.

All the examples and discussion in this book work on the assumption that you are using a two-floppy system with the recommended VPI.CNF file. They work just as well if you have a hard disk with the floppy set up as your work disk.

INSTALLING VP-Info ON A HARD DISK SYSTEM If you have a hard disk system, you must have a proper CONFIG.SYS file on your root menu. If you already have a CONFIG.SYS file that specifies 20 or more files and buffers, it will work fine. If it specifies fewer than 20, use EDLIN or a word processor that generates ASCII files to modify the values so that the lines read:

```
FILES = 20
BUFFERS = 20
```

If you do not have a CONFIG.SYS file in your root directory, create one using the COPY command with the CON option that allows you to create a file directly from the DOS prompt:

1. At the DOS prompt type **COPY CON CONFIG.SYS** and press **Return**.

NOTE

The <cr> represents Return; the ^Z is produced by pressing and holding Ctrl while typing Z. This key sequence is represented by Ctrl-Z in text.

2. Type the two following lines, ending each line by pressing **Return**.

```
FILES = 20<cr>
BUFFERS = 20 ^Z<cr>
```

Notice the "1 file(s) copied" message.

When you turn on your computer, the CONFIG.SYS file configures your system for proper operation with VP-Info. The FILES = 20 command allows 20 files, including the VP-Info program files and your database and command files, to be in use (or open) at the same time. This lets you take advantage of VP-Info's ability to have an application work simultaneously with six different databases in addition to program files. Command files (also called programs and procedures) contain a series of VP-Info commands that are prepared and used to perform common routines automatically.

The BUFFERS = 20 line speeds up VP-Info operation. Buffers are temporary storage locations in your computer's memory. During VP-Info operation, data is temporarily stored in memory rather than being written to and read from disk. Memory activity is much faster than inputting and outputting data to and from your disk, so multiple buffers speed up VP-Info operations.

You can copy VP-Info to your hard drive (usually drive C) as follows:

3. From your root directory, make a VP-Info subdirectory on your hard disk by typing **MD VPI** and pressing **Return**.
4. Switch to this new directory by typing **CD VPI** and pressing **Return**.
5. Place VP-Info Program disk in drive A.
6. Type **COPY A:*.*** and press **Return**.
7. When the copying concludes, remove the disk in the A drive.
8. Place the Sample Files disk in drive A.
9. Type **COPY A:*.*** and press **Return**.
10. To create the necessary VPI.CNF file, first type **RENAME VPI.CNF VPICNF.SEC** to retain the CNF file provided by Paperback Software.
11. Type **COPY CON VPI.CNF** and press **Return**.
12. Type the following lines, carefully proofreading each line before you press **Return**, and conclude the last line by pressing **Ctrl-Z** to create the "^Z," then press **Return** a final time to save the file. (Notice the drive activity after you type ^**Z<cr>**.) Proofreading is important, because COPY CON only allows you to correct mistakes on your current line. If you have a system with two floppy disks rather than a hard disk, remember to change all the A:\ drive references to B:\ instead.

```
SET MEMORY TO 64<cr>
FILES<cr>
*.DBF,A:\<cr>
*.NDX,A:\<cr>
*.PRG,A:\<cr>
*.TXT,A:\<cr>
*.LIB,A:\<cr>
*.CPL,A:\<cr>
*.FRM,A:\<cr>
ENDFILES^Z<cr>
```

13. Type **TYPE VPI.CNF** and press **Return** to confirm that your file was written and is correct. Compare your screen to the following:

```
C:\VPI>TYPE VPI.CNF
SET MEMORY TO 64
FILES
*.DBF,A:\
*.NDX,A:\
*.PRG,A:\
*.TXT,A:\
*.LIB,A:\
*.CPL,A:\
*.FRM,A:\
ENDFILES
C:\VPI>
```

Your VP-Info program is now ready to run. If you had to create a new CONFIG.SYS file, you must reboot with your Reset button or the key combination Alt-Ctrl-Del to install the new configuration.

RUNNING A SAMPLE VP-Info SESSION To start VP-Info, switch your DOS prompt to the drive (or subdirectory) containing the VP-Info program (A: on a two-floppy system, C:\VPI on a hard disk), type VPI and press Return. When the *prompt* (a number, usually 1, followed by an angle bracket — "1>") is displayed, then VP-Info is ready for a command.

Because VP-Info is a large program, there's not enough disk space left on your floppy disk for working files. If you are using a system with two-floppy disks, you will want to use drive B as your working diskette. If you created the VPI.CNF file as described, most of your files are automatically placed on drive B, where you should keep the data disk that includes the VPI.HLP file.

If you have a hard-disk system, you can use VP-Info without having to use an alternate working disk, but you should use the VPI.CNF file to place data or command files on floppy disks in drive A.

Once you have VP-Info in operation and have settled on your working disk, you are ready to create a database structure, or, if one already exists on the data disk, you can bring it into use and add (called *append*), edit, or delete records.

In the following sample session, you create a database called PHONE. Each instruction you are to type begins with the prompt supplied by VP-Info, a number followed by an angle bracket (>); do not type the prompt. Remember to press Return to enter each command. Where considered helpful, explanatory remarks are provided after command lines, separated from them with a semicolon. Do not type the explanatory remarks.

As with DOS commands, VP-Info commands, variables, and field names are typed in either lower- or uppercase. However, if you are trying to match a string within a database field, the exact uppercase and lowercase appearance of the string is required.

NOTE

VP-Info commands are abbreviated by typing the first four characters of the command. For example, DISPLAY can be typed DISP.

1. Create a database called PHONE by typing the following boldfaced characters (do not type the remarks):

NOTE

Entries are typed and then accepted by pressing the Return key, represented by <cr>. Field types require the initial letter only. The cursor jumps automatically to the next appropriate column when you finish an entry or press Return. If you make an entry error (for example, too large a width or decimal value), then an error message interrupts the entry. If you make a typo, back space and correct it. Pressing End in a still blank field name area ends the CREATE function.

```
                                                  Remarks
1>CREATE PHONE                              Creates a new database

PARTY<cr>      C      30      ; Field name PARTY, type Char/text, width 30.
NUMBER<cr>     C      14      ; Field name NUMBER, type Char/text, width 14.
<End>                         ; Pressing End in blank field ends creation.

Save as Type 1, 2, or 3?  2   ; Pressing Return saves as Type 2.
```

2. Now enter a few records. To do this, type **APPEND** and press **Return**. The following display is presented, with a 30-space reversed video field for PARTY and a 14-space field for NUMBER:

```
                                                      Remarks

Record No       1                         ; First blank record of the database.
PARTY    [                              ] ; Blank field named PARTY.
NUMBER   [              ]                 ; Blank field named NUMBER.
```

3. Type the following information into the PARTY and NUMBER fields for five records. Typing the last character of the NUMBER field causes the next record to be displayed.

```
Record No     1
PARTY   [Smith, John         ]
NUMBER  [(408) 232-1210]
```

```
Record No     2
PARTY   [Jones, Paul         ]
NUMBER  [(813) 267-9500]
```

```
Record No     3
PARTY   [Hood, J.T.              ]
NUMBER  [(405) 343-1090]
```

```
Record No     4
PARTY   [Maxwell, Mary           ]
NUMBER  [(214) 232-4545]
```

```
Record No     5
PARTY   [Jackson, Lois           ]
NUMBER  [(201) 599-6111]
```

```
Record No     6
PARTY   [End                     ]
NUMBER  [              ]
```

4. Press **End** when blank Record No. 6 is displayed to end the data entry session and return to the prompt.

Now that you have a database with five records, you can use it to look up phone numbers. Before you list the database to the screen, clear the screen of unnecessary text. This is done with the ERASE command.

5. To erase the screen, type **ERASE** and press **Return.**
6. To list the database, type **LIST** and press **Return**. Compare your screen to the following:

```
1>LIST
00001  Smith, John                    (408) 232-1210
00002  Jones, Paul                    (813) 267-3500
00003  Hood, J.T.                     (405) 343-1090
00004  Maxwell, Mary                  (214) 232-4545
00005  Jackson, Lois                  (201) 599-6111
```

If you wish to omit the record numbers from the display, type **LIST OFF** rather than LIST, and press **Return**.

```
1>LIST OFF
Smith, John                    (408) 232-1210
Jones, Paul                    (813) 267-3500
Hood, J.T.                     (405) 343-1090
Maxwell, Mary                  (214) 232-4545
Jackson, Lois                  (201) 599-6111
```

7. It may be handy to sort your phone list alphabetically. To do this, sort on the party field to a new database named ALPHA. Then use this new database and display it to see the list in alphabetical order. Type **SORT** and press **Return**.

```
                                         Remarks
1>SORT ON PARTY TO ALPHA        ; Alphabetically sorts the records on the
     5 RECORDS READ             ; party field to a new database named "alpha."
     5 COPY(S)
```

Notice the three messages "5 RECORDS READ," "5 RECORDS INDEXED," and "5 COPY(S)." (The copy message is written on top of the index message, which is only visible for a few seconds.) These are examples of VP-Info's *automatic conversation* which tells you what is happening. These messages always appear when you are working at the 1> prompt. A command covered later explains how to suppress them in command files.

8. To print the sorted phone list, put the ALPHA database in use and turn on the printer with the SET PRINT ON command. Then, everything that is displayed on the screen is listed to the printer. Conclude by turning off the printer with the SET PRINT OFF command. Type the commands as follows:

CAUTION

Do not issue print commands if you do not have a printer or if the printer is not ready to use. Either of these errors can cause the computer to lock up and require restarting.

```
                                              Remarks
1>USE ALPHA                           ; Puts ALPHA in use.
1>SET PRINT ON                        ; Directs displayed text to the printer.
1>LIST OFF                            ; Lists the database without record numbers.
Hood, J. T.                 (405) 343-1090
Jackson, Lois               (201) 599-6111
Jones, Paul                 (813) 267-9500
Maxwell, Mary               (214) 232-4545
Smith, John                 (408) 232-1210
1>?                                   ; Send a blank line to clear printer.
1>SET PRINT OFF                       ; Turns printing off.
1>ERASE_                              ; Clears the display screen.
```

There are two ways to speed up operations that require many steps. While working at the 1> prompt, you can recall each of the last five commands by pressing the Up Arrow until you see the one you want. Once the command is on the line with the cursor, you can edit it with the arrow keys, the Ins key, and the Del and Backspace keys and execute it by pressing Return. If you change your mind, you can clear the command line by pressing the Esc key.

If the steps are an operation you do often, you can consolidate them into a *command file*, which is a list of the commands used to perform patterned activity with your database. This procedure eliminates the time required to enter each command individually. It is also helpful for inexperienced VP-Info users, who only need to type a simple command to put a complex procedure to work.

The WRITE instruction followed by a filename puts VP-Info into the file editing mode. In the file editing mode, you can type in your command lines. You may wish to refer to the end of this module to read about VP-Info's full-screen editor, and how other editors can be used to create database command files.

9. At this point, you can enter the command file editing mode by typing the following command:

```
                                      Remarks
1>WRITE PHONELST                    ; Opens a file named "phonelst"
•                                     you are now ready to begin typing
•                                     the command file.
```

Before creating the procedure, you should be familiar with a few of VP-Info's editing keys. You can see a list of these keys at any time while you are in the editor by pressing Alt-H. For now, you can get by with the following keys:

NOTE

The expression Ctrl-key means that the Ctrl key is held down while the designated *key* is typed. This is like pressing and holding the Shift key to type a capital letter.

Arrows	Move cursor in the direction of the arrow.
Ctrl-Left Arrow	Moves the cursor to the beginning of the line.
Ctrl-Right Arrow	Moves the cursor to the end of the line.
PgUp	To previous page (or PgDn to next page).
Ctrl-Home	Top of file.
Ctrl-End	Bottom of file.
Ins	Turn the Insert Character function on or off.
Ctrl-N	Insert a line at the cursor position.
Del	Delete the character at cursor position.
Backspace	Delete character to left of cursor position.
Ctrl-T	Delete the line at the cursor position.
Ctrl-P	Print the file.
Alt-H	Display Help screen of WRITE editing keys.
Ctrl-W	Write (or save) the command file and end the editing session. Pressing End has the same effect.
Esc	Cancel a Save request.
Ctrl-Q	Quit the editing session without saving.

10. Now combine the commands used previously into a command file that uses the PHONE database, alphabetically sorts it into the ALPHA database, and then lists the alphabetized database to the printer. Type the boldfaced words into the editor. (Do not type the explanatory remarks.)

```
                                      Remarks
* TELEPHONE LIST PROGRAM            ; A line beginning with an asterisk is a comment and it does
* PHONELST.PRG                        not affect command file operation. Also, a semicolon can
*                                     separate a command from a comment.
SET TALK OFF                        ; Turns off VP-Info's message conversation.
ERASE                               ; Clears the screen.
USE PHONE                           ; Opens the PHONE database.
SORT ON Party TO ALPHA              ; Alphabetically sorts on the Party field to a
*                                     database named ALPHA.
USE ALPHA                           ; Opens ALPHA.
*     The IF . . . ENDIF structure, checks for a ready printer and doesn't allow you to
*     accidentally lock up the computer if the printer is off.
IF PRINTER( )                       ; Checks for ready printer.
SET PRINT ON                        ; Activates printer only if it's ready.
ENDIF                               ; Signals end of IF structure.
LIST OFF                            ; Lists database to screen, and to the printer if
*                                     it's ready, with record numbers invisible (OFF).
?                                   ; Clears the last print line from printer.
SET PRINT OFF                       ; Makes sure printing is off.
USE                                 ; Closes ALPHA.
DELE FILE ALPHA.DBF                 ; Deletes ALPHA database (command words can be
*                                     abbreviated to their first four letters).
RETURN                              ; Closes command file; returns to the prompt.
```

11. Before saving the file, proofread it carefully, then press **Alt-F**. Notice that the line between IF and ENDIF is automatically indented. The Alt-F feature in the editor helps you proofread for command structure.
12. Press **End** and then **Return** to save the command file to disk.
13. To run the command file, type **DO PHONELST** and press **Return**.
14. Once a database is created, it must be maintained. You can edit, add, and delete records. In this portion of our sample session, we'll edit record number 3 by changing the phone number. We'll also add a new record to our database, and we'll delete one.

    a. Edit record number 3 as follows:

```
                          Remarks
1>USE PHONE             ; Places the phone database in use.
1>EDIT 3                ; Displays record number 3 at the top of the screen for editing.

Record No      3
PARTY      [Hood, J.T.                    ]
NUMBER     [(405) 343-1090]
```

Move the cursor down to the number field, press **Down Arrow**, and then type **(408) 221-3454**. The next record is automatically displayed. Press **End** to save the change and return to the VP-Info prompt.

b. Add a new record as follows:

```
                                                  Remarks
1>APPEND                     ; This command displays the next available record number, which is 6.
Record No        6
PARTY        [Acme Brick Company                 ]   NUMBER     [(512) 960-1415]
```

Enter the text as shown. After the number is typed, a blank record 7 is automatically displayed; press **End** to exit the append mode.

c. Delete a record as follows:

```
                                                  Remarks
1>DELETE RECORD 2            ; Marks record 2 for deletion.
      1 DELETES              ; VP-Info conversation indicates one record marked for deletion.
1>PACK                       ; Completes deletion of marked record and resequences
      5 TOTAL PACKED         ; record numbers, then announces the number of records remaining.
```

15. You can quit VP-Info by typing **QUIT** and pressing **Return**. If you want to experiment with the full-screen editor commands described in the next few paragraphs, use the QUIT command later.

USING THE VP-Info FULL-SCREEN EDITOR

The VP-Info full-screen editor is easy to use. It creates a line at a time and lets you insert and delete characters or lines using a set of simple control key sequences. A partial list of control keys is included in step 9 of the preceding sample session. A complete list is contained in Module 71, on the WRITE command.

To start the VP-Info editor, begin at the prompt. Type:

```
1>WRITE myfile.txt
```

and press Return. The file *myfile.txt* can be any legitimate one- to eight-character filename with a one- to three-character optional extension. For now, actually use the name "MYFILE.TXT." If you don't type an extension, VP-Info assumes that the file being edited is a command file and assigns the extension PRG.

An editing screen is displayed with a status line at the top:

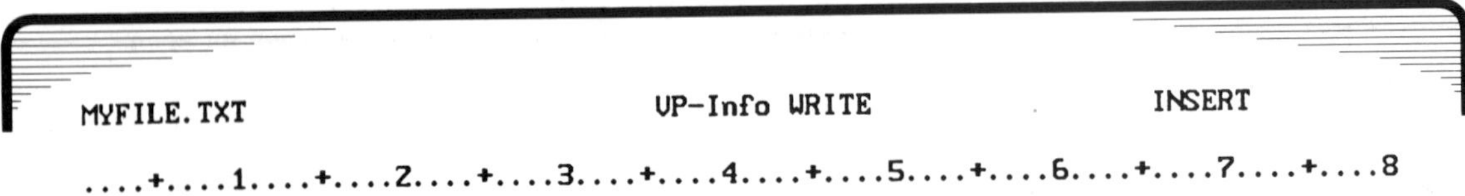

Think of the blank screen as a blank sheet of paper — just waiting for you to start typing text. So start typing. If you make a typographical error, back space and retype your text. If you type beyond the 76th character on a line, an automatic word wrap occurs. When you press Return, a triangle symbol appears at the end of the line.

To delete a character, you can use either the Backspace or the Del key. You can delete an entire line by pressing Ctrl-T. To replace a character, simply move the cursor to it, delete it, and type the correct character. The editor always begins in Insert mode, so that what you type pushes existing text aside. To use *Overwrite* or strikeover mode, press Ins to go from the Insert mode to the Overwrite mode.

Once you are through preparing your text file, press End to save it. VP-Info asks " Save this file as " and offers the filename you started with. If you want to change the name, type a new one. When the name is correct, press Return and the file is saved under the filename and extension that you assigned.

If you decide to throw away the text because it was only a practice session, press Ctrl-Q instead of End to quit without saving. VP-Info asks you if you really want to "Abandon these changes? (Y/N)." Type Y for yes and the VP-Info prompt is displayed. If you type N for no, you can continue editing your file.

There are also times when a series of statements is repeated several times within the same command file. For times like this, VP-Info offers a set of block copy functions:

Alt-B	Mark beginning and end of block.
Alt-C	Copy block to cursor position.
Alt-D	Delete block.
Alt-K	Kill (cancel) block marking.
Alt-M	Move block to cursor position.

USING ANOTHER EDITOR TO CREATE AND TEST COMMAND FILES

Although the VP-Info full-screen editor is quite satisfactory for creating most command files, you may wish to use a full-featured word processor, a program editor, or a pop-up utility to write your command files. Only those programs that create pure ASCII files are useful.

"Pop-up" notepad utilities, like Sidekick or Homebase, are convenient, because you do not have to leave the VP-Info operating environment. You can pop up the editor, make changes to a command file, write the file back to disk, escape from the editor, and run the program.

For information on using outside editors concurrently with VP-Info, see Module 53, Run.

Module 3

RECOMMENDED LEARNING SEQUENCE

INTRODUCTION

This module provides a checklist of the modules within this book. The checklist is arranged in a simple-to-complex learning sequence. The checklist provides a roadmap, suggesting where to begin and how to progress through the VP-Info commands. The sequence begins with the fundamental, easy-to-use, and easy-to-understand commands. As your knowledge of the fundamental VP-Info commands increases, you will find the advanced commands easier to understand. Within a matter of hours, you will be using VP-Info to solve real problems of your own. You will find that one of the attractive features of VP-Info is that you can do useful things with only a half-dozen or so commands.

If desired, you can study the use and form of VP-Info commands by simply reading this book. However, learning by doing is strongly recommended. There is simply no substitute for actually trying out commands on your computer as you read about them. You will get immediate feedback about how they work, and more importantly, how you can apply them to your own needs.

THE LEARNING SEQUENCE

If you follow the sequence contained in Table 3-1 at the end of this module, you will begin by building a real database of information. You will start with commands that let you create and use databases. You'll then learn how to add, edit, insert, and delete records, move around within the database, list the database to the screen or printer, and display selected information.

Next you learn how to create, store, and use memory variables, which are like temporary "storage bins" in memory. Then you learn how to incorporate these commands into command files, which let you save a command sequence in a file for automatic operation. You also learn how to design reports for either screen display or hardcopy.

As you work your way through the early modules, you get "sneak previews" of more VP-Info commands. In other words, you use new commands in conjunction with the ones you are learning so that things work properly. When used in command files, the commands are explained so you understand their purpose. If you are curious about some of the new commands, you can find out more about them by looking them up in this book's modules or in your VP-Info manual. You can also review commands by using the built-in VP-Info HELP utility.

By the time you finish this book, you will have built and edited databases, written procedures to display menus and prompts, entered and retrieved data, and designed and produced reports. So if you follow the recommended sequence, you will have models for VP-Info applications that really work.

Once you are finished, you can use these models as a basis for applications of your own. In fact, you may want to copy some of the practice files, make slight modifications, and then enter and process your own information.

Commands are described by category in the following list. If you want to know which commands are used to edit database information, create memory variables, display and print information, and so on, you can refer to this list. All command forms are not included in the list, but it does contain a respectable sampling to help you locate commands according to their purpose.

Database Creation Commands

COPY TO *filename*	—Copies database in use to named database file.
COPY STRUCTURE TO *filename*	—Copies structure of database in use to named database file.
CREATE	—Creates a new database.
SORT ON *fieldname* TO *filename*	—Sorts on named field to named database file.
TOTAL ON *fieldname(s)* TO *filename*	—Stores total of values in named field(s) to database file.

Database Editing Commands

BROWSE	—Displays database and allows editing.
DELETE	—Marks records for deletion.
EDIT *n*	—Edits record n of database in use.
FLUSH	—Updates file copy of database.
MODIFY	—Modifies database structure.
PACK	—Deletes marked records.
RECALL	—Unmarks records marked for deletion.
REPLACE *fieldname* WITH *expression*	—Replaces contents of named field with the expression.

Commands Used to Add Records

APPEND	—Appends (adds) records to database in use.
APPEND BLANK	—Adds a blank record to the bottom of the database.
APPEND FROM *filename*	—Adds records from named database file.

Record Pointer Positioning Commands

GO BOTTOM	—Positions record pointer to the last record.
GO TOP	—Positions record pointer to the first record.
GO *n*	—Positions record pointer to record n.
SKIP	—Positions record pointer to next record.
SKIP +*n*	—Moves record pointer down n records ("+" optional).
SKIP −*n*	—Moves record pointer up n records.

Commands for Finding (or Locating) a Specific Record

CONTINUE	—Used with LOCATE to find the next matching record.
FIND *expression*	—Finds first record with an indexed field matching expression.
LOCATE FOR *expression*	—Positions record pointer to record matching expression.

Commands Used to Display Information (Can be used to print with SET PRINT ON or SET FORMAT TO PRINT)

BOX *row,col,row,col*	—Draws a box on screen.
CLS or ERASE	—Clears the screen.
CURSOR *row,col*	—Moves cursor to specified row and column.
COUNT	—Displays number of last record in database.
DISPLAY	—Displays current record.
DISPLAY ALL FOR *expression*	—Displays specified records.

Command Used to Display Information (Continued)

HELP	—Displays on-screen information about VP-Info.
LIST	—Lists all records.
LIST FOR *expression*	—Lists specified records.
NOTE or *	—Used at beginning of line to insert remark within a command file.
REPORT *filename*	—Displays named file in preset report format.
SPOOL	—Sends print commands to a disk file.
SCREEN	—Saves image of screen.
SET *expression*	—Sets various system parameters that affect display, printing, colors, etc.
TEXT . . . ENDTEXT	—Allows continuous text entry into command file.
WINDOW *row,col,row,col*	—Creates a window using the coordinates.
@ *row,col* GET field	—Displays contents of specified field at row and column position.
@ *row,col* SAY 'text'	—Displays text within quotes at row and column position.
? #	—Displays current record number.
? DATE( )	—Displays system date and saves it as :DATE.
? *field1, field2, . . .*	—Displays named fields.
? *'text'*	—Displays text within quotes or brackets.
? TIME( )	—Displays system time and saves it as :TIME.
Shift-PrtSc	—Prints current display screen.

Commands Used to Create, Delete, Save, and Recall Memory Variables

ACCEPT *'text'* TO *memvar*	—Stores character-type string to named memory variable; displays text in quotes or brackets.
AVERAGE TO *memvar*	—Stores average value of selected data to designated memory variable.
CLEAR ALL	—Clears all active memory variables and open files.
DIM	—Creates a matrix variable type.
INPUT *'text'* TO *memvar*	—Stores numeric-type input to named memory variable; displays text in quotes or brackets.
RELEASE *memvar*	—Deletes named memory variable.
RESTORE FROM *filename*	—Recalls saved memory variables from disk.
SAVE TO *filename*	—Saves memory variables to disk.
STORE *expression* TO *memvar*	—Stores expression to named memory variable; the form *memvar = expression* also used.
SUM *expression* TO *memvar*	—Stores sum of expression to named memory variable.
WAIT TO *memvar*	—Pauses operation; character pressed is saved to named memory variable.

Commands for Running, Pausing, and Terminating Command File Operation

CANCEL	—Stops Operation; returns control to prompt.
CHAIN *filename*	—Starts a program from inside another.
COMPILE *filename*	—Creates a permanent compiled file.
DO *filename*	—Starts a program file.
Esc	—Pressing Esc cancels command files or exits from EDIT/BROWSE operations.
ON ERROR	—Intercepts errors to allow special error handling.
ON ESCAPE	—Intercepts pressing Escape key.
RETURN	—Stops operation; returns control to command file from which current file was called.
WAIT	—Pauses operation until a key is pressed.
WRITE	—Opens editor to write or modify command file.

Branching and Looping Commands

CASE *expression* OTHERWISE	—Part of the DO CASE statement; command lines associated with each CASE command operate if expression is true. If no CASE is true, OTHERWISE may be used to provide an alternate action.
DO CASE . . . ENDCASE	—Used to begin and end the DO CASE statement; contains embedded CASE and OTHERWISE commands.
DO WHILE *expression* . . . ENDDO	—Causes continuous operation while the expression is true or until RETURN, CANCEL, or BREAK is encountered.
ELSE	—Used within an IF statement to provide an alternate action if the IF expression is false.
IF *expression* . . . ENDIF	—Checks expression; commands embedded within the IF statement operate if the expression is true. ENDIF completes the IF statement.
REPEAT . . . ENDREPEAT	—Creates a structure that repeats a controlled number of times.

File Commands

CLEAR ALL	—Closes all files and clears all memory variables.
CLOSE *file n*	—Closes designated file.
CLOSE ALL	—Closes all open files.
DELETE FILE *filename*	—Deletes named file.
DIR	—Displays a DOS-like file directory.
LIST FILES LIKE *expression*	—Lists files matching the expression.
PERFORM *procedure*	—Activates the named procedure.
PROCEDURE . . . ENDPROCEDURE	—Designates a small command file that can be called by other command files.
QUIT	—Stops VP-Info program; returns to operating system.
RENAME *filename* TO *filename*	—Renames a file.
RUN	—Runs COM or EXE program; requires more than 256K of memory to operate.
SELECT *n*	—Allows selection of one of six possible databases, where n is 1 through 6.
SET ALTERNATE TO *filename*	—Displayed information is written to a file with the extension .TXT, when SET ALTERNATE ON command is issued.
USE *filename*	—Opens database file for use.
USE	—Used alone, closes active database file.

HOW TO GET STARTED

You should recall how you started in the sample VP-Info session in Module 2. If you don't, turn back to Module 2 and review it. Use the operating and startup information for the kind of system you have (two-floppy drives or a hard disk system). Then move through the modules in the following sequence.

Table 3-1 Recommended Learning Sequence Checklist

	Sequence	*Command(s)*	*Module*	*Page*
□	1	About This Book	1	1
□	2	VP-Info Overview	2	4
□	3	Recommended Learning Sequence	3	18

Recommended Learning Sequence (Cont.)

	Sequence	Command(s)	Module	Page
□	4	QUIT	48	186
□	5	DIR	23	90
□	6	RENAME	49	188
□	7	HELP	36	137
□	8	CREATE	17	68
□	9	DISPLAY, LIST, SYSTEM VARIABLES	24	92
□	10	MODIFY	42	162
□	11	ERASE, CLS	30	117
□	12	STATUS	62	240
□	13	USE	68	264
□	14	CLOSE	13	56
□	15	CLEAR	12	54
□	16	APPEND	5	27
□	17	FLUSH	33	125
□	18	EDIT	28	112
□	19	BROWSE, BROWSE OFF	8	42
□	20	EJECT	29	114
□	21	Interactive Mode (?), # (Record Number)	39	152
□	22	GO, GOTO, GO BOTTOM, GO TOP, SKIP	35	135
□	23	DELETE, RECALL, PACK	21	82
□	24	ZAP	72	281
□	25	REPLACE	51	192
□	26	COPY	15	61
□	27	SORT	61	238
□	28	INDEX, REINDEX	38	147
□	29	LOCATE, CONTINUE	41	158
□	30	FIND	32	122
□	31	SCOPE	55	207
□	32	STORE, RELEASE, SAVE, RESTORE, VARIABLE	63	242
□	33	DIM	22	87
□	34	SUM	64	248
□	35	AVERAGE	7	40
□	36	COUNT	16	65
□	37	ACCEPT, INPUT	4	24
□	38	WRITE	71	273
□	39	FILES, SET DEFAULT TO	31	119
□	40	RUN	53	200
□	41	DO	25	98
□	42	CHAIN, GLOBAL	10	49
□	43	CANCEL, RETURN	9	45
□	44	WAIT, WAIT TO	69	267
□	45	PERFORM, PROCEDURE	45	174
□	46	COMPILE	14	58
□	47	NOTE, *, ;	43	167
□	48	Print Statement (?)	47	180
□	49	AT (@ *row,col*), BOX, ROW( ), COL( ), Positioning Text and Data	6	34

Recommended Learning Sequence (Cont.)

	Sequence	*Command(s)*	*Module*	*Page*
□	50	SAY, SAY GET, SAY USING, CLEAR GETS, READ	54	202
□	51	TEXT, TEXT. . .ENDTEXT	65	252
□	52	LIBRARY, SET LIBRARY TO, REMLIB( )	40	156
□	53	WINDOW, COLOR	70	270
□	54	SCREEN	56	210
□	55	CURSOR, MENU( )	18	72
□	56	SCROLL	57	214
□	57	GET, GET PICTURE, CLEAR GETS, READ, ON FIELD	34	127
□	58	DO CASE, CASE, OTHERWISE, ENDCASE	26	103
□	59	IF, ELSE, ENDIF	37	141
□	60	DO WHILE, BREAK, LOOP, ENDDO, EOF	27	106
□	61	REPEAT	50	190
□	62	Sequential and Non-sequential Files	59	224
□	63	SELECT, SET RELATION TO, SET LINK TO	58	216
□	64	TOTAL	66	257
□	65	UPDATE	67	260
□	66	POST	46	177
□	67	CHR( ), RANK( )	11	51
□	68	DATE( ), TIME( )	19	74
□	69	SET Functions	60	232
□	70	ON ERROR, ON ESCAPE, INKEY( )	44	169
□	71	REPORT, REPORT FORMS, SPOOL	52	195
□	72	DEBUGGING COMMAND FILES	20	78

Turn to Module 48 to begin the learning sequence.

Module 4

ACCEPT, INPUT

DESCRIPTION

The ACCEPT and INPUT commands are used in command files. Both are used to display prompts and to pass text or numbers directly from your keyboard to a memory variable. Once text or numbers are typed, pressing Return completes the entry.

There is one important distinction between the two commands. The ACCEPT command accepts any character-type variables, while the INPUT command only lets you input numeric-type variables.

The form for these commands is:

```
ACCEPT   "Type the member's ID number " TO MId
INPUT    'Enter the membership fee ' TO MFee
```

The text within quotes is displayed as a user prompt. The TO MId and TO MFee statements transfer your typed response to memory variables named MId and MFee.

If you wish to use an apostrophe (or "single quote") within the user prompt text, use double quotes around the prompt. If you want to use a double quote within the prompt text, enclose the prompt in single quotes.

The space between the last character of the prompt text and the trailing quote is optional and only used to ensure adequate separation between the text of the displayed prompt and the cursor position.

Using the above lines in a command file results in a display similar to the following:

```
Type the member's ID number_

Enter the membership fee_
```

The typed response to the ACCEPT and INPUT commands is always completed by pressing Return. When Return is pressed, the typed value is stored to the named memory variable.

APPLICATIONS

The ACCEPT and INPUT statements are excellent ways to allow a user to enter either a character- or numeric-type value to a memory variable. Typed values are used in many ways. A common use is to search for records containing a "match." For example, if you want to find a record containing the name Jones in the NAME field of the active database, you could use the ACCEPT command to store the name to a memory variable. The command might read:

```
ACCEPT   'Enter the name to look up ' TO MName
```

There is nothing magic about what you call a memory variable, but it is advisable to use a meaningful "handle." In the preceding example, the memory variable name is the same as the field name preceded with the letter "M" (for "memory"). This is an easy way to remember that the memory variable MName is associated with the NAME field. As you work your way through the development of a command file, you can remember what you called the memory variable containing the name value. An ADDRESS field might be associated with MAddress, AMOUNT with MAmount, and so on.

TYPICAL OPERATION

In this illustration the ACCEPT and INPUT commands are used in a command file to display prompts and store keyboard inputs to memory variables. Begin at the VP prompt.

1. Type **WRITE PEOPLE** and press **Return** to use the VP-Info editor.
2. Type the following command file. (Do not type explanatory remarks.)

```
                                           Remarks
* PEOPLE.PRG - Prints information about people.
ERASE                                      ; Clears the screen.
SET TALK OFF                               ; Turns off VP-Info conversation.
?
? "  ENTER YOUR NAME"                      ; Displays text within quotes.
ACCEPT '    AND PRESS RETURN:  ' TO MName    ; Stores entry to MName.
ERASE                                      ; Clears screen.
?
? ' TYPE YOUR AGE'                         ; Displays text within single quotes.
INPUT '    AND PRESS RETURN:  ' TO MAge    ; Stores entry to MAge.
ERASE                                      ; Clears screen.
?
? 'YOUR NAME IS ' ,MName                   ; Displays text and contents of MName.
?
? ' and YOUR AGE IS ',PIC(MAge, '999' )    ; Displays text and contents of MAge.
?
WAIT                                       ; Pauses operation until a key is pressed.
ERASE                                      ; Clears screen.
CANCEL                                     ; Returns control to VP prompt.
```

3. Press **End** and then **Return** to write the command file to disk.
4. To run the command file, type **DO PEOPLE** and press **Return**.
5. Respond to the following screen prompt by typing your name and pressing **Return**.

```
ENTER YOUR NAME
AND PRESS RETURN:
```

6. Respond to the next screen prompt by typing your age and pressing **Return**. Notice the following display.

```
YOUR NAME IS MICK MCALLISTER

 and YOUR AGE IS 24

WAITING
```

7. Press any key to return to the VP prompt.
8. When you are finished experimenting, erase the practice file by typing **DELETE FILE PEOPLE.PRG** and pressing **Return**.
9. Turn to Module 71 to continue the learning sequence.

Module 5

APPEND

DESCRIPTION

The APPEND commands are used to add records to the database in use. The command is either issued from the VP prompt or used as a statement in a command file. The general form of the command is

```
APPEND FROM filename FOR expression
```

An "SDF DELIMITED WITH *delimiter*" clause is also available.

Some forms of the APPEND command include:

APPEND BLANK	Appends a blank record to the bottom of the database.
APPEND FROM *filename*	Appends records from another (closed) database file.
APPEND FROM *filename* FOR *expression*	Appends selected records from another database file, but only records with data that matches the expression.
APPEND FROM *filename* SDF	Appends records from a matching text file.

APPEND When APPEND is used alone, a screen is displayed that includes the record number, field names, and record lengths, similar to the one shown in the following screen illustration. The record lengths are indicated by a highlighted, or *reverse video*, block which shows you the field boundaries.

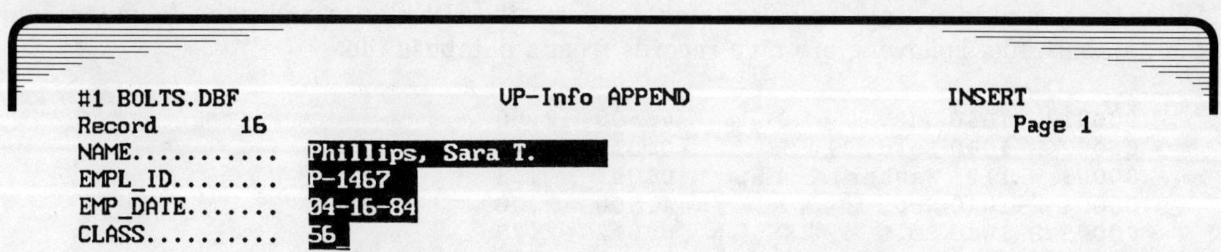

To exit the APPEND process, press Ctrl-W, End, or Esc to write the added records, including the one that is currently displayed. Press Ctrl-Q to quit without saving the present record. If you press any Exit key before entering any data in the current record, that record is not saved. In the APPEND mode, you can move between fields by using the cursor control keys. To include a box describing the control keys at the top of the APPEND screen, type SET MENU ON at the VP prompt.

APPEND BLANK The APPEND BLANK command adds a blank record to the end of the database in use and positions the record pointer to the new blank record. You can edit the blank record at a later time with EDIT, BROWSE, REPLACE, or from within a command file. Often, the APPEND BLANK command is used within command files. Data entry is guided by a set of explanatory prompts. The form for the APPEND BLANK command is

```
1>APPEND BLANK
```

APPEND FROM The APPEND FROM *filename* command is used to add data from the named, closed database to the one in use. If you attempt to append from an open database, VP-Info closes it before doing the append. You can create the structure of a new database, using the CREATE command, and fill it from an existing one. The form for the APPEND FROM command is

```
1>APPEND FROM filename
```

If you want to add only a certain class of records, say ones that have zip codes in the range of 70000 to 79999, use

```
1>APPEND FROM FILENAME FOR ZIP >= 70000 .AND. ZIP <= 79999
```

Each record in the named database is checked. Those records with 70000 to 79999 in the ZIP field are appended to the database in use.

The APPEND FROM command is also used in conjunction with the SDF (System Data Format) clause. This tells VP-Info that the FROM file is a standard ASCII (text) format file. It is read into a database as long as the appended fields are equal to or smaller in size than those in the target database. An example of this command looks like the following:

```
1>APPEND FROM filename SDF
```

When the records are copied into the database in use, the SDF clause copies the delimiters into the database file. Following are nine records from a database file.

```
00001 N-1040 Nut, 1/4 X 1         4.500  12.00
00002 B-1040 Bolt, 1/4 SS         0.012    .29
00003 W-1125 Washer, 1/4 SS       0.002    .05
00004 N-1040 Nut, 1/4 X 1         4.500  12.00
00005 B-1040 Bolt, 1/4 SS         0.012    .29
00006 W-1125 Washer, 1/4 SS        .002    .05
00007 N-1040 NUT, 1/4 X 1         4.500    .00
00008 B-1040 Bolt, 1/4 SS         0.012   0.29
00009 W-1125 Washer, 1/4 SS        .002    .05
```

The above database originally contained records 1 through 3. These three records were copied to a temporary file using

```
1>COPY TO filename SDF
```

Records 4 through 6 were then appended to the database using

```
1>APPEND FROM filename SDF
```

When field lengths of a FROM file are shorter than those of the database being appended, they are "padded" with trailing blanks. If the field lengths are longer, the characters that won't fit are discarded.

The APPEND FROM command can also be used with the DELIMITED clause. This adds a delimited text file (with the extension .TXT) to the database in use. This type of file is created with an ordinary word processor that produces standard ASCII files. Records 7 through 9 of the above example were copied using

```
1>COPY TO filename SDF DELIMITED
```

and then appended to the database using

```
1>APPEND FROM filename SDF DELIMITED
```

This tells VP-Info that the FROM file is a text file with single quotation marks separating the fields. The single quotation marks interfere with the accurate reading of numeric fields; notice that in Record 7, the value "12.00" has been lost.

VP-Info provides an alternate mechanism for writing sequential files with many more commands and functions, described in Module 59.

APPEND TO The APPEND TO *file number* command copies the current record of the file in use into the open destination file, with the field options of APPEND FROM. For keeping one file open at a time, see Module 58. The command takes the form

```
1>APPEND TO file number
```

If your file in use was HARDWARE.DBF, containing the nine records listed in the APPEND FROM example, and with the record pointer on #3, and a second file, INVENTORY.DBF was in use as file number 2, then

```
1>APPEND TO 2
```

would copy record #3 (W-1125 Washer, ¼ SS 0.002 .05) as a new record in INVENTORY.DBF.

APPLICATIONS

There are a number of uses for the APPEND commands. The APPEND command used alone allows the addition of records directly from the keyboard of your computer. The APPEND BLANK command is used to enter an empty record to the bottom of the active database for field entry with the EDIT, BROWSE, or REPLACE commands. The APPEND BLANK command is also used in command files to add new records in conjunction with programmed user prompts. This process is described with the SAY . . . GET commands in Module 54.

The APPEND FROM command is a powerful tool that is often used to build new databases from existing ones. Selected information is added by either using a certain number of fields, or by using the FOR statement as illustrated in the Description section of this module. Finally, the APPEND FROM command is often used to enter ASCII format data files that are appropriately structured into a database. This means that a data file prepared with a word processor or a spreadsheet can be added to a VP-Info file.

For example, you can use your word processor to prepare a data file with a TXT file extension. Be sure your fields are organized in the proper sequence, and their widths are identical to the field widths of the VP-Info database file. Once the data file is created and saved, then start VP-Info and put your database file in use. Finally, type the command

```
1>APPEND FROM filename SDF
```

This adds the records from the word processed data file to the bottom of your database file.

TYPICAL OPERATION

In this operation you use the APPEND and APPEND FROM commands in the interactive mode, and the APPEND BLANK command in a command file that requests data entry by displaying prompts. Although you have not encountered the command file design process yet, following along in this exercise provides a brief introduction. Begin at the VP prompt.

1. Type **CREATE ABC** and press **Return**. The database create structure screen is displayed.
2. Type the name, type, and width information as shown.

```
Thursday, June 25, 1987
                          VP-Info Create                       ABC.DBF

Name      Type   Width   Dec        Name       Type   Width   Dec

NAME       C      20      0
EXTN       C       4      0
MAIL       C       4      0
                   0      0
```

3. Press **End** to end Create and then press **Return** to save the database as a type 2 database.
4. Type **APPEND** and enter these records:

```
Record No.      1
NAME            Sergio, Vincent
EXTN            3596
MAIL            84
_______________________________
Record No.      2
NAME            Bishop, Sam
EXTN            2234
MAIL            430
_______________________________
Record No.      3
NAME            Collins, Arthur
EXTN            4554
MAIL            323
_______________________________
Record No.      4
NAME            Harris, Robert
EXTN            3353
MAIL            2230
_______________________________
Record No.      5
NAME                                          -Press End to stop.
EXTN
MAIL
_______________________________
```

5. Type **APPEND** and press **Return**; then enter the following record contents.

```
Record No.      5
NAME            Alexander, T.G.
EXTN            1104
MAIL            84
_______________________________
Record No.      6
NAME                                          -Press End to stop.
EXTN
MAIL
_______________________________
```

6. Type **CREATE XYZ** and press **Return** to create a new database. A database create structure screen is displayed.

7. Type the field contents as shown.

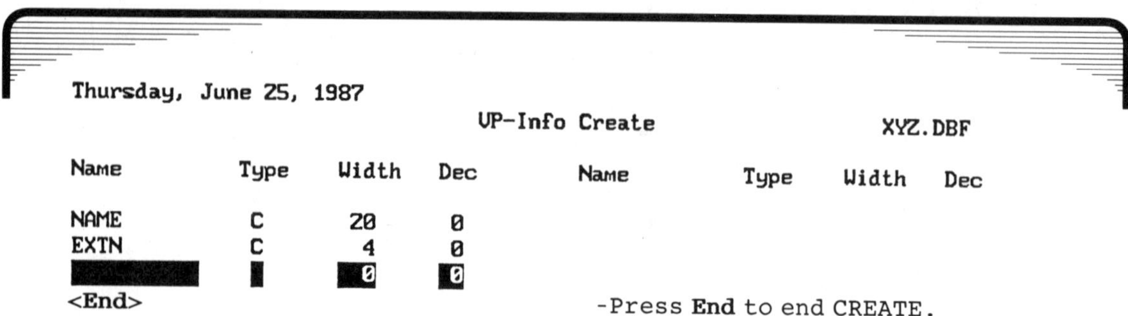

8. Press **Return** to save this as a type 2 database.
9. Type **APPEND FROM ABC** and press **Return**. Notice that the VP-Info conversation indicates "5 APPEND(S)."
10. Type **LIST** and press **Return** to verify that the name and extension fields have been transferred.

NOTE

In the following steps, a command file is prepared that uses the APPEND BLANK command. The ; (semicolon) notation lets you place comments on a command line without having them be interpreted as part of the command. However, do not type the remarks.

11. Type **WRITE PBX** to enter the VP-Info full-screen editor.
12. Type the following command file. (Don't type the explanatory remarks.)

```
                                        Remarks
ERASE                       ; Clears the screen.
USE ABC                     ; Puts ABC database in use.
APPEND BLANK                ; Adds blank record to bottom of database.
@ 3,20 SAY 'Enter the directory name ' GET NAME     ; Displays NAME prompt.
@ 5,20 SAY 'Enter the phone extension ' GET EXTN    ; Displays EXTN prompt.
@ 7,20 SAY 'Enter the mail drop number ' GET MAIL   ; Displays MAIL prompt.
READ                        ; Reads typed field contents into blank record.
?
?                           ; Question marks enter two blank lines.
WAIT                        ; Pauses and displays prompt until a key is pressed.
CLS                         ; Clears the screen.
CANCEL                      ; Returns to VP prompt.
```

13. When the command file is complete, press **End** and then **Return** to save it.
14. Type **DO PBX** to run the command file.
15. To respond to the following screen prompts, type a name, a telephone extension, and a mail drop. Then press any key to return to the VP prompt.

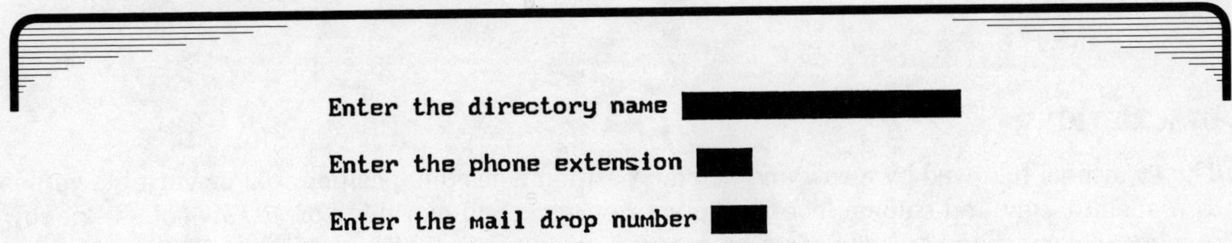

16. To verify that the record you typed was added to the database, type **LIST** and press **Return**.
17. Type **CLEAR** to close all files. This concludes the APPEND operation.
18. Turn to Module 33 to continue the learning sequence.

Module 6

AT (@ *ROW,COL*), BOX, ROW( ),COL( ) POSITIONING TEXT AND DATA

DESCRIPTION

The @ symbol followed by a row and column position is used to position text or variable values at a specific row and column location on your screen. You can think of @ *row,col* as "at row number, column number" say something, get a value, or both. The SAY and GET statements, individually or in combination, are used with @ row,col. Some examples of how the @ row,col statement is used follow. The line numbers are for reference only and are not used as part of the command lines.

```
1.      @ 7,10 SAY "WHAT'S YOUR NAME? "
2.      @ 7,40 GET NAME
3.      @ 9,10 SAY "      PHONE NUMBER? "
4.      @ 9,40 GET PHONE PICTURE '(999) 999-9999'
5.      READ
```

or

```
6.      @ 7,10 SAY "WHAT'S YOUR NAME?  " GET NAME
7.      @ 9,10 SAY "      PHONE NUMBER?  " GET PHONE PICTURE '(999) 999-9999'
8.      READ
```

Line 1 displays the question (or "prompt"), "WHAT'S YOUR NAME? " beginning at row 7, column 10 of the display screen. Keep in mind that VP-Info begins numbering rows and columns at 0,0 and ends with 24,79 (the lower right corner of the screen).

Line 2 allows data entry from the keyboard into the NAME field of the database in use beginning at row 7 column 40.

Lines 3 and 4 are similar to lines 1 and 2, except that line 4 makes use of the PICTURE clause, which controls the format of typed information.

Line 5 contains the READ command. This command reads your typed response to the GET statement into the specified field of a corresponding database. For example, GET NAME lets you type a name; READ reads the typed name into the NAME field of the open database file. Of course, the database must be in use for these operations to work.

Lines 6 and 7 are alternate forms of lines 1 through 4, except the exact position of data entry is not controlled. Data entry takes place to the right of the prompts. You can add leading or trailing spaces within the quotation marks following the SAY statement to control horizontal text placement.

Another command, CLEAR GETS, is used in place of READ to prevent data entry. What this command says is, "Keep the GET statements clear." The following example shows how the NAME field is displayed, but protected from data entry, while the PHONE field accepts input.

```
6.          @ 7,10 SAY "WHAT'S YOUR NAME? " GET NAME
6a.         CLEAR GETS
7.          @ 9,10 SAY "      PHONE NUMBER? " GET PHONE PICTURE '(999) 999-9999'
8.          READ
```

ROW-COLUMN NOTATION The row-column notation starts at 0,0, which is the first row and first column. Therefore, rows are 0 to 24 for a 25-line screen, and columns are 0 to 79, which provides for 80-column coverage.

ROW( ),COL( ) Using the ROW( ),COL( ) specification with the @ sign allows you to print on the next column in the current row. This allows you to use SAY and GET as movable or *floating point* instructions.

Consider the following command lines:

```
Number1 = '1234567890'
@ 10,10 say Number1
@ ROW( ),COL( ) say 'X1234567890'
```

which would print "1234567890X1234567890" on the screen, beginning at row 10, column 10. If Number1 is going to vary in length, then @ ROW( ),COL( ) allows you to keep the displayed image together.

USING, PICTURE AND PIC( ) The USING clause is used with @ *row,col* SAY to control the format of displayed and printed information. Look at this example:

```
@ 11,38 SAY AMOUNT USING '$9999.99'
```

Here, the contents of the AMOUNT field of the active database begin displaying at row 11 column 38. The display includes a dollar sign, four number places (which are controlled by the 9's), a decimal point, and two number places. The value 125.765 is displayed as $ 125.76.

Alternatively, the command

```
@ 11,38 SAY PIC(AMOUNT,'$9999.99')
```

results in the same display.

The PICTURE clause is used when the field or variable is subject to a GET rather than a SAY, as in this pair of commands:

```
@ 11,38 SAY "PRICE: " GET MPrice PICTURE '$9999.99'
READ
```

The GET . . . PICTURE clause is used to control information as it is typed into a database record. Look at the following example.

```
@ 12,60 GET FRACTION PICTURE '999/999'
```

Other forms of the PICTURE clause are described in Modules 34 and 54.

OTHER STATEMENTS Besides positioning text and fields, there are a number of other uses for the @ row,col statement. Some are described in the remaining paragraphs of this section.

The @ *row,col* SAY CHR(*ASCII code number*) Statement You can use the @ SAY statement with CHR(*number*) to print symbolic characters on the screen. It does not execute the command associated with the ASCII code, however. For example, the statement, @ 12,1 SAY CHR(17) causes a left-facing triangle (the symbol used to represent carriage returns in the VP-Info editor) to appear on the screen. This means that you cannot use the command @ 12,1 SAY CHR(7) to "beep" the computer's speaker. To produce a beep, use ? CHR(7) instead.

Positioning Memory Variables You can also control the position of memory variables with the @ row,col statement. The following command file lines show a memory variable GW being created and then displayed.

```
STORE 'GEE WHIZ!' TO GW
CLS
@ 12,24 SAY 'The little kid said '+GW
```

This sequence prints "The little kid said GEE WHIZ!" beginning at row 12, column 24.

SET Statements Used with @ *row,col* There are several SET statements that are commonly used with @ row,col. These are summarized in the following list. In each case, the default setting is listed first.

SET BELL ON/OFF	When on, causes a "beep" when you type illegal entries (letters in a numeric field, for example) or when you fill a field.
SET CONFIRM OFF/ON	When on, forces you to end every entry in the APPEND, BROWSE, EDIT screen by pressing Return. This is to prevent accidents after entries that fill the field.
SET DATE TO *format*	Sets the format of the DATE( ) string. See Module 19 for more information.
SET FORMAT TO *device*	Directs @ displays to either the screen or the printer.
SET INTENSITY ON/OFF	This displays half-intensity (or reverse video) text. To eliminate half-intensity, simply enter the command line SET INTENSITY OFF. This only works on computers supporting half-intensity display.

SET UPPER OFF/ON	When on, it functions like the Caps Lock key, turning all entries into uppercase. Using this avoids problems with case in INDEX and FIND functions.
SET ZERO ON/OFF	When on, the number 0 is displayed; when off, values of zero are represented with blank spaces.

Storing Row-Column Positions to Memory Variables You can store screen position numbers to memory variables and use them in place of numbers. For example, you might store 5 to Y as the vertical line position, and 15 to X as the horizontal column position. Then you can use "@ Y,X" instead of "@ 5,15."

You can use a continuous loop in which the row value (Y) is incremented (or increased) by 1 each time a line is displayed or printed. This is accomplished by storing Y + 1 to the present value of Y. In other words, if Y starts out being 5, then 5 + 1 changes the value of Y to 6. With a DO WHILE loop, this process can continue until the value of Y reaches some predetermined number, like 55, the bottom line of your printer. At this point, you can cause a page eject (form feed), reset the value of Y back to 5, and start over on the next page. The Typical Operation section of this module provides an example.

Field values are displayed in "reverse video" (black on a white background) when @ row,col GET is used. If you wish to eliminate this effect, you can add SET INTENSITY OFF to your command file or type it at the VP prompt.

Drawing Boxes The BOX command draws a box whose upper left and lower right corners are specified by a series of row and column numbers as follows:

	Remarks
`BOX 4,15,17,60`	;Draws a box beginning at Row 4, Col 15 and extending to Row 17, Col 60.
`BOX 0,0,24,79 DOUBLE`	;Draws a box enclosing the entire screen in a double line.

APPLICATIONS

As you can see from the examples, @ row,col SAY is a powerful formatting tool. It is used to position text on either the screen or printer. The SET FORMAT TO PRINT command routes data to the printer; SET FORMAT TO SCREEN routes the same data to the screen. You can use @ row,col SAY to format lists, mailing labels, reports, or any other information from database fields or memory variables.

TYPICAL OPERATION

In the following illustration, @ row,col SAY is used in a command file that uses the ABC database created in Module 5 and modified in Module 38. Begin at the VP prompt.

1. Type **WRITE PHDIR** and press **Return** to use the VP-Info editor.

2. Type the following command file. (Don't type the explanatory remarks or the indentations.)

```
                                  Remarks
* PHDIR.PRG                       Lists all records in the ABC database.
CLS
*                                 The following lines are printed to the screen.
*
@  7,20 SAY 'THIS PROGRAM PRINTS A TELEPHONE LIST.'
@  9,20 SAY 'BE SURE YOUR PRINTER IS READY.'
@ 11,20 SAY 'PRESS P TO PRINT THE LIST, OR'
@ 13,20 SAY 'PRESS Q TO QUIT.'
ACCEPT TO Choice                  ; Pause and store response to Choice.
CLS
IF !(Choice)='Q'                  ; Look for Q in upper or lower case.
   CANCEL                         ; If Choice = 'Q' or 'q,' return to prompt.
ENDIF                             ; Pass control to next command line.
*
SET FORMAT TO PRINT               ; Direct @ row,col output to printer.
Y = 5                             ; Store 5 to memory variable Y.
X = 15                            ; Store 15 to memory variable X.
USE ABC                           ; Put ABC database in use.
*
DO WHILE .NOT. EOF                ; Continue operation until end-of-file.
   IF Y >= 55                     ; Look for Y greater than or equal to 55.
      EJECT                       ; If Y > = 55, perform a form feed.
      STORE 5 TO Y                ; If Y > = 55, reset Y to 5.
   ENDIF                          ; Pass control to next command line.
   *
   @ Y,X SAY NAME                 ; Place NAME field contents at row Y, column X.
   @ Y+1,X SAY EXTN               ; Place PHONE field contents at row Y + 1, column X.
   Y = Y+3                        ; Add 3 to current value of Y to advance 3 lines.
   SKIP                           ; Position record pointer to next record.
   *
   IF EOF                         ; Check for end-of-file condition.
      EJECT
      SET FORMAT TO SCREEN        ; Direct @ row,col output to screen.
      WAIT                        ; Pause and display "WAITING" prompt.
      CLS                         ; Clears screen.
      CANCEL                      ; Returns control to VP prompt.
   ENDIF                          ; Passes control to next command line.
ENDDO                             ; Ends DO WHILE statement.
RETURN                            ; Terminates program.
```

NOTE

If you would rather print the phone list to your screen, change the SET FORMAT TO PRINT to SET DEVICE TO SCREEN and place an asterisk at the right margin in front of EJECT (two places).

3. Before saving the file, press **Alt-F** to insert the indentation, and proofread for missing ENDs.
4. Press **End** and **Return** to save the command file.
5. Run the command file by typing **DO PHDIR** and pressing **Return**.
6. Respond to the following screen prompt by typing **P** to continue or **Q** to quit.

```
THIS PROGRAM PRINTS A TELEPHONE LIST.

BE SURE YOUR PRINTER IS READY.

PRESS P TO PRINT THE LIST, OR

PRESS Q TO QUIT.
```

7. Notice that the command file prints names and telephone extensions.
8. When you finish experimenting with this command file, delete it from your disk by typing **DELE FILE PHDIR.PRG** and pressing **Return**.
9. Turn to Module 54 to continue the learning sequence.

Module 7
AVERAGE

DESCRIPTION

The AVERAGE command is similar to the SUM command, except instead of summing the values of one or more numeric fields within a database, it finds the average (or *arithmetic mean*). The result is either displayed or stored to a memory variable. Forms of the AVERAGE command and corresponding examples are shown in the following list.

1. AVERAGE *field name* Averages the contents of the specified field name and displays the result.

```
1>AVERAGE QTY
   13 AVERAGE(S)
    168.00
```

2. AVERAGE *field1,field2* . . . Averages specified field names and displays the results.

```
1>AVERAGE QTY,COST,PRICE*1.05
  105 AVERAGE(S)
   2309.00 34523.48 74560.86
```

3. AVERAGE *fieldname(s)* TO *memory variable(s)* Averages named field name to the named memory variable.

```
1>AVERAGE QTY TO MQTY
1>AVERAGE QTY,COST TO MQTY,MCOST
```

4. AVERAGE *fieldname* TO *memory variable* FOR *expression* Averages named field to named memory variable for those records that match the expression.

```
1>AVERAGE QTY TO MQTY FOR COST > .99
```

5. AVERAGE *fieldname* TO *memory variable* WHILE *expression* Averages named field to named memory variable while expression is valid. If expression becomes invalid, averaging ceases.

```
1>AVERAGE QTY TO MQTY WHILE COST <= 100.00
```

APPLICATIONS

The AVERAGE command is used to store the arithmetic mean of one or more fields within a database file to one or more memory variables for later use, or to display an arithmetic mean in response to a direct user inquiry. The AVERAGE command is used both in command files and in the interactive mode.

TYPICAL OPERATION

In this illustration the AVERAGE command is used with the PICNIC database created in Module 64. Begin at the VP prompt.

1. Type **USE PICNIC** and press **Return**.
2. Type **AVERAGE GUESTS,AMOUNT TO Mgu,Mam** and press **Return**. Notice the following:

```
1>AVERAGE GUESTS,AMOUNT TO Mgu,Mam
   13 AVERAGE(S)
       3.23        3.23
1>
```

3. Type **? MGu, MAm** to confirm the contents of the variables.
4. Type **CLEAR ALL** to close all files and to release all memory variables.
5. Turn to Module 16 to continue the learning sequence.

Module 8

BROWSE, BROWSE OFF

DESCRIPTION

BROWSE The BROWSE command lets you examine records, edit them, mark or unmark records for deletion, and even add new records.

Typing BROWSE from the VP prompt displays the database in a manner similar to the following screen illustration.

```
#1 BOLTS.DBF                          VP-Info BROWSE
         ITEMNO NAME                      COST PRICE
00001    N-1040 Nut, 1/4 X 1              4.500 12.00
00002    B-1040 Bolt, 1/4 SS              0.012   .29
00003    W-1125 Washer, 1/4 SS             .002   .05
```

You can display a command menu bar at the top of the screen by typing SET MENU ON at the prompt before typing the BROWSE command.

You can type the BROWSE command with the FIELDS option:

```
BROWSE FIELDS NAME, ADDRESS    ; Displays only the named fields.
```

If the database fields cannot fit on the 80-column screen, VP-Info displays as many as can fit, in the order that the fields occur in the record. Use the FIELDS option to read other fields.

You can move around in a database while browsing by using the cursor control keys. Edit with the following control keys which are active in the BROWSE mode.

Up Arrow	Cursor right one field
PgUp	Cursor up one record
Dn Arrow	Cursor left one field
PgDn	Cursor down one record
Left Arrow	Cursor left one character
Backspace	Erase character left of cursor
Right Arrow	Cursor right one character
Ins	Turn insert/strikeover mode on/off
Del	Delete character at cursor position
Ctrl-Home	Go to first record
Ctrl-End	Go to last record
Ctrl-PgDn	Append record to end of file

Ctrl-Y	Delete field contents from cursor position
Ctrl-U	Mark/unmark record for deletion
Ctrl-Q	Quit the BROWSE mode without saving changes
Ctrl-W, Esc or End	Write (save) changes to the database and return to the VP prompt.

The BROWSE screen does not allow you to move beyond the last record.

As you can see, the BROWSE mode uses a large number of control keys to allow moving from field to field or from record to record within a database. The available editing keys make changing the information within a database easy.

The BROWSE mode displays each record on a single line. If the record has more than 80 characters, only the first *n* fields that fit on the screen are displayed. If the first field is more than 80 characters wide, BROWSE does not work. To view the hidden fields, specify them in a BROWSE FIELDS option.

You can alter the contents of a record by simply moving the cursor to the field to be changed and typing in the new information. You can use Del to delete characters and Ctrl-Y to delete from the cursor position to the end of the field. You can insert text by pressing Ins. When the insert mode is active, the word INSERT is displayed at the top of the screen. When text is typed, following text is displaced to the right.

Once you have finished modifying a database using BROWSE, you can save your changes by pressing End, which "writes" the changed records to disk. If you decide to abandon the changes in the last modified record, press Ctrl-Q to quit without saving the changes. Both the Ctrl-W (write changes) and Ctrl-Q (quit without saving) commands take you back to the VP prompt.

BROWSE OFF The BROWSE OFF command can be used in a command file to create a GET TABLE (see Module 34) and allow editing of data presented in a user-designed format. For example, the following command file creates a browsing window with a small menu of commands:

```
*BROWSE.PRG
USE MEMBERS
ERASE
WINDOW 5,5,10,60
TEXT
USE <PG UP> and <PG DN> to scan.
Press <End> to select a record.
Name                          Joined
@Name                        @Joined
ENDTEXT
BROWSE OFF
WINDOW
ERASE
DISPLAY
RETURN
```

APPLICATIONS

The BROWSE command is used to view and update the contents of a database. It is perhaps the most "direct" way to view and edit. The EDIT and LIST commands provide an alternative to the BROWSE command. However, there are several advantages to use of the BROWSE command.

Several records are viewed simultaneously using BROWSE, while only one record is displayed at a time when EDIT is used. When you use the LIST command to view a database, the records cannot be edited. Finally, with LIST, records wrap at the 80th column. This often clutters the data display, making it difficult to distinguish one field from another. BROWSE displays the information in a structured manner. Records are on a single, continuous line. Fields are aligned in columns beneath their field names, which are displayed at the top of each column.

TYPICAL OPERATION

In this operation the BROWSE command is used to display the contents of the database named XYZ, which you created in Module 5. Begin at the VP prompt.

1. Type **USE XYZ** and press **Return**.
2. Type **BROWSE** and press **Return**.
3. Move around in the database with the PgUp, PgDn, and cursor control keys.
4. Move to record 5 and press **Ctrl-U** to mark the record for deletion. Notice that an "*" signals the mark.

```
#1 XYZ.DBF                                 VP-Info BROWSE
           NAME                  EXTN
00001   Sergio, Vincent          3596
00002   Bishop, Sam              2234
00003   Collins, Arthur          4554
00004   Harris, Robert           3353
00005  *Alexander, T.G.          1104
```

5. Press **End** to leave the Browse screen.
6. Type **LIST** and press **Return**. Notice that record 5 includes an asterisk. The record is marked for deletion.
7. Type **PACK** and press **Return**. Notice that 4 records are copied. Record 5 has been deleted.
8. Type **DELETE FILE XYZ.DBF** and press **Return** to remove the XYZ.DBF file from your disk.
9. Turn to Module 29 to continue the learning sequence.

Module 9

CANCEL, RETURN

DESCRIPTION

The CANCEL and RETURN commands are used to end command file operation. Both commands close the active command file and transfer control out of it.

CANCEL When the command CANCEL is encountered in a command file, command file execution ceases and the VP prompt is displayed. At that point, you can enter commands directly from your keyboard.

RETURN RETURN is used in a DO file to take you back to the point of command file origin. The form for the RETURN command is:

```
RETURN
```

If the active command file was called from the VP prompt with the DO *filename* command, then RETURN operates like CANCEL. It stops command file operation, closes the active command file, and redisplays the VP prompt. If the command file was called by another command file, then RETURN passes control back to the calling command file.

RETURN is often used as the last line in a command file. If RETURN or CANCEL is not used at the end of a command file called with the DO command, operation passes through the last line of a called command file and returns to the command file from which it was called automatically. However, files remain open until either the CLEAR ALL or QUIT command is used. Open files can be damaged if a computer reset, as might be induced by a power failure, causes your computer to "crash." Therefore, it is best to terminate command files with either RETURN or CANCEL.

APPLICATIONS

The CANCEL command is frequently used in command files to give you the opportunity to stop command file operation. For example, you might use a series of command lines similar to these to provide an "exit" option.

```
? 'Type X to exit, any other key to continue...'
WAIT TO EXIT
IF !(EXIT)='X'
    CANCEL
ENDIF
```

If an X is typed, the CANCEL command displays the VP prompt, and control is returned to your keyboard. Pressing any other key bypasses the IF statement and command file operation continues. The !( ) function allows either an upper- or lowercase X in response to the WAIT command.

The RETURN command is used inside a DO file in the same way as the CANCEL command, except that the result is slightly different. In fact, you can substitute RETURN for CANCEL in the previous example if you want to return to a command file called with the DO command. As previously mentioned, if the current command file was called from the VP prompt, control returns to the prompt.

The RETURN command is treated as a CANCEL in a file called with the CHAIN command rather than with DO, taking you back to the VP prompt. The only way to "RETURN" from a CHAIN file is to chain back to the calling file, with the understanding that you start that file over from the beginning.

TYPICAL OPERATION

In this illustration the CANCEL and RETURN commands are used in three small command files called DEMO1, DEMO2, and DEMO3. These command files pass control back and forth to demonstrate the use of CANCEL and RETURN. Begin at the VP prompt.

1. Type **WRITE DEMO1** and press **Return** to access the full-screen editor.
2. Type the following command file. (Don't type the explanatory remarks.)

```
                                   Remarks
* DEMO1.PRG — Uses DEMO2 and DEMO3 to demonstrate CANCEL and RETURN.
DO WHILE T                   ; Continues operation while true.
?
? 'This is the DEMO1 command file.'
? '     Press 2 to run the DEMO2 command file,'
? '     Press 3 to run the DEMO3 command file,'
? ' or Press X to eXit.'
WAIT TO WHAT                 ; Pauses and stores keyed character to
*                              memory variable WHAT.
DO CASE                      ; Begins CASES keyed to value of WHAT.
   CASE !(WHAT)='X'          ; Checks for WHAT equals "X" or "x."
      CANCEL                 ; Cancels command file if WHAT = X.
   CASE WHAT='2'             ; Checks for WHAT equals "2."
      DO DEMO2               ; Runs DEMO2 command file if WHAT = 2.
   CASE WHAT='3'             ; Checks for WHAT equals "3."
      DO DEMO3               ; Runs DEMO3 command file if WHAT = 3.
ENDCASE                      ; Passes control to following command line.
? 'DEMO1'
ENDDO                        ; Completes DO WHILE statement.
RETURN                       ; Always end with a RETURN command.
```

3. Press **Alt-F** to format the file and press **End** and **Return** to write the command file to disk.
4. Type **WRITE DEMO2** and press **Return** to type the following command file.

```
                                Remarks
• DEMO2.PRG — Uses DEMO1 and DEMO3 to demonstrate CANCEL and RETURN.
DO WHILE T                ; Continues operation while true.
?
? 'This is the DEMO2 command file.'
? '     Press 1 to RETURN to the DEMO1 command file,'
0 '     Press 3 to run the DEMO3 command file,'
? ' or Press X to eXit. '
WAIT TO WHAT              ; Pauses and stores keyed character to the
•                           memory variable WHAT.
DO CASE                   ; Begins CASES for value of WHAT.
  CASE !(WHAT)='X'        ; Checks for WHAT equals "X" or "x."
    CANCEL                ; Back to prompt if WHAT = "X."
  CASE WHAT='1'           ; Checks for WHAT equals "1."
    ? 'BACK TO DEMO1.'
    RETURN                ; Continues with DEMO1 command file if WHAT = "1."
  CASE WHAT='3'           ; Checks for WHAT equals "3."
    DO DEMO3              ; Runs DEMO3 command file if WHAT = "3."
ENDCASE                   ; Passes control to following command line.
? ' DEMO2'
ENDDO                     ; Completes DO WHILE statement.
RETURN                    ; Should never get here.
```

5. Press **Alt-F** to format the file and press **End** and **Return** to write the command file to disk.
6. Type **WRITE DEMO3** and press **Return** to type the following command file.

```
                                Remarks
• DEMO3.PRG — Uses DEMO1 and DEMO2 to demonstrate CANCEL and RETURN.
?
? 'This is the DEMO3 command file.'
? '     Press Spacebar to return to the previous command file,'
? 'or Press X to eXit. '
WAIT TO WHAT              ; Pauses operation; keyed character is
•                           stored to memory variable WHAT.
DO CASE                   ; Begins CASES for value of WHAT.
  CASE !(WHAT)= 'X'       ; Checks for WHAT equals "X" or "x."
    CANCEL                ; Cancels command file operation if WHAT = "X."
  CASE WHAT= ' '          ; Checks for spacebar.
    ? 'BACK TO DEMO2.'
    RETURN
ENDCASE                   ; Ends CASES. Control passes to next line.
? "How'd you get here?"
RETURN                    ; An incorrect input could get you here.
```

7. Press **Alt-F** to format the file and press **End** and **Return** to write the command file to disk.
8. Now type **DO DEMO1** and press **Return**. Notice the following displays and respond to the prompts by typing the number shown on each WAIT line.

NOTE

The customary ERASE commands have been omitted for this demonstration, resulting in what may seem peculiar behavior by the cursor. Press the correct number or letter, regardless of the location of the cursor. Notice that the screen begins to scroll once it is full.

```
1>DO DEMO1
   DO DEMO2
      DO DEMO3
   DO DEMO3

This is the DEMO1 command file.
    Press 2 to run the DEMO2 command file,
    Press 3 to run the DEMO3 command file,
 or Press X to eXit.
WAITING                                                     Type 2

This is the DEMO2 command file.
    Press 1 to RETURN to the DEMO1 command file,
    Press 3 to run the DEMO3 command file,
 or Press X to eXit.
WAITING                                                     Type 3

This is the DEMO3 command file.
    Press Spacebar to return to the previous command file,
 or Press X to eXit.
WAITING                                                     Press Spacebar
BACK TO DEMO2.
 DEMO2

This is the DEMO2 command file.
    Press 1 to RETURN to the DEMO1 command file,
    Press 3 to run the DEMO3 command file,
 or Press X to eXit.
WAITING
    Press 1 to RETURN to the DEMO1 command file,
BACK TO DEMO1.
DEMO1                                                       Type 1

This is the DEMO1 command file.
    Press 2 to run the DEMO2 command file,
    Press 3 to run the DEMO3 command file,
 or Press X to eXit.
WAITING                                                     Type X
```

9. Experiment with command file operation until you understand how it works. Do not erase the three Demo files, because they are used again in Module 14.
10. Turn to Module 69 to continue the learning sequence.

Module 10
CHAIN, GLOBAL

DESCRIPTION

The CHAIN command is used to start the operation of a VP-Info command (or program) file. It is used as a statement within a command file, like the DO command, but its operation is somewhat different and generally programs should not include both commands. Do not CHAIN out of a program file that you got into with DO. The form of the CHAIN command is:

```
CHAIN filename
```

The named command file operates until:

1. The end of the file is reached, which passes control back to the VP prompt.
2. A CANCEL command is encountered, passing control back to the VP prompt.
3. The Esc key is pressed, which interrupts program operation and returns to the prompt.
4. A command file error is encountered, such as not closing an IF with an ENDIF or a DO WHILE with an ENDDO.
5. An error message is displayed.

DO and CHAIN The CHAIN command does not operate like the DO command in the existing file and variable environment. Its first act is to clear the memory of all variables and close all files — in both the immediate and the command file mode. In fact, since the function of CHAIN is to link two command files together, there is no point in using it from the immediate mode at all.

The second difference between the two commands is that you cannot RETURN from a CHAINed file. This feature has advantages and disadvantages. On the one hand, it means that you must think of a CHAIN as a one-way street. If you chain from MAINMENU.PRG to MENU3.PRG, when you finish MENU3 you do not go back to MAINMENU. Actually, if you conclude MENU3 with the command CHAIN MAINMENU you can go back, keeping in mind that you arrive with all variables cleared and all files closed, ready to start MAINMENU over from scratch, whereas a DO/RETURN combination allows you to go back to MAINMENU and pick up where you left off. The advantage of chaining is that chained programs, unlike programs called with DO commands, are not compiled until they are needed, so you can keep the size of a program file down by using CHAIN.

GLOBAL VARIABLES Although CHAIN clears variables and closes files, you can pass variables across a CHAIN command with the command line, GLOBAL *variable name1,variable name2 . . .*, listing all the variables to be passed. The GLOBAL command must be at the beginning of the source file and all the files the variables are to be passed into. GLOBAL can pass any variable except a matrix (Module 22).

APPLICATIONS

Use CHAIN when it is all right to clear the file environment and variables, and when command file size is a problem. If a Main Menu called MENU.PRG does not open any databases, you can use CHAIN to create a variety of independent paths into various command files that each open various files, and then link all the paths back to the Main Menu by concluding each path with the command CHAIN MENU to restart the Main Menu file.

TYPICAL OPERATION

In this illustration the pair of command files used in Module 25 to illustrate the DO command is revised to demonstrate differences in the CHAIN command. Begin at the VP prompt.

1. Type **WRITE Level1** and press **Return** to use the VP-Info editor.
2. Modify the command file by changing the command "DO DLevel2" to read

   CHAIN DLevel2
3. Press **End** but not Return. Instead, respond to the Save prompt by typing the new filename:

   CLEVEL1.PRG

   and then press **Return**.
4. Type **DO CLEVEL1** and press **Return** while comparing operation to the results in Module 25. Notice:
   a. that the variable LVL2 is not listed as an Unknown variable when the STAT command is executed.
   b. that going to Level2 requires lengthy disk access while DLEVEL2 is compiled.
   c. that although the message "ABC still open" is displayed, in fact the database is not still open, because the ABC record is not displayed as it was before.
   d. that although the message "Going back to Level1 . . ." is displayed, the program terminates, ignoring the RETURN entirely and stopping at the prompt.
5. Type **DELE FILE CLEVEL1.PRG** and press **Return**, then type **DELE FILE DLEVEL2.PRG** and press **Return** to clear space on your work disk.
6. Turn to Module 9 to continue the learning sequence.

Module 11

CHR( ), RANK( )

DESCRIPTION

The RANK( ) function returns the ASCII equivalent of a character within the parentheses. For example, the command:

```
1>? RANK('A')
```

returns the number 65, which is the ASCII code for capital A. The CHR( ) function reverses the process, returning the character equivalent to the ASCII code typed within the parentheses. For example, the command:

```
1>? CHR(65)
```

returns the character A. Here is a more detailed look at these handy functions.

CHR( ) If you have ever played with the BASIC programming language, you probably know about the CHR$( ) function, which displays the ASCII character equivalent to the number within parentheses. VP-Info's CHR( ) function is similar. On your computer you should find that a CHR(7) outputs a "beep" on the speaker. The ASCII value for a carriage return is CHR(13); a line feed is CHR(10). Special graphic symbols are also displayed using the CHR( ) function. You may want to use these functions in command files to display special symbols or to mark areas within a window.

To determine the ASCII characters contained in your computer, a command file is included in the Typical Operation section of this module that displays the character number and character for the entire ASCII set in your computer. Some forms of the CHR( ) command are shown in the following list.

```
1>? CHR(64)              ; Displays the @ (AT) sign.
@
1>? CHR(75)              ; Displays the character K.
K
1>STORE 72 TO X          ; Stores 72 to the memory variable X.
1>STORE 73 TO Y          ; Stores 73 to the memory variable Y.
1>? CHR(X),CHR(Y)        ; Displays the character equivalents
HI                       ; of the specified variables.
```

RANK( ) If you want to check the ASCII code for a certain character, you can use a statement similar to the first example in this module. If several characters are used in the string within parentheses, only the value of the first character is returned. Look at the following command line.

```
1>? RANK('Hello')
   72.00
```

This is the same as:

```
1>? RANK('H')
```

APPLICATIONS

You can use the CHR( ) function to add special effects to menu screens. You can also use the CHR(7) to cause your speaker to "beep" during data entry or to get attention during command file operation. As shown in the preceding list of examples, the CHR( ) function is also used to store values to memory variables for later use. The CHR( ) function can be used to send special command codes to your printer. For example, if the code to cause your printer to output 15- or 17-pitch compressed type was 29 and the code for the default typesize was 28, then the following sequence of commands would demonstrate compressed type and then return to the default:

```
1>SET PRINT ON
1>STORE "123456789012" TO Elite
1>? Elite
1>?                       ; Causes printing (printer is one step behind).
1>? CHR(29)+Elite+CHR(28) ; Switches pitch, prints, switches back.
1>? Elite                 ; Prints string again.
1>?                       ; Clears last string from printer.
```

There are times when you want to underline printed text. The CHR(13), which is a carriage return (without a line feed), is often used to move the print head back to the beginning of the printed line without causing a line feed. Next, you can space over and print the underline character at the desired location. To continue the example above, if you type

```
1>? Elite+CHR(13)+ "____"
1>?
1>SET PRINT OFF
```

the first four digits of the demonstration string are printed with an underline.

TYPICAL OPERATION

In this illustration the CHR( ) function is used in a command file that displays all ASCII characters between 1 and 254. Begin at the VP prompt.

1. Type **WRITE CHR** and press **Return** to use the editor.
2. Type the following command file. (Do not type the explanatory remarks.)

```
                                        Remarks
* CHR.PRG – Displays character set and corresponding numbers.
CLS                                     ; Clears the screen.
SET TALK OFF                            ; Turns off conversation.
? '           CHR   VALUE'              ; Displays heading.
X = 1                                   ; Stores the value 1 to memory variable X.
DO WHILE X < 255                        ; Causes continuous operation until X = 255.
* Main structure displays the value of X and the ASCII character, using
* three places and no decimal for the value of X.
   ? PIC(X,'999'),' ',CHR(X)
   X = X + 1                            ; Adds 1 to X (increments X by 1).
   IF MOD(X,23)=0                       ; If X is divisible by 23, the screen is full.
      WAIT                              ; Stop for a key.
      CLS                               ; Erase screen.
   ENDIF                                ; Screen full.
ENDDO                                   ; Ends DO WHILE loop; passes control on.
CANCEL                                  ; Returns control to VP prompt.
```

3. Press **Alt-F** to format the file, proofread it, and then press **End** and then **Return** to write the command file to disk.
4. Type **DO CHR** and press **Return** to run the command file.
5. When you are through with the command file, you may wish to save it for future reference. However, it is not used again in this book.
6. Turn to Module 19 to continue the learning sequence.

Module 12

CLEAR

DESCRIPTION

The CLEAR command resets VP-Info to a "clear" state. All files are closed and all active memory variables are released from memory, as if the RELEASE ALL command (described in Module 63) had been given. The command form is:

```
1>CLEAR
```

The word "CLEAR" also appears in the CLEAR GETS command described in Modules 34 and 54. CLEAR GETS is not related to CLEAR, which is the subject of this module.

APPLICATIONS

There are three situations where you may wish to use the CLEAR command. First, you can issue it and then the ERASE command at the VP prompt to close all files, release all memory variables, and wipe the screen clean, giving you a "clean slate" on which to work.

Second, you can use CLEAR at the beginning of a command file. Used at the beginning of a command file, it releases any memory variables that may exist and closes all files. This makes all memory variables available for use. It also assures you that only those files needed are open, eliminating unwanted surprises during operation.

Third, used at the end of a file, CLEAR eliminates all memory variables and closes all files so that following activity is predictable. If you call one command file from another, and the first command file requires a memory variable for operation, you can list the variable as a GLOBAL memory variable and use CHAIN (Module 10) as your connecting command.

TYPICAL OPERATION

In this illustration the CLEAR command is used to demonstrate its effect on an open database file and memory variables. The MEMBERS database, created in Module 17 and modified in Module 42 is used in the following procedure, but any database file can be used. Begin at the VP prompt.

1. Type **USE MEMBERS** and press **Return.**
2. Type **LIST NAME OFF** and press **Return**. Compare your screen to the following:

```
1>LIST NAME OFF
Williams, David
Phillips, George W.
Galvin, Theodore A.
1>
```

3. Type **STORE 45 TO MVAR1** and press **Return.**
4. Type **STORE 'Hello' TO MVAR2** and press **Return.**
5. Type **STORE T TO MVAR3** and press **Return.**
6. Type **LIST MEMO** and press **Return.** Notice the following:

```
1>LIST MEMO

Name          Type    Width    Contents
MVAR1           N       8      45
MVAR2           C       5      Hello
MVAR3           L       2      .T.
** Total **  3  variables, 15  bytes
1>
```

7. Type **CLEAR** and press **Return.**
8. Verify that CLEAR deleted all memory variables by typing **LIST MEMO** and pressing **Return.** Notice that the conversation reports "0 variables, 0 bytes."
9. Verify that CLEAR closed the database file by typing **LIST NAME OFF** and pressing **Return.** Notice that the conversation reports that no database is in use.
10. Turn to Module 5 to continue the learning sequence.

Module 13

CLOSE

DESCRIPTION

The CLOSE command is used to close one or more data (DBF) files and related files. There are three forms for the CLOSE command:

1. CLOSE — Closes the selected file and its indexes.
2. CLOSE#*file number* — Closes the data file and related indexes assigned that file number.
3. CLOSE ALL — Closes all open data and index files.

Other commands used to close files include CLEAR and QUIT. Type USE and press Return to close the active database.

APPLICATIONS

The CLOSE command is used to close files during VP-Info operation. It may be issued from the VP prompt or included in a command file. This command allows you to close a selected database while leaving others open. Without the ability to close specific files, you would have to use the CLOSE ALL command and then selectively reopen the ones needed.

TYPICAL OPERATION

In this illustration the MEMBERS database, modified in Module 42, is used. Next, the PHONE database from Module 2 is opened as a secondary database. Finally, the CLOSE command is used to close the MEMBERS database while the PHONE database stays open. Begin at the VP prompt.

1. Type **USE MEMBERS** and press **Return**.
2. Type **USE#2 PHONE** and press **Return** to open a second database.
3. To display the status of open files, type **STATUS** and press **Return**. Notice the display at the top of the screen:

```
Thursday, June 25, 1987          VP-Info STATUS

Rec #              File name     Indexed by
00001 *File 1 ... MEMBERS.DBF
00001  File 2 ... PHONE.DBF
00000  File 3 ...
00000  File 4 ...
00000  File 5 ...
00000  File 6 ...
```

4. Press **Esc** to return to the prompt.
5. Type **CLOSE** and press **Return** to close the MEMBERS database.
6. Type **STAT** to confirm that PHONE is still open but MEMBERS is closed. Compare the resulting screen display to this:

```
Thursday, June 25, 1987              VP-Info STATUS

Rec #             File name          Indexed by
00001 *File 1 ...
00001  File 2 ... PHONE.DBF
00000  File 3 ...
00000  File 4 ...
00000  File 5 ...
00000  File 6 ...
```

7. Press **Esc** to return to the prompt.
8. Now type **CLOSE ALL** and press **Return**.
9. Type **STATUS** and press **Return** to verify that the database is closed. Notice that no database name is displayed.
10. Turn to Module 12 to continue the learning sequence.

Module 14

COMPILE

DESCRIPTION

The COMPILE command takes a PRG file and creates a compiled file from it. When VP-Info uses a program, the program is always compiled first, for faster operation. A compiled program is one rewritten into machine-readable code and stored in a CPL file with the same filename as its PRG. The PRG file is retained, since the CPL file is — to the human reader — a jumble of meaningless symbols. VP-Info always makes a CPL file when you type DO *filename* from the VP prompt, and it always looks first for an existing CPL file before settling for a PRG file.

The CPL file made automatically in response to a DO command is erased after the operation is completed, but if the program crashes while being debugged, the automatic erasure may be bypassed. This can lead to some confusing effects. If you are working on a program and you make modifications after it crashes, and the modifications don't seem to be happening when you rerun the program, then the chances are that the CPL version of the program was not erased. Since VP-Info chooses the CPL version over your modified PRG version, you must manually delete the CPL file or it will be selected to run, rather than your modified file. A way around this phenomenon is to type SET DO OFF before running an untested program. Then the CPL is almost always erased automatically.

To see the benefits of compiling your program, consider these statistics: it takes roughly ten seconds to compile a program, which means 10+ seconds of load time every time you use a PRG file, and an additional ten seconds for each DO command in the file. Loading a CPL program of one to five thousand bytes (1 to 5K, or 200 to 1000 words) takes less than four seconds. A 5K PRG file is only about one to two kilobytes long after compiling. The length depends on the amount of display text included in the file. Display text, such as the actual menu in MENU.PRG, is not compressed when compiled. (This is another argument for using the text-handling features discussed in Modules 65 and 40.)

The form of the COMPILE command is COMPILE *filename*, where *filename* is a PRG file. The conversation responds

```
Compile program filename
1>
```

If you have SET DO OFF, then any DO commands inside the specified program are ignored temporarily. (VP-Info keeps track of them in ENV files with their filenames.) This is handy if you are debugging a program and do not want to wait for the entire elaborate compile process each time you rerun it; it also lessens the chance that a crash will leave behind a troublesome

CPL file. However, if DO is OFF, then the COMPILE command must be warned if it is to produce a proper CPL file at the end of the revision process. At that point, either type SET DO OFF or add the command LINK to your COMPILE command like this:

```
1>COMPILE filename LINK
```

Unlike other compilers, such as Turbo PASCAL, VP-Info does not produce independent programs that can run from the DOS prompt. To run a CPL file, you must be in the VP-Info environment. Paperback Software provides a Runtime System which licensed users may purchase and redistribute with their own VP-Info applications. The Runtime System is only that part of VP-Info needed to run CPL files.

All of the programming limitations discussed in Modules 25 and 10 also apply to CPL programs, of course.

APPLICATIONS

You can create economical applications by compiling your files, which makes them both smaller and faster. Ideally, an application's final form would be twofold: it would exist as a heavily commented PRG file, documented for easy modification, and as a small, compact CPL file, stripped by the compiler of all comments, its texts set aside in libraries or text files. If you are selling applications or writing them for office staff with little computer expertise, distributing CPL files protects your programs, which cannot be modified in that form.

TYPICAL OPERATION

In this illustration the MENU program from Module 71 is compiled and run to compare its size and speed to the original. Begin at the VP prompt.

NOTE

If you are not set up for the RUN COMMAND /C command, then make the required copy of MENU at the DOS prompt and then restart VP-Info.

1. Type **RUN COMMAND /C COPY MENU.PRG MENUCOMP.PRG** and press **Return.**
2. Type **COMPILE MENUCOMP** and press **Return.**
3. When the VP prompt reappears (about ten seconds later), type **DO MENU** and begin counting (or timing on your watch) until the full-screen menu appears. On a PC with a standard clock, this takes about 13 seconds. If you have an AT or a turbocharged system, the time is much less, and the CPL program is similarly accelerated.
4. When the screen requests a selection, respond by typing **7** to exit to VP prompt.
5. Back at the prompt, type **DO MENUCOMP** and press **Return**, timing until the menu screen appears. Notice that the screen is produced roughly three times as fast (4 seconds on a PC).
6. Type **7** again to exit from the program.

7. Type **RUN COMMAND /C DIR B:menu*.*** to examine the sizes of the two files (or exit to DOS and examine them). Compare your screen to the following:

```
1>RUN COMMAND /C DIR B: MENU*.*
1>_lume in drive B: has no label
  Directory of B:\

MENUCOMP PRG        1632  11-17-87     6:16a
MENUCOMP CPL        1303  12-01-87     3:18p
        2 File(s)       188416 bytes free
```

Notice that the VP prompt and the cursor are positioned after the RUN command so that the first line of the directory is partially erased.

The reduction here is only about 20%, but more than half of the MENU.PRG file is the text screen that makes the menu, and none of that has been compressed. The actual programming commands, about 750 bytes of the file, have been compressed by nearly fifty per cent.

8. Watch the screen messages as you create a compiled version of the DEMO files used in Module 9 by typing: **COMPILE DEMO1**.

As the file is compiled, each nested DO file is also compiled as needed. Notice that DEMO3 is compiled twice, once when it is called by DEMO2 and again when it is called by DEMO1.

9. To examine the results, type **RUN COMMAND /C DIR B:dem*.*** and press **Return**. Compare your screen to the following:

```
1>RUN COMMAND /C DIR B:DEM*.*
1>_lume in drive B has no label
 Directory of B:\

DEMO3     PRG       771   11-26-87     1:48a
DEMO1     PRG      1100   11-26-87     1:44p
DEMO2     PRG      1011   11-26-87     1:45p
DEMO1     CPL      1306   11-26-87     2:42p
        4 File(s)      186368 bytes free
```

Notice that even though the CPL program contains two copies of the DEMO3 program, so that it represents a total of 3653 bytes of PRG files, it is a little more than a third as many bytes.

10. If you have other PRG files available, try compiling them and making this comparison.
11. When you are finished experimenting with compiled files, type **QUIT** to return to the DOS prompt and erase the compiled files and DEMO files by typing the following DOS commands:

    DELETE B:*.CPL
    DELETE B:DEMO*.PRG

12. Turn to Module 43 to continue the learning sequence.

Module 15

COPY

DESCRIPTION

The COPY command lets you copy either an entire database file or selected records within the active database to a new database file. You can assign a filename of your choice to the copied file. A number of clauses are available with the COPY command. These include:

```
STRUCTURE
SDF
SDF DELIMITED WITH
```

All of these let you control the format of the newly created (copied) file.

The STRUCTURE clause lets you copy all or part of a database structure without the contents.

The SDF DELIMITED WITH clause formats the copied file with a field separator (delimiter), such as a single quotation mark.

The SDF clause lets you copy the database in standard data format, which produces an ASCII text file that is readable by most word processing programs.

The following list shows forms of the COPY command accompanied by explanations and an example of each.

1. COPY TO *filename* Copies database structure and contents to the named file. If the named file does not exist, it is created; if it exists, its previous contents and structure are erased.

```
1>COPY TO NEWFILE
```

2. COPY NEXT *n* TO *filename* Copies database structure and contents of next n records to the named file.

```
1>COPY NEXT 10 TO NEWFILE
```

3. COPY TO *filename* FOR *expression* Copies database structure and contents to the named file for those records matching the expression.

```
1>COPY TO NEWFILE FOR AGE >= 18
```

4. COPY FIELDS *name1,name2,. . .* TO *filename* Copies structure and contents of specified fields to the named file.

```
1>COPY FIELDS NAME,ADR,CSZ TO NEWFILE
```

5. COPY FIELDS *name1,name2* TO *filename* FOR *expression*   Copies structure and contents of specified fields to the named file for those records matching the expression.

```
1>COPY FIELDS NAME, AGE TO NEWFILE FOR AGE >= 18
```

6. COPY STRUCTURE TO *filename*   Copies database structure (without its contents) to the named file.

```
1>COPY STRUCTURE TO NEWFILE
```

7. COPY STRUCTURE TO *filename* FIELDS *name1,name2*   Copies database structure of the named fields (without contents) to the named file, without copying any other fields.

```
1>COPY STRUCTURE TO NEWFILE FIELDS NAME, AGE
```

8. COPY TO *filename* SDF   Copies database contents to the named file as a sequential (ASCII) text, with a carriage return at the end of each record. All trailing blanks are retained, and there are no spaces or markers of any kind separating the fields.

```
1>COPY TO NEWFILE.LST SDF
```

9. COPY TO *filename* SDF DELIMITED WITH *character*   Copies the database contents in sequential format to the named file, separating the fields with commas and placing the specified character at the beginning and end of each field.

```
1>COPY TO NEWFILE SDF DELIMITED WITH '
```

The DELIMITED and SDF clauses are also used with the APPEND command to add standard ASCII data files to a VP-Info database. This application is described in Module 5.

CAUTION

The creation and use of SDF files, a feature provided primarily for dBASE programmers, is complicated by exceptions and limitations. VP-Info provides its own alternate set of commands for writing sequential files which are much easier to work with. See Module 59.

APPLICATIONS

The ability to COPY an entire database, selected records, or selected fields of only certain records makes the COPY command extremely flexible. And the ability to copy a database as a sequential (ASCII) file allows the user to prepare the contents of a database for use with other programs.

You can also use the SDF options to create files usable by a conventional word processing program. This means you can prepare word processed reports from database files. This is an extremely valuable capability for several reasons.

First, you can output selected fields and records to the word processor file using FIELD and FOR *expression* as described in the above list. This provides a file that is automatically "preprocessed" to save manual editing of unwanted records and fields. Second, you can use VP-Info's SORT command (Module 61) to alphabetize the output using a field of your choice as the object of the sort.

If you wish to view, or view and "touch up," a file that has been copied with DELIMITED or SDF, you can use VP-Info's full-screen editor by typing WRITE *filename*.TXT and pressing Return. (Be sure to specify the TXT extension, or VP-Info mistakenly assumes you want to write *filename*.PRG.) The copied file is displayed. If it's all right the way it is, press Ctrl-Q to quit. If editing is necessary, make your changes, and then press End to save the changed file. Both Ctrl-Q and End take you back to the VP prompt.

TYPICAL OPERATION

In this illustration the COPY command is used to transfer data from a sample database in several file formats. The copied files are displayed using the TEXT command. Begin at the VP prompt.

1. Type **CREATE STOCK** and press **Return.**
2. Prepare the following file structure, pressing **End** and then **Return** when the seventh field space appears after you type the information for QTY_OUT.

Name	Type	Width	Dec
PART_NO	C	15	0
DESCRIP	C	20	0
COST	N	7	2
PRICE	N	7	2
QTY_IN	N	7	0
QTY_OUT	N	7	0
<End>			

3. Type **APPEND** and enter this data as the first four records, pressing **End** when the entry fields for Record 5 appear:

PART_NO	DESCRIP	COST	PRICE	QTY_IN	QTY_OUT
TX-345-02	BOOT, TIRE	2.76	4.95	20	11
GG-4544-15	TUBE, INNER	6.55	11.95	48	23
BR-78R-14	TIRE, RADIAL	33.45	56.55	24	14
FS-3455-120W	BATTERY, MAINT. FREE	22.47	34.95	12	7
<End>					

4. Type **COPY FIELDS PART_NO, DESCRIP, PRICE TO TEMP** and press **Return.**
5. Type **USE TEMP** and press **Return.**

6. Type **LIST OFF** and press **Return** and examine the contents.

```
1>LIST OFF
TX-345-0Z        BOOT, TIRE               4.95
GG-4544-15       TUBE, INNER             11.95
BR-78R-14        TIRE, RADIAL            56.55
FS-3455-120W     BATTERY, MAINT.FREE     34.95
```

7. Type **USE STOCK** and press **Return**.
8. Type **COPY FIELDS PART_NO, DESCRIP, COST FOR COST > 10 TO TEMP SDF** and press **Return**.
9. Type **TEXT TEMP.TXT** and press **Return**. Notice the records in this file.

```
1>TEXT TEMP.TXT
BR-78R-14        TIRE, RADIAL            33.45
FS-3455-120W     BATTERY, MAINT.FREE     22.47
1>
```

10. Type **COPY FIELD PART_NO, DESCRIP, COST TO TEMP SDF DELIMITED WITH #** and press **Return**.
11. Type **WRITE TEMP.TXT** and press **Return**. Notice the appearance of the records in this file; notice also that the COPY command wrote over (erased) the first TEMP.TXT file.

```
TEMP.TXT                                 VP-Info WRITE                    INSERT

....+....1....+....2....+....3....+....4....+....5....+....6....+....7....+....8
#TX-345-0Z        #,#BOOT, TIRE           #,    2.76◄
#GG-4544-15       #,#TUBE, INNER          #,    6.55◄
#BR-78R-14        #,#TIRE, RADIAL         #,   33.45◄
#FS-3455-120W     #,#BATTERY, MAINT.FREE  #,   22.47◄
```

12. Press **Ctrl-Q** and type **Y** to exit from the Editor.
13. Type **DELE FILE TEMP.TXT** and press **Return**. The TEMP.TXT file is deleted.
14. Type **DELE FILE TEMP.DBF** and press **Return**. The TEMP.DBF file is deleted.
15. Type **CLEAR ALL** and press **Return** to close all files.
16. Turn to Module 61 to continue the learning sequence.

Module 16
COUNT

DESCRIPTION

The COUNT command is used to return the number of records in a database file. Used alone, the COUNT command returns a numeric value equal to the number of records in a database. If the FOR expression is used, then it returns a number equal to the number of records meeting the expression. The COUNT value, which is an integer (whole number), can also be saved to a designated memory variable. Some forms of the COUNT command are shown in the following list.

1. COUNT — Counts the number of records in the database in use and displays the number.

```
1>COUNT
   13 COUNT(S)
```

2. COUNT FOR *expression* — Counts the number of records in the database meeting the expression.

```
1>COUNT FOR AMOUNT > 2
```

3. COUNT TO *memory variable* — Stores the number of records in the database to the designated memory variable.

```
1>COUNT TO MVCT
1>? MVCT
      13.00
```

4. COUNT FOR *expression* TO *memory variable* — Stores the number of records in the database meeting the expression to the designated memory variable.

```
1>COUNT FOR AMOUNT = 3 TO MVCT
1>? MVCT
       3.00
```

APPLICATIONS

The COUNT command is convenient for determining the number of records that contain a certain value. The value returned by the COUNT command is useful in computations that require the number of records as part of an arithmetic expression. The COUNT command is often used in the interactive mode, and it is also used in command files. It is often used to determine the last record number in the active database.

TYPICAL OPERATION

In this illustration the COUNT command is used in a command file. You use it to display statistical information about the PICNIC database file created in Module 64. Begin at the VP prompt.

1. Type **WRITE COUNT** and press **Return** to use the VP-Info editor.
2. Type the COUNT command file. (Do not type the explanatory remarks.)

```
                                                    Remarks
* COUNT.PRG — Uses COUNT to produce statistical information.
CLS                             ; Clears the screen.
USE PICNIC                      ; Puts PICNIC database in use.
COUNT TO MRecs                  ; Counts number of records to memvar MRecs.
SUM GUESTS TO MGst              ; Sums GUESTS fields to memvar MGst.
COUNT FOR GUESTS = 1 TO M1      ; Stores count for the number of records
COUNT FOR GUESTS = 2 TO M2      ; which contain each possible value for
COUNT FOR GUESTS = 3 TO M3      ; the number of guests into a memory
COUNT FOR GUESTS = 4 TO M4      ; variable whose name is keyed to the
COUNT FOR GUESTS = 5 TO M5      ; appropriate number.
? '      DESCRIPTION                    NUMBER'  ; Lines beginning
? '      -----------                    ------'  ; with ? print the text
? ' MEMBERS WITH 1 GUEST        :   ', M1        ; in quotes followed by the
? ' MEMBERS WITH 2 GUESTS       :   ', M2        ; indicated memory variable.
? ' MEMBERS WITH 3 GUESTS       :   ', M3
? ' MEMBERS WITH 4 GUESTS       :   ', M4
? ' MEMBERS WITH 5 GUESTS       :   ', M5
? ' AVERAGE GUESTS PER MEMBER :   ', MGst/MRecs
? ' TOTAL MEMBERS               :   ', MRecs
? ' TOTAL GUESTS                :   ', MGst
? '                                   ------'
? '        TOTAL ATTENDANCE     :   ', MGst + MRecs
? '                                   ======'
?
WAIT                            ; Pauses operation until key is pressed.
ERASE                           ; Clears the screen.
CLEAR ALL                       ; Closes database and clears memory variables.
CANCEL                          ; Returns control to VP prompt.
```

3. Press **End** and then **Return** to write the command file to disk.
4. Run the command file by typing **DO COUNT** and pressing **Return**. Notice the information displayed by the command file.

```
    DESCRIPTION                        NUMBER
    -----------                        ------
  MEMBERS WITH 1 GUEST        :          0.00
  MEMBERS WITH 2 GUESTS       :          2.00
  MEMBERS WITH 3 GUESTS       :          6.00
  MEMBERS WITH 4 GUESTS       :          5.00
  MEMBERS WITH 5 GUESTS       :          0.00
  AVERAGE GUESTS PER MEMBER   :          3.23
  TOTAL MEMBERS               :         13.00
  TOTAL GUESTS                :         42.00
                                       ------
      TOTAL ATTENDANCE        :         55.00
                                       ======

 WAITING
```

5. When you are through experimenting with the command file, type **DELETE FILE COUNT.PRG** and press **Return**.
6. Turn to Module 4 to continue the learning sequence.

Module 17

CREATE

DESCRIPTION

The CREATE command is used to build a database from scratch. If you followed the sample session in Module 2, you used the CREATE command to create the PHONE database file. To create a new database, type: CREATE *filename* and press Return at the VP prompt. The filename may have from one to eight characters in it. When you press Return, VP-Info displays:

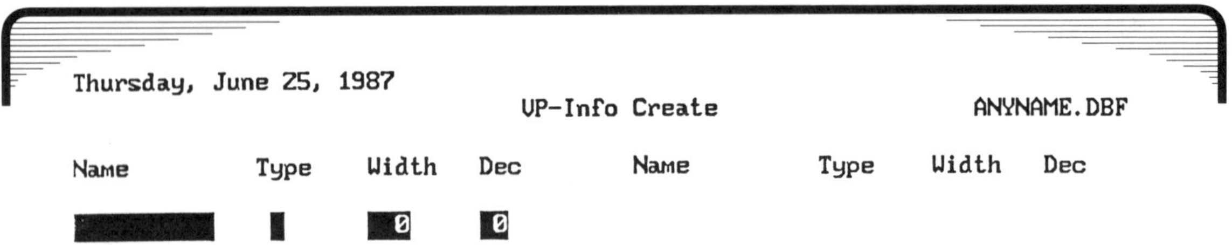

At this point, VP-Info is waiting for you to assign field names, field types, field widths, and the number of decimal places if the field is a numeric type. The following list provides information about names, types, widths, and decimal places.

Field Name — A field name can be up to ten characters in length, must start with an alphabetical character, and may contain numbers or underscores, but no spaces. Your field name should identify the contents as clearly as possible to make it easy to remember.

Type — The type may be C for character, L for logical, or N for numeric. Character type fields can contain letters, numbers, punctuation marks, or spaces. Logical type fields can contain a true (T) or false (F), yes (Y) or no (N), or a blank. Numeric type fields can only contain numbers and a decimal point.

Width — The maximum widths of fields are:

Character	—	254 characters (or bytes)
Logical	—	1
Number	—	20 (including the decimal point if one is used)

Dec — This is the number of decimal places for a numeric field. For dollars and cents values, you should type 2 in this field. Keep in mind that the number you specify is used to set aside that many places of the value you typed for width, plus one for the decimal point itself. In other words, if you specify width of 7 and 2 decimals in a dollar and cents field, the highest value allowed in the field is $9999.00. The maximum allowable number of decimal places is 6.

A typical (Type 2) database record can have up to 32 fields, and no single character field can exceed 254 bytes.

A sample database structure follows. Notice that the field parameters, which you type when you create your database structure, are displayed directly beneath the appropriate headings. You can delete an unwanted field by putting the cursor on the desired line and pressing Ctrl-T. To insert a field line, position the cursor and press Ctrl-N. If your database has more than 12 fields, VP-Info jumps to the second column automatically, then on to the third after 24 fields. To move across these 12 field columns, press Ctrl-L to go left or Ctrl-K to go right.

NOTE

You can add a boxed menu of editing keys to the bottom of the screen by typing SET MENU ON at the VP prompt.

```
Thursday, June 25, 1987
                              VP-Info Create                         ANYNAME.DBF

Name         Type    Width   Dec      Name         Type      Width   Dec
```

Name	Type	Width	Dec	Remarks		
PRODUCT	C	20	0	Type PRODUCT <cr>	C	20 <cr>
PRICE	N	6	2	Type PRICE <cr>	N	6 2 <cr>
IN_STOCK	L	1	0	Type IN-STOCK <cr>	L	1 <cr>
		0	0	Press End to end CREATE.		

Pressing End displays the prompt:

```
Save this file as type 1 or 2 or 3 ... 2
```

Type 2 or press Return (or any key except 1, 3, or Esc) to create a standard, dBASE II-type file with a maximum of 32 fields per record. Pressing Esc cancels the creation process, discarding the work. Typing 1, 2, or 3 saves the file in the specified type. Type 1 is exclusive to VP-Info and can use 256 fields per record. Type 3 is the same as dBASE III files, allowing 128 fields. Types 1 or 3 can only be used after a SET FIELDS TO command has modified the computer's data table to allow more than 32 fields.

To add data to your new database, you type APPEND, which presents you with a blank record to edit, with each field in reverse video. You can then type the new contents in the fields of your sample database. While appending, if you make a typographical error, you may return to it with the cursor keys and retype (until you complete that record). Use the Backspace or Del key to erase. Once you enter a value in the last field, a new blank record is displayed for data entry.

Completed records cannot be edited in the APPEND mode. The APPEND process continues until you press End. Pressing End takes you back to the VP prompt.

The structure of your database can be changed using the MODIFY command described in Module 42. The contents of a record are edited using the BROWSE, EDIT, or REPLACE commands (Modules 8, 28, or 51).

APPLICATIONS

The CREATE command is the first command used by most VP-Info users. With it you can assign a filename and design the structure of a new database. Your choice of both filename and field names should be meaningful to you, the user. In fact, the very structure of the database including field types and lengths can be tailored to fit your personal needs. Therefore, the flexibility of the CREATE command makes VP-Info a powerful tool for use with custom applications.

TYPICAL OPERATION

In this illustration the CREATE command is used to design a database that contains information about each member in a professional organization. The information includes name, address, professional affiliation, birth date, age, dues status, and general information. Go ahead and CREATE this database, because it is used later with other commands. Begin at the VP prompt.

1. Type **CREATE MEMBERS** and press **Return**. VP-Info displays the following:

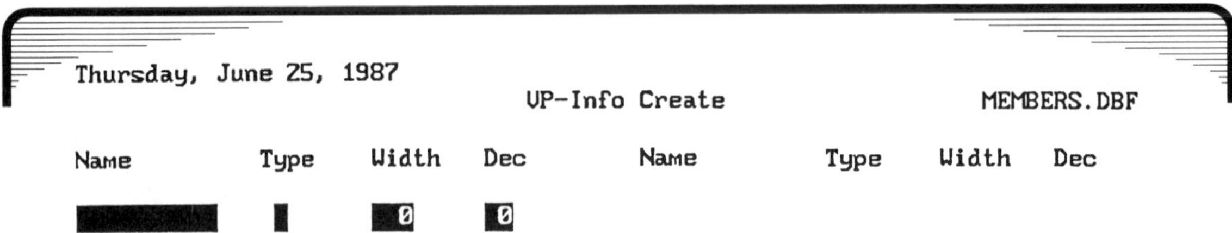

2. Create the database structure by typing the following. (Notice that the cursor jumps automatically to the Width after you type a single letter representing the Type, and it skips the Decimal for Character or Logical Types.)

Thursday, June 25, 1987

VP-Info Create MEMBERS.DBF

Name	Type	Width	Dec	Name / Type / Width / Dec — *Remarks*
NAME	C	25	0	Type NAME <cr> C 25 <cr>
ST_ADR	C	25	0	Type ST_ADR <cr> C 25 <cr>
C_S_Z	C	25	0	Type C_S_Z <cr> C 25 <cr>
AFFIL	C	25	0	Type AFFIL <cr> C 25 <cr>
JOINED	C	8	0	Type JOINED <cr> C 8 <cr>
AGE	N	2	0	Type AGE <cr> N 2 <cr>
PAID_UP	L	1	0	Type PAID_UP <cr> L 1 <cr>
INFO	C	50	0	Type INFO <cr> C 50 <cr>

3. Press **End** to end CREATE and then press **Return** to save the file as a Type 2.
4. Type **APPEND** and enter the data as shown.

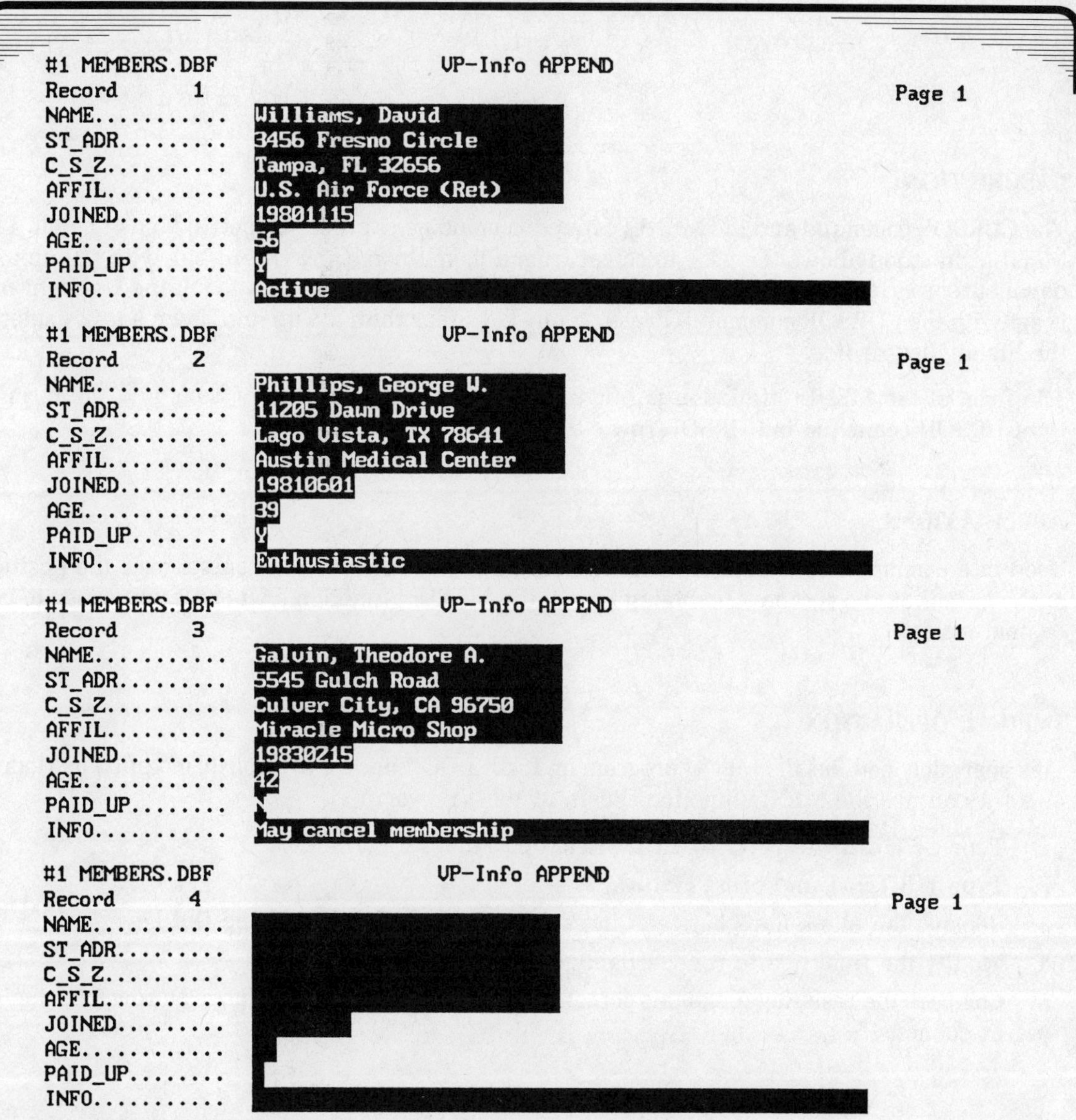

```
#1 MEMBERS.DBF                VP-Info APPEND
Record      1                                              Page 1
NAME..........  Williams, David
ST_ADR........  3456 Fresno Circle
C_S_Z.........  Tampa, FL 32656
AFFIL.........  U.S. Air Force (Ret)
JOINED........  19801115
AGE...........  56
PAID_UP.......  Y
INFO..........  Active
#1 MEMBERS.DBF                VP-Info APPEND
Record      2                                              Page 1
NAME..........  Phillips, George W.
ST_ADR........  11205 Dawn Drive
C_S_Z.........  Lago Vista, TX 78641
AFFIL.........  Austin Medical Center
JOINED........  19810601
AGE...........  39
PAID_UP.......  Y
INFO..........  Enthusiastic
#1 MEMBERS.DBF                VP-Info APPEND
Record      3                                              Page 1
NAME..........  Galvin, Theodore A.
ST_ADR........  5545 Gulch Road
C_S_Z.........  Culver City, CA 96750
AFFIL.........  Miracle Micro Shop
JOINED........  19830215
AGE...........  42
PAID_UP.......  N
INFO..........  May cancel membership
#1 MEMBERS.DBF                VP-Info APPEND
Record      4                                              Page 1
NAME..........
ST_ADR........
C_S_Z.........
AFFIL.........
JOINED........
AGE...........
PAID_UP.......
INFO..........
```

5. Press **End** when record 4 appears to end the entry.

The database structure is created, three records have been added, and you are back at the VP prompt, with your new database in use.

6. To close the database file, type **CLOSE** and press **Return**.
7. Turn to Module 24 to continue the learning sequence.

Module 18

CURSOR, MENU( )

DESCRIPTION

The CURSOR command and the MENU( ) function combine to create a special kind of menu. The MENU( ) function allows the user to select from a menu by moving a light bar with the up and down cursor keys until the desired choice is highlighted. The initial position of the highlight bar is set with the CURSOR command. Pressing any key other than the up and down arrows selects the highlighted choice.

The form of the MENU( ) function is MENU(*number of choices,width of bar*), and the form of the CURSOR command is CURSOR(*row,col*).

APPLICATIONS

Used in a command file, the CURSOR command allows you complete control over the position of the cursor on the screen. Combining it with the MENU( ) function, you can create easy-to-use custom menus.

TYPICAL OPERATION

This operation modifies the MENU program and ADRBOOK library previously modified in Module 40 so it can use the MENU function. Begin at the VP prompt.

1. Type **SET LIBRARY TO ADRBOOK** to open the library file.
2. Type **WRITE .1** and press **Return**.
3. Remove the blank lines between the selections with **Ctrl-Y** and the **Del** key.
4. Modify the final line to read "Highlight your selection."
5. Compare the resulting file to this screen. Notice that the first selection is on row 6 beginning at column 15.

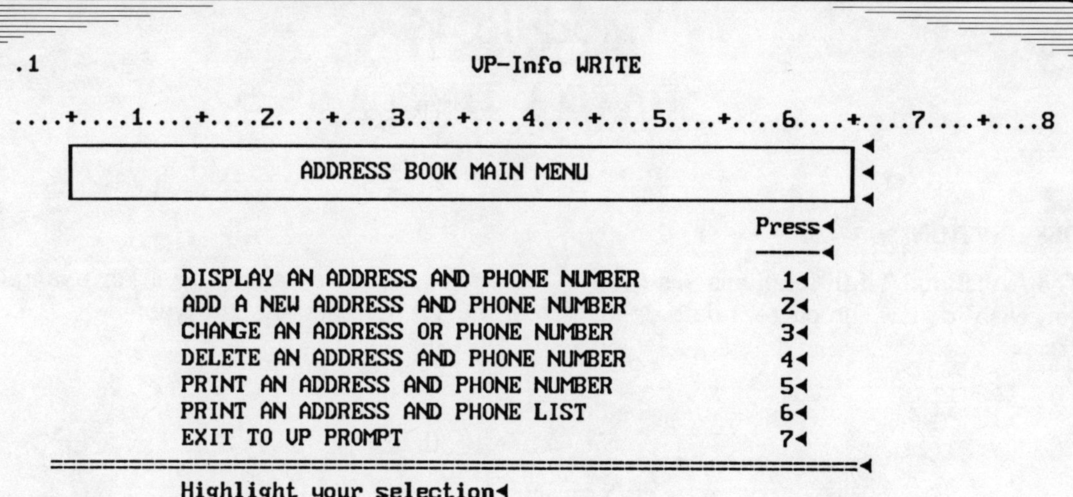

```
.1                              VP-Info WRITE
....+....1....+....2....+....3....+....4....+....5....+....6....+....7....+....8
                        ADDRESS BOOK MAIN MENU

                                                        Press
                                                        -----
            DISPLAY AN ADDRESS AND PHONE NUMBER           1
            ADD A NEW ADDRESS AND PHONE NUMBER            2
            CHANGE AN ADDRESS OR PHONE NUMBER             3
            DELETE AN ADDRESS AND PHONE NUMBER            4
            PRINT AN ADDRESS AND PHONE NUMBER             5
            PRINT AN ADDRESS AND PHONE LIST               6
            EXIT TO VP PROMPT                             7
============================================================
            Highlight your selection
```

6. Press **End** and then **Return** to save the library volume.
7. Type **WRITE MENU** and press **Return** to edit the MENU program.
8. Modify the first eleven lines to read as follows (remarks and boldface indicate changed lines):

```
* MENU.PRG – A command file for displaying the address book menu.
ERASE
SET LIBRARY TO ADRBOOK
SET TALK OFF
* Use a DO WHILE loop to sustain operation.
DO WHILE T
    STORE 0 to Select           ; MENU( ) takes numerical arguments.
    TEXT .1
CURSOR 6,15                     ; Delete the READ command.
Select=MENU(7,50)               ; Reading the light bar position.
Choice=STR(Select,1)            ; Convert the position to a string.
* Use series of CASE statements to run the selected command file,
* exit to the VP prompt, or exit to the operating system.
```

9. Go to the CASE Choice = '7' portion of the program and add the following command line before the RETURN:

```
SET LIBRARY TO                  ; Closes Library on exit.
```

10. Press **End** and then **Return** to save the new file.
11. Type **DO MENU** and experiment with the new menu functions. When you are through experimenting with the program, do not delete it; save it for later modules.
12. Turn to Module 57 to continue the learning sequence.

Module 19

DATE( ), TIME( )

DESCRIPTION

The DATE and TIME functions are used to return the system date and time. For example, if you wish to view the current date or time from the VP prompt, you can type:

```
1>? DATE( )
19871201
1>? TIME( )
06:23:21
```

Each time you use the system date or time, its current value is stored to the :DATE or :TIME system variable as a character string in the format requested. This means that you can also use ? :DATE to print the date, but :TIME always contains the last time you asked for rather than the current time. You can store the date or time to a memory variable using:

```
X = DATE(number)
```

or

```
STORE DATE(number) TO X
```

where the number refers to a series of formats covered later in this section. In either case, the date is ready for use. You can also print the date and time on a report using a command like:

```
? 'Report Date:  ',DATE(4)
? 'Report Time:  ',TIME( )
```

You can store a date string in a variety of formats, and then you can display a date in a variety of formats with X = DATE(n), where n is a number representing one of nine display formats. Similarly, T = TIME(n) permits you to choose from three display formats.

The date and time formats are listed and described in Appendix D.

Do not confuse the display format operations with the input format operations described in Module 60 under SET DATE TO. The number included in a DATE( ) function controls the format for displaying a date string. However, for DATE( ) to read a date string, you must have SET DATE TO selected for the format in which that string was stored. The default, or startup, format is YYYYMMDD. This format is useful for sorting on dates or doing mathematical functions on the date's value. If you type SET DATE TO 'MMDDYY' you are telling the program that the string "100211" means October 2, 2011. If you change the date setting to 'YYDDMM,' the string remains the same, but it is read as November 2, 2010, and displayed in the format specified in the DATE( ) function. An example should clarify this:

First, you can recall the current input setting, to find out how dates are read by typing

```
1>? date(7)                       ; The SET DATE input format is choice 7.
```

You can adjust the setting with the following sequence:

```
1>set date to 'yymmdd'
1>ok=date(7)                      ; Initialize :DATE to fit new format.
```

Once you have done that, the following commands return these results:

```
1>? :DATE
120287
1>Today = '100206'                ; Any one of three dates.
1>? DATE(4,Today)
Saturday, February 6, 2010        ; Output current read format (4).
1>SET DATE TO 'DDMMYY'            ; Change reading of date strings
1>? DATE(4,Today)
Tuesday, February 10, 2006        ; Format 4, but a new read format.
1>? DATE(7)                       ; Print today's date as DDMMYY, initialize :DATE.
021287                            ; :DATE changed
1>? DATE(4,:DATE)
Tuesday, December 2, 1987         ; If :DATE had not been initialized, the read format would have
                                    forced the DDMMYY format on the old :DATE, giving a result
                                    of "Wednesday, February 12, 1987."
```

Failing to reset :DATE with the new input format causes the following results:

```
1>SET DATE TO 'MMDDYY'
1>? DATE(4,:DATE)                 ; The string in :DATE is '021287'
February 12, 1987
1>? DATE(7)                       ; Print and save the system date in the new format.
1>? DATE(4,:DATE)
Tuesday, December 2, 1987
```

You cannot change the system date and clock from inside VP-Info. Both DATE( ) and DATE(7) change the string in :DATE, but only DATE(7) creates a :DATE compatible with the current SET DATE command. Any DATE(n) function call changes the string in :DATE. To use :DATE without changing it, use the form

```
1>? DATE(n,:DATE)
```

or store :DATE to a memory variable.

DATE AND TIME MATH VP-Info provides functions for doing mathematical operations involving numbers of days. Time math can be performed using the TIME(3) format, which displays time as seconds expired since midnight, and the VAL( ) function to convert the Time string to a number. This operation was demonstrated in Module 50.

Date math requires three special operators; they are:

1. DAYS(*date string1,date string2*), which returns the number of days between the first and second date as a positive or negative number.

```
1>? days('19840226','19850226')
     366.00
1>? days('19850226','19860226')
     365.00
1>? days('19880226','19860226')
    -730.00
```

2. DAYS(*date string,number*), which returns the date before or after the specified date. If today is December 1, 1987, then:

```
1>? date(4,days(today,37)
Wednesday, January 7, 1987
1>? date(2,days(today,-37)
10/25/87
```

3. MONTHS(*date string1,date string2*), which returns the number of whole months between the first and second date.

```
1>? months(today,'19871101')
        -1.00
1>? months(today,'19871130')
        -1.00
```

Since these are pure math functions, entering irrational dates can yield unexpected, if predictable results. For example, on December 1, 1987, DAYS(Today, '19871130') gives a – 1.00 result, and DAYS(Today,'9871132') gives a + 1.00 — December 2 is the 32nd day of November.

APPLICATIONS

The most common application of the DATE( ) and TIME( ) function is to display or print the current date and time on reports. This makes the DATE( ) and TIME( ) functions important, and you should familiarize yourself with them as well as with the other functions described in Appendix D.

You may wish to store the date or time to a memory variable, as shown in the previous examples, and then display the contents of the memory variable each time the date is needed. The alternative is to use the DATE( ) and TIME( ) functions directly. An example of a command file using both of these approaches is contained in the Typical Operation section of this module.

TYPICAL OPERATION

In this illustration the DATE( ) function is used in a command file. Begin at the VP prompt.

1. Type **WRITE DATE** and press **Return** to use the editor.
2. Type the following command file. (Do not type the explanatory remarks.)

```
                                         Remarks
* DATE.PRG – Show uses of the DATE( ) function.
CLS                               ; Clear the screen.
SET DATE TO 'yymmdd'              ; Set input format.
Ok=DATE(7)                        ; Initialize :DATE.
Mdate=DATE(4,:DATE)               ; Store a display format without changing :DATE.
? " TODAY'S DATE IS",DATE(4,:DATE) ; Display text followed by :DATE.
? " THE TIME IS",TIME( )          ; Display text and system time, set :TIME.
?                                 ; Display blank line.
? ' USE',Mdate,'ON ALL REPORTS.'    ; Display text and memory variable Mdate.
? ' USE :DATE ('+:DATE+') FOR Math and Sorting.'
If $(:DATE,3,4)>'1225'            ; If :DATE is after Christmas
Target=($(STR(VAL(:DATE)+10000,6),1,2)+'1225') ; Next year.
ELSE
Target=$(:DATE,1,2)+'1225'                              ; This year.
?
? ' Only',PIC(DAYS(:DATE,Target),'999'),' days till Christmas+'
CANCEL                            ; Returns control to VP prompt.
```

3. Press **Alt-F** to format the program, proofread it, and then press **End** to write the command file to disk.
4. Type **DO DATE** and press **Return** to run the command file; compare your screen to the following display.

```
TODAY'S DATE IS Tuesday, December 2, 1987
THE TIME IS 09:21:15

USE Tuesday, December 2, 1987  ON ALL REPORTS
USE :DATE (871202) FOR Math and Sorting.

Only 23 days till Christmas!
1>
```

5. Erase the DATE.PRG file by typing **DELE FILE DATE.PRG**.
6. Turn to Module 60 to continue the learning sequence.

Module 20

DEBUGGING COMMAND FILES

DESCRIPTION

VP-Info provides some special commands and settings whose function is to ease the process of writing, testing, and correcting command files. The following settings are useful while testing files:

1. SET LINE ON — This toggle switch is usually on. It includes line numbers in compiled files, so that VP-Info can use them to identify problem points. When you are ready to create a final program file, you can compress the CPL file by another couple of bytes per line if you SET LINE OFF before compiling the file.
2. SET STEP ON — Normally off, this switch holds execution of each line of the program, waiting for a keystroke. The line about to be executed is reported by number in the upper left corner of the screen. With a printout of the file, you can follow along and try to locate the spot that is causing trouble.
3. SET DEBUG ON — Normally off, this switch determines whether variables listed as part of a DEBUG command are listed. It allows you to track the changes in a variable as the file operates. In versions of VP-Info numbered 1.1 or higher, it also erases the current CPL file automatically if the program crashes.
4. SET ECHO ON — Normally off, this switch forces the printing of command lines while they are being compiled.
5. SET DO OFF — When turned off, this switch suppresses the compilation of nested DO commands, making it easier to debug selected portions of a file.

THE DEBUG COMMAND The DEBUG command itself looks like the VARIABLE command used to establish a variable table at the beginning of a file, and it functions like a switchable print (?) command. Here is the form of the DEBUG command:

```
DEBUG expressions
```

where the list of expressions is set up just like a line for the ? command.

With SET DEBUG OFF, the commands are ignored; with DEBUG ON, they are printed just like normal ? commands.

OTHER COMMANDS THAT CAN HELP WITH DEBUGGING Many of the commands in VP-Info are helpful during the testing and debugging process.

Adding the STATUS command to a file allows you to check files, indexes, settings, and the contents of variables.

Judiciously placed SET PRINT ON commands can produce hardcopy records when needed. The SET ALTERNATE and SPOOL commands can redirect information into a file for later examination.

IF . . . ENDIF structures triggered by unexpected results can help. For example, an IF EOF structure at a spot where the processing of records seems to run out of data unexpectedly could trigger the printing of some variables or simply issue the SET DEBUG ON command.

The ON ERROR structure can be used in commands keyed to specific types of errors to trigger messages.

Note and * markers can be used to temporarily disable portions of the debugging commands or problem areas, particularly to disable printer commands that would waste paper while debugging.

The Alt-F formatting command in the editor helps catch one of the most common errors, the failure to provide enough ENDs for your structures. If the file's last line is indented, there is definitely something wrong; even if it is not, check the nested structures to confirm that each one ends where and when it should.

COMMON ERRORS IN PROGRAM FILES There are surely as many ways to foul up a command file as there are commands, but some are fairly common and easy to check for. If a file does not work, chances are VP-Info will report the offending line and a relevant error message. Typing WRITE puts you back in the editor, positioned at the problem line. First check it for misspellings. If you call the variable holding the contents of a NAME Field "Mname," then mistype the variable as Nmame, VP-Info has no idea what you mean, and if you ask it to print NAME when you mean Mname, you are guaranteed peculiar results.

If the problem is not a typo, then check for errors related to the error message. Did you try to INPUT a character variable rather than a numerical one? INPUT only takes numbers. Did you store a field as a character variable and then try to divide it? Math functions only work on numeric variables. Did you ACCEPT a "Y/N" response as a character, and then try to use it as a logical type?

If neither simple procedure solves the problem, then print the file out (by putting it in the editor and then pressing Ctrl-P), and then SET STEP ON and run it again, to see which line is causing the problem. If you can, stop the file at the error point by pressing Esc instead of Return at a given line to cancel execution, and then use STAT or LIST MEMO to check current values.

If the trouble is a variable whose value is not behaving, add a DEBUG command to the beginning of the file, referencing the offending variable, and SET DEBUG ON to print its changing value.

APPLICATIONS

Getting a new command file to work can be the most maddening aspect of working with a relational and programmable database. That the error is often some trivial typing mistake or minuscule oversight is no consolation, especially if the result was a locked up computer or a scrambled data disk.

Use the DEBUG facilities liberally while writing your programs, and you can save yourself some grief and frustration.

TYPICAL OPERATION

In this illustration, a command file is developed and debugged for use with the MENU program last modified in Module 18. Begin at the VP prompt.

1. Type **WRITE MENU** and press **Return** to use the editor.
2. Between the DO CASE command and the CASE Choice = '2' command, type these two lines:

   ```
   CASE Choice='1'
       DO SHOW
   ```

   and then press **End** to save the modified file.
3. To use the ADRBOOK itself, first add yourself, some friends if you like, and these three sample records, using the APPEND command:

Name	St_Adr	CSZ	HPhone
Custer, George A.	123 Rue Daie	Crow Agency, MT 58111	123-4567
Jefferson, Thomas	333 Monticello Dr.	Arlington, VA 12122	890-1234
McAllister, Mick	1260 E. Stratford	SLC, UT 84106	999-9999

   (Leave the WPhone and Notes fields blank in the three sample records.)
4. Next, type **INDEX ON Name to NAMEBOOK** and press **Return** to create this index.
5. Type the following command file. (Do not type the explanatory remarks.)

   ```
   * SHOW.PRG – Displays existing AdrBook records.
   ERASE
   Mname="                              "
   USE ADRBOOK INDEX NAMEBOOK
   @ 2,10 Say "Type Name to find: " GET Mname
   DEBUG "Name: ",Mname, "RecNo: ",#
   IF EOF
   ? "Not Found"
   WAIT
   CANCEL
   ENDIF
   ? Mname"'s Record: "
   DISP OFF
   ```

6. Press **Alt-F** to format the file and proofread it, then press **End** to save the file and, back at the VP prompt, type **DO SHOW** to run it. Notice that it doesn't stop for you to input a name. That may suggest what is wrong with the program, which contains one of the commonest VP-Info programming errors.
7. To isolate the error, type **SET DEBUG ON** and press **Return**, then type **SET STEP ON** and press **Return** again. From here on, the STEP command requires its own triggering keystroke for every command, whether in immediate or file mode.

8. Type **DO SHOW** and press **Return**. Notice that the message "line 0" appears at the top of the screen, and nothing else happens.
9. Press **Return** again to trigger the next step, which is compilation. Now the drive operates, and the line number changes to "1."
10. Press **Return** to trigger line 1. Continue pressing **Return**, following along with the notes below, keyed to the line about to be executed:

    4: Line 3 cleared the screen.
    6: Line 5 opened the file and index.
    7: Line 6 wrote the SAY message. Try to type a name.
    8: Attempting to type moved the line counter. Try again.
    9: It happened again, and somehow our line counts are all out of whack. However, the DEBUG command presents us with a message.
    14: We jumped straight to the ENDIF. Where is our input line?
    15: Line 13 printed the Record message, which is fouled up. The next Return concludes the program.

11. Type **WRITE** and press **Return** to go back to editing the SHOW program.
12. The necessary READ command is missing. Insert it on the line below the SAY command and press **End** to save the file.
13. Type **Do SHOW** and step through the program again. Now it stops to allow you to input a name when you press **Return** after the STEP command reports Line 6. Notice that pressing Return creates the familiar reverse video input field.
14. Type **Custer** and press **Return** (twice). Continue stepping through the program. Notice that it now works. Pressing **Return** for Line 8 causes DEBUG to print the variables specified. Pressing **Return** three more times causes the record itself to display.

You may wish to continue refining the SHOW program, using the skills you have acquired as a VP-Info programmer. To polish the program, you might TRIM the Mname so the apostrophe comes up next to the name. This is the last learning module; the appendixes present more information on various technical aspects of using VP-Info, including suggested training exercises, a complete list of all VP-Info functions, a glossary, and a discussion of networking with VP-Info.

Module 21

DELETE, RECALL, PACK

DESCRIPTION

This module describes commands used to mark and unmark records for deletion and the command that actually removes marked records from the active database. The deletion process begins with marking one or more records for deletion, using the DELETE command. The RECALL command unmarks records; the PACK command eliminates the marked records from the active database. Each of these commands is described in the following paragraphs.

DELETE The DELETE command can take the following forms:

1. DELETE	Marks the current record for deletion.
2. DELETE RECORD *n*	Marks record n for deletion.
3. DELETE NEXT *n*	Marks the next n records for deletion.
4. DELETE ALL	Marks all records in the database for deletion.
5. DELETE FOR *expression*	Marks current record for deletion if it matches the expression. May be used with ALL or NEXT.
6. DELETE WHILE *expression*	Marks all records for deletion, beginning at the current record, until it reaches a record not matching the expression. May be used with ALL or NEXT.
7. DELETE FILE INV	Deletes INV.DBF from the .DBF disk.
8. DELETE FILE SOME.DAT	Deletes SOME.DAT from the boot disk.
9. DELETE FILE B:TEMP.TXT	Deletes TEMP.TXT from the B disk.

When a database is listed using either the LIST or DISPLAY ALL command (Module 24), an asterisk appearing after the record number indicates that the record is marked for deletion. You can also mark a record for deletion when a database is displayed using the BROWSE command (Module 8). When using BROWSE, pressing Ctrl-U marks and unmarks (recalls) the current record.

When records are marked for deletion, they are not transferred during APPEND FROM, COPY, or SORT operations, nor are they included in AVERAGE, COUNT, POST, SUM, or TOTAL operations. If you type SET DELETE ON, then they are excluded from all operations except GO, EDIT, DISPLAY, or BROWSE commands that explicitly call their record numbers.

The FOR or the WHILE clause may be added to a DELETE, DELETE ALL, or DELETE NEXT *n* command to specify only records whose fields match a given expression. For example, if you want to delete all records that contain an AGE value less than 50, you can use this command:

```
DELETE ALL FOR AGE < 50
```

This command tells VP-Info to mark every record in the database that has an age field value between 0 and 49.

Similarly, if you have your records indexed by the year and you wish to delete all records prior to 1983, you may use this command:

```
DELETE WHILE YEAR < 1984
```

VP-Info deletes all records from the current record until it reaches a record with a year field of 1984 or higher. The difference between DELETE FOR and DELETE WHILE is that FOR searches from its starting point through the specified range (ALL, NEXT 100, etc.), deleting any matching records; WHILE stops at the first failure to match.

You may list deleted records before discarding them by typing:

```
LIST ALL FOR *.
```

The DELETE FILE command may be used to delete one specific file (no wild card symbols are allowed). If you wish to delete a backup file with the filename INVREC.BAK from the B drive, use this command:

```
DELETE FILE B:INVREC.BAK
```

If you have specified a default drive for the file in a FILES . . . ENDFILES structure (Module 31) in your CNF file, or if the file is on the logged drive, then you may leave off the drive identifier in the command.

RECALL The RECALL command is used to unmark those records that were marked for deletion. As with DELETE, RECALL has several forms:

1.	RECALL	Unmarks the current record.
2.	RECALL RECORD *n*	Unmarks record n.
3.	RECALL NEXT *n*	Unmarks any deleted records in the next n records.
4.	RECALL ALL	Unmarks all records in the database.
5.	RECALL FOR *expression*	Unmarks the current record if it matches the expression. May be used with ALL or NEXT.
6.	RECALL WHILE *expression*	Unmarks all deleted records from the current record until it finds one not matching the expression. May be used with ALL or NEXT.

The clauses work with RECALL in much the same way that they do with DELETE. RECALL NEXT might seem a little different, since it looks for deletions in the next *n* records rather than recalling the next *n* deletions.

Given the following list of data, with record #1 current, the command RECALL NEXT 2 results in 0 RECALL(S) because VP-Info only checks record #1 and record #2.

```
00001  Smith, John              (408) 232-1210
00002  Jones, Paul              (813) 267-9500
00003 •Hood, J.T.               (408) 221-3454
00004 •Maxwell, Mary            (214) 232-4545
00005 •Jackson, Lois            (201) 599-6111
00006  Acme Brick Company       (512) 960-1415
```

For RECALL to work with a scope, you must have DELETED set OFF (Module 60), or RECALL cannot see the records previously deleted.

PACK The PACK command deletes the marked records from the database in use and resets the record numbers. For example, if you have three records marked for deletion in a ten-record database, the PACK command eliminates the marked records and renumbers the remaining records from 1 to 7. Don't PACK a database until you are ready to eliminate the marked records, because they are gone for good once the database is packed.

If you PACK an indexed file (Module 38), the marked records are eliminated from both the index and the database simultaneously, a lengthy process on a larger database. The automatic reindexing takes a little longer than the actual packing process. If you are doing a number of delete and pack tasks in the same session, you may want to close the index during the process, and then reindex after all the packs are done. In general, you can save processing time by only packing the database when necessary, rather than routinely after any delete.

APPLICATIONS

One obvious application for the DELETE and PACK commands is eliminating unwanted records. The DELETE FILE command is a "housekeeping tool" for eliminating unwanted files from your disks. For example, when you modify a command file, VP-Info creates a backup copy with the BAK extension. You can recover the disk space used by the backup file with the DELETE FILE command. For wildcard deletions use the DOS DELETE command. (See Module 53 on running DOS commands from inside VP-Info.)

A convenient application of the DELETE command is "aging" your data files. If you wish to remove year-old accounts from a disk at the beginning of 1988, you can copy those records to an OLDCUST archive file and then delete them using these commands:

```
1>USE CUSTOMER                               ; Puts database in use.
1>COPY TO OLDCUST FOR $(LastSaleDt,1,4)<1986
• Transfers customers who have not purchased anything since 1986 into
• the archive.
1>DELETE FOR $(LastSaleDt,1,4)<1986          ; Deletes them from CUSTOMER.
1>PACK                                       ; Removes the records permanently.
```

All of these commands are used either interactively or in command files. Frequently they are used with the LOCATE (Module 41) or FIND (Module 32) commands to delete records containing specified information.

The DELETE FILE command is also used in command files to remove temporary files created to sort and display information. Deleting temporary sort files and "scratch pad" files restores valuable disk space for future use.

TYPICAL OPERATION

In this illustration a command file is prepared that deletes records from the MEMBERS database with an unpaid status (PAID = .F.). The command file makes use of the DELETE and PACK commands. Begin at the VP prompt.

1. Type **WRITE DELREC** and press **Return**. You are in VP-Info's editor.
2. Type the following DELREC.PRG command file. (Do not type the explanatory remarks or the indentation.)

```
* DELREC.PRG    Deletes all unpaid members from MEMBERS database.
ERASE                           ; Clears the screen.
? '          CHECK TO SEE IF ANY MEMBERS ARE UNPAID.'
? '          (UNPAID RECORDS ARE TAGGED ".F.")'       ; Displays message.
WAIT                            ; Pauses until a key is pressed.
ERASE                           ; Clears the screen.
USE MEMBERS                     ; Opens MEMBERS database.
DISPLAY ALL Name, Paid          ; Displays Name and Paid fields of MEMBER database.
?                               ; Prints a blank line.
?
? '          To Delete Unpaid Member Records, Press "D"'
? '            or Press Any Other Key to Quit.'        ; Displays message.
?
WAIT TO Option                  ; Pauses operation, stores next keystroke to memory
*                                 variable Option.
ERASE                           ; Clears screen.
IF !(Option) = 'D'              ; If Option is 'd' or 'D', do following commands.
DELETE All FOR .NOT. Paid       ; Marks all records that have a logical
*                                 False (or No) in the Paid field.
PACK                            ; Eliminates marked records.
ENDIF                           ; Concludes conditional commands.
RETURN                          ; Returns to the VP prompt.
```

3. Proofread the program, and then press **Alt-F** to format the command file. (Notice that the conditional commands in the IF. . .ENDIF structure are automatically indented.)
4. Press **End** and then **Return** to write the command file to disk.
5. Type **DO DELREC** and press **Return**.
6. The following message is displayed. Press **Return** to respond.

```
     CHECK TO SEE IF ANY MEMBERS ARE UNPAID.
     (UNPAID RECORDS ARE TAGGED ".F.")
WAITING
```

7. The following information is displayed on the screen.

```
00001  Williams, David          F
00002  Phillips, George W.      Y
00003  Galvin, Theodore A.      N


        To Delete Unpaid Member Records, Press "D"
           or Press Any Other Key to Quit.
WAITING
```

8. Type **D** to delete the unpaid records. Williams' and Galvin's records are marked for deletion, deleted, and packed, and then the prompt reappears.
9. Turn to Module 72 to continue the learning sequence.

Module 22

DIM

DESCRIPTION

The DIM command is used to declare a matrix variable. A matrix is an array, or table, of values stored as a single variable. All elements in a matrix must be of the same type, and each is identified by up to three numbers indicating its location in the table. Here are some sample array declarations:

DIM CHAR 20 NAME[5,5]	; Here, a character variable NAME is declared, which is to be stored as a table with 25 locations ranging from 1,1 to 5,5.
DIM NUM PRICE [2,10], COST [2,10]	; Two numerical variables are declared, each with its values stored in a table with 20 locations.
DIM LOG GATES[8,5,4]	; A logical variable is declared; its values are to be stored in a three dimensional table (a cube), in four layers with room for forty values per layer.

Notice that GATES only counts as one variable, yet it can hold 160 values, in effect functioning as a set of 160 variables, and leaving you another 127 memory variables to work with if you need them.

A matrix may take up to 64K of memory, and you may have as many as 20 matrix variables declared at once.

APPLICATIONS

A matrix offers two features: first, it allows you to increase the limits on memory variables by storing information in tabular form; second, information that is naturally tabular — prices and costs, for example — can be stored and then accessed easily.

TYPICAL OPERATION

In this illustration tables of products and prices are created, and products and prices are matched through references to array locations. Begin at the VP prompt.

1. Type **DIM CHAR Prod[2,3]** and press **Return**.
2. Type **DIM NUM Price[2,3]** and press **Return**.
3. Type **PROD[1,1] = 'STEAK'** and press **Return**.

4. Press the **Up Arrow**. Notice that the last line you typed reappears for editing.
5. Use the cursor keys to move the cursor to the second 1 and type **2** to change it, then move the cursor to "S" of "STEAK" and type **ROAST**. Your new line now reads:

```
1>PROD[1,2] = 'ROAST'
```

6. Press **Return** to execute the new command.
7. Press the **Up Arrow** again to retrieve the last command. Continue this process until you have entered all the following commands:

```
1>PROD[1,3] = 'HAMBURGER'
1>PROD[2,1] = 'DRUMSTICKS'
1>PROD[2,2] = 'BREAST'
1>PROD[2,3] = 'LIVERS'
```

8. Type **? PROD** and press **Return**. Compare your screen to this:

```
1>? PROD
STEAK      ROAST      HAMBURGER
DRUMSTICKS BREAST     LIVERS
```

9. Type **PRICE[1,1]=4.48** and press **Return**.
10. Press the **Up Arrow** and edit the command line to enter the following series of commands:

```
1>PRICE[1,2]=2.48
1>PRICE[1,3]=1.48
1>PRICE[2,3]=0.48
1>PRICE[2,2]=1.48
1>PRICE[2,1]=0.98
```

11. Type **? PRICE** to see the price array, which should look like this:

```
1>? PRICE
      4.48      2.48      1.48
      1.08      1.48      0.48
```

12. Type **CHICKEN = 2** and press **Return.**
13. Type **BREAST = 2** and press **Return.**
14. Type **? PRICE[Chicken,Breast]** and press **Return**. Notice that VP-Info reports the price as $1.48.
15. Type **? 'Chicken ',prod[2,3],' cost ',price[2,3],' per lb.'** and press **Return**, then compare your screen with the following:

```
1>? 'Chicken ',prod[2,3],' cost ',price[2,3],' per lb.'
Chicken  LIVERS      cost          0.48  per lb.
```

16. Type **Release all** and press **Return** to clear the matrix variables from memory.
17. Turn to Module 64 to continue the learning sequence.

Module 23

DIR

DESCRIPTION

The DIR command is similar to the DOS DIR command. It is used to list a directory of files on the screen. Typing DIR by itself and then pressing Return lists the files on the logged drive. A typical listing might resemble the following:

```
.              <DIR>  11-03-87  7:05a   ..             <DIR>  11-03-87  7:05a
REVISION.VPI    1169 03-24-88 12:03a   VPI.EXE       258240 09-30-87  1:40a
VPI.ERR        10624 09-30-87  1:40a   VPI.CNF          384 09-30-87  0:00a

270417 bytes in 4 files.
19456704 bytes remaining.
```

You can also use the DOS wild card (*) to list selected files. For example, if you want to list all filenames having the extension PRG, you can use the command form:

```
1>DIR B:*.PRG
```

Every filename on B having the extension PRG is listed.

Notice that these two command forms are identical to those used by DOS. The only difference between the VP-Info DIR command and the DOS DIR command is that VP-Info reports files having no extension when you type: DIR R*.

APPLICATIONS

The DIR command is used to review filenames on the specified disk drive.

TYPICAL OPERATION

In this illustration the DIR command is used to check all filenames having the extension PRG. Start at the VP prompt.

1. Type **DIR B:*.PRG** and press **Return**.
2. Notice the display.

```
1>DIR B:*.PRG
PHONELST.PRG


169 bytes in 1 files.
122128 bytes remaining.

1>
```

3. Turn to Module 49 to continue the learning sequence.

Module 24

DISPLAY, LIST, SYSTEM VARIABLES

DESCRIPTION

This module describes the DISPLAY and LIST commands, which are used to display the contents of a database. The # function (where # stands for *record number*) is also introduced. The # function is used to display or store database record numbers. The term *current record* represents the current location of the record pointer. BROWSE is another command used to display the contents of a database. However, BROWSE allows you to edit the contents. The BROWSE command is described in Module 8.

Before the DISPLAY or LIST commands or the # function is used, a database must be opened with the USE command. Once the database is open, you can position the record pointer to records within the database using the GO and SKIP commands, which are described in detail in Module 35.

DISPLAY The DISPLAY command is used to perform a number of tasks. It can:

1. Display the contents or structure of a database.
2. Display the system settings.
3. Display the active memory variables and their contents.
4. Display and print database information simultaneously.

Here is a list of sixteen typical forms of the DISPLAY command:

1.	DISPLAY	; Displays current record's number and content.
2.	DISPLAY OFF	; Displays contents of current record; omits record number display.
3.	DISPLAY #	; Displays current record's number.
4.	DISPLAY NEXT *n*	; Displays record number and contents of the specified next *n* records.
5.	DISPLAY ALL	; Displays all records (similar to LIST, except that DISPLAY ALL pauses each time the screen fills, waiting for you to press a key before the display is continued).
6.	DISPLAY *field1, field2, . . .*	; Displays contents of specified fields in current record.
7.	DISPLAY ALL FOR *expression(s)*	; Displays all records matching the specified expression(s).
8.	DISPLAY ALL *fieldname(s)* FOR *expression(s)* OFF	; Combines forms 2, 6, and 7 above.

9. DISPLAY ALL FOR @('*expression*',*fieldname*)>0 ; Displays contents of records which have strings within the specified field that match the string in the expression.
10. DISPLAY WHILE *expression* ; Displays records while expression is true.
11. DISPLAY STRUCTURE ; Displays database structure.
12. DISPLAY MEMORY ; Displays active memory variables.
13. DISPLAY FILES ; Displays all database files on the logged disk drive.
14. DISPLAY FILES ON B: ; Displays all database files on the B drive.
15. DISPLAY FILES LIKE B:*.PRG ; Displays all files on drive B with the extension PRG. (The * wildcard can be substituted to represent all filenames and extensions.)
16. DISPLAY FILES LIKE B:MENU2-*.* ; Displays all files on drive B whose filenames begin "MENU2-" and who have extension names (used to check for BAK files).

Most of the forms in the above list are self explanatory; however, a few can use some examples for clarification. *Current record* means the record at which the record pointer is located. Instead of DISPLAY # you can use:

```
1> ? #
```

In form 6, *field1*, *field2* . . . represents one or more field names, as in:

```
1> DISPLAY NAME, ST_ADR, PAID_UP
```

Assuming the open database contains the indicated fields, this command displays the record number followed by the contents of the NAME, ST_ADR, and PAID_UP fields for the current record. If you want to display this information for all records, you can use:

```
1> DISPLAY ALL NAME, ST_ADR, PAID_UP
```

The same command followed by the OFF clause suppresses the display of the record numbers. If there is more data than one screen can show, the display stops when the screen is full and the cursor appears on the 24th line waiting for you to press any key (except Esc, which cancels the display) before showing the next screenful.

In forms 7-10, an expression is one or more values that match one or more fields within a record. For example, you could use:

```
1> DISPLAY ALL FOR $(JOINED,3,2)>= '81'.AND. .NOT. PAID_UP
```

This command displays the records with a year value greater than or equal to '81' in the JOINED field, and a false value (logical .F.) in the logical field PAID_UP.

The substring function — $( ) — tells VP-Info to look at the 3rd and 4th character in the JOINED field.

You can combine forms 2, 6, and 7 in an expression like the one shown in entry 8 to display certain information. Let's say you want to display the NAME, ST_ADR, and C_S_Z (city, state, zip) fields for all records that contain a logical true (T) in the PAID_UP field. You also want to suppress the record number display. The command

```
1>DISPLAY ALL NAME, ST_ADR, C_S_Z FOR PAID_OFF
```

Displays the contents of the named fields for all records that have a logical true (T) in the PAID_UP field.

Form 9 is a powerful command form can find all records having the specified expression anywhere in the specified string. If you wish to display all records having a partial match, the @( ) function can specify a string expression which has a position other than 0 in the field string. For example, DISPLAY ALL @('MN',C_S_Z)>0 will find "MN" anywhere in the C_S_Z (city, state, zip code) string, regardless of the length of the city name preceding it.

This command displays all record numbers followed by T or F (for true or false), where T indicates that the record contains the expression "TX" in the C_S_Z field. The expression can be located at any position within the C_S_Z field. This is handy when the expression is not always found at the same position in the field. The position of the state and zip code in the string is determined by the length of the city name:

```
Bozeman, MN 83331     ["MN" is the tenth and eleventh letter]
Hardin, MN 83331      [the ninth and tenth]
Miles City, MN 83331 [the thirteenth and fourteenth]
```

Here is another example. Suppose you wish to find all members with a first name beginning with 'G.' Since in the MEMBERS database, names are stored alphabetically by last name, the following command displays the name and age of anyone fitting the expression:

```
1>DISPLAY ALL NAME, AGE FOR @(', G',NAME)>0
```

where NAME and AGE are field names. Thanks to the comma and space specification, this command finds records containing first names beginning with G, like Matton, George and Boone, Gerta, but not Green, Will or Potts, Tom G. The display includes record numbers and the contents of both the Name and Age fields.

Forms 13 through 16 are variations of the DISPLAY command that can be used to list files. You cannot combine an "ON" specification with a "LIKE" specification; the ON clause only works for database files with the DBF extension.

LIST The LIST command is almost the same as DISPLAY ALL. You can use LIST in place of DISPLAY in LIST FILES, LIST STRUCTURE, and LIST MEMORY. You can also use the FOR, LIKE, ON, and OFF clauses.

The primary advantage of the LIST command is that it is shorter to type than DISPLAY ALL. If you type LIST, the contents of the database are displayed on the screen, scrolling to the end of the file; ALL is understood. DISPLAY ALL automatically pauses and waits for you to press a key each time the screen fills, but LIST displays the entire file without pausing. However, you can stop the listing by pressing Esc.

SYSTEM VARIABLES The LIST SYSTEM command displays a list of 23 preset variables, called system variables. System variable names always begin with a colon. Many of them are demonstrated in the learning modules. Here is a list of the system variables with a brief explanation of each one.

Name	Type	Width	Current Contents	
:F1	C	5	HELP	Pressing the function key causes
:F2	C	10	LIST STRU;	the contents to appear on the
:F3	C	6	WRITE	command line. A semi-colon is
:F4	C	10	LIST MEMO;	a carriage return, causing the
:F5	C	7	BROWSE;	command to execute immediately.
:F6	C	5	STAT;	The control codes can also be
:F7	C	12	^ WCONT;EDIT;	programmed to the keys, such as
:F8	C	11	LOCATE FOR	the ^ W on the F8 key, standing
:F9	C	5	FIND	for Ctrl-W or the End key.
:F10	C	5	EDIT;	
:TIME	C	8	14:41:37	Time string format.
:DATE	C	8	19861103	Date string format.
:VERSION	C	3	1.1	Version of VP-Info in use.
:SERIAL	C	14	M123456789	Serial No. of disk.
:COMPANY	C	1		Programmable variables
:TITLE	C	1		used in reports.
:PICTURE	C	10	9999999.99	Default number format.
:TERMINAL	C	1		For use with ANSI.SYS.
:KEY	N	8	13	ASCII code of last key pressed.
:AVAIL	N	8	1	Next empty volume's number.
:FIELD	N	8	1	Position of next variable.
:ERROR	N	8	0	Stores error number and related
:MESSAGE	C	1		messages for ON ERROR.
:RETRY	N	8	25	Networking variable.
:USER	N	8	1	Networking variable.
** Total **		25	variables. . .199 bytes	

The use of :DATE and :TIME is covered in Module 19.

The :VERSION and :SERIAL variables are strictly informational and should never be changed.

Using :COMPANY and :TITLE is covered in Module 52.

Changing the default number format with :PICTURE is described in the Applications section of this module.

The :TERMINAL variable is for networked operations using ANSI.SYS.

The :KEY variable can be used to reference keystrokes for menu selections.

The use of :AVAIL is covered in Module 40.

Module 34 describes the use of :FIELD.

Using :ERROR and :MESSAGE is covered in Module 44.

Using :RETRY and :USER is covered in Appendix E.

APPLICATIONS

The DISPLAY and LIST commands are used in a number of ways. First, they are used to simply "dump" the contents of a database to the screen. You can simultaneously route displayed data to your printer if you type SET PRINT ON before using the DISPLAY or LIST commands. If you use SET PRINT ON, be sure to enter SET PRINT OFF when printing finishes.

Being able to display information selectively begins to show the real power of VP-Info. With the DISPLAY and LIST commands, you can limit the display to certain fields and specify that only those records which match certain parameters are displayed.

The # function is more than just a way to determine the current position of the record pointer. You can use # to store the number value of the current record number to a memory variable for future use. The command: STORE # TO Rn stores a number equal to the current record number to the memory variable Rn. This little trick is used to save the number of a record that contains some needed information for later use. Memory variables are described in detail in Module 63.

All of the commands described in this module can be entered at the VP prompt or placed in command files.

The system variables may be used to store frequently used information, like a company name or report title. You can reprogram many of the system variables by typing the variable name and setting it equal to a new string. For example, the command: F8 = "CLEAR" assigns the CLEAR command to that key. If you assign "CLEAR;" to the key, then it executes automatically — not a good idea with a potentially destructive command like CLEAR, but handy if used as it is with :F2, so you can press F2 to get a display of the current database's structure.

If you are working with numbers that are too large for the current :PICTURE, which only displays values below ten million, the command: :PICTURE = '9999999999' will change the display to show numbers below ten billion (without decimal portions). Since numbers are only accurate to seventeen places, there is no point in declaring a :PICTURE variable larger than that.

TYPICAL OPERATION

In this illustration the LIST and DISPLAY commands are used to view certain records in the MEMBERS database created in Module 17. Begin at the VP prompt.

1. Type **USE MEMBERS** and press **Return**.
2. Type **LIST NAME, C_S_Z, PAID_UP** and press **Return**. Compare your screen to the following:

```
1>USE MEMBERS
1>LIST NAME, C_S_Z, PAID_UP
00001  Williams, David          Tampa, FL 32656          Y
00002  Phillips, George W.      Lago Vista, TX 78641     Y
00003  Galvin, Theodore A.      Culver City, CA 96750    N
```

3. Type **LIST FOR # = 1** and press **Return**. Notice the following:

```
1>LIST FOR # = 1
00001  Williams, David           3456 Fresno Circle          Tampa, FL 32656
 U.S. Air Force (Ret)       19801115 56 Y Active
```

4. Type **DISPLAY STRUCTURE** and press **Return**. Check the display:

```
1>DISPLAY STRUCTURE
Data file:             MEMBERS.DBF
Number of records:          3
File number:               #1
Field    Name       Type   Width  Dec
  1      NAME        C      25
  2      ST_ADR      C      25
  3      C_S_Z       C      25
  4      AFFIL       C      25
  5      JOINED      C       8
  6      AGE         N       2
  7      PAID_UP     L       1
  8      INFO        C      50
** Record Length **        162
```

5. Type **DISPLAY NAME, JOINED FOR .NOT. PAID_UP OFF** and press **Return**. Compare your screen to the following illustration.

```
1>DISPLAY NAME, JOINED FOR .NOT. PAID_UP OFF
Galvin, Theodore A.        19830215
```

6. Type **STORE # TO REC** and press **Return**; then type **DISPLAY MEMORY** and press **Return**. Notice the following:

```
1>STORE # TO REC
1>DISPLAY MEMORY

Name          Type    Width    Contents
REC             N       8      3
** Total **   1  variables, 8  bytes
```

7. Type **CLEAR** to close all files and to clear all memory variables.
8. Turn to Module 42 to continue the learning sequence.

Module 25

DO

DESCRIPTION

The DO command is used to start the operation of a VP-Info command (or program) file. The DO command is used either from the VP prompt or as a statement within a command file. The form of the DO command is: DO *filename* where *filename* is the name of a command file. When you type the command, VP-Info compiles the specified file, creating a new file with the same filename but the extension CPL, and then the new compiled command file is run and its commands executed. The DO *filename* command is also used as a statement in a command file. When used as a statement within a command file, the DO command causes the named command file to be compiled and then to begin operation. The named command file operates until:

1. The end of the file is reached, which passes control back to the VP prompt.
2. A CANCEL command is encountered, which passes control back to the VP prompt.
3. A RETURN command is encountered, which returns control to the command file from which the present command file was called. If the DO command originated at the VP prompt, RETURN passes control back to the prompt.
4. The Esc key is pressed, which interrupts program operation and returns to the prompt.
5. A command file error is encountered, such as not closing an IF with an ENDIF or a DO WHILE with an ENDDO. In this case, unless you have typed the command SET DO OFF, the CPL file with the same name remains on the disk, causing problems if it is not erased with the DELETE FILE command.
6. An error message is displayed.

You can also start operation of a command file directly from the DOS prompt by typing: VPI *filename* where the filename is the name of a command file.

VP-Info and dBASE The operation of the DO command is very different from that of its dBASE counterpart. VP-Info is a compiler, which means that it rewrites its command files in compact, impressively fast machine-readable form. The tradeoff is that it must treat variables, files, and macros differently than an interpreter like dBASE would.

Here are some of the most significant differences:

1. When a DO program is called, any DO programs it contains are compiled along with it into one complete file. If you have a DO subroutine that you refer to in six different places in the text of the first DO command, that entire subroutine is added to the complete compiled file six times. Thus, calling subroutines can result in very large files. Size is not likely to create a noticeable loss of speed, because compilers are very fast, but the size limit for a DO file is about 25K.

Avoid this problem by placing often-used DO subroutines inside PROCEDURE structures if they are short, and then calling them with the PERFORM command (Module 45). You can also avoid it by typing SET DO OFF, but this slows down operation while the computer compiles each DO file as needed.

2. The compiler checks whether the command lines are "do-able" while it rewrites them. If it finds a reference to a non-existent DBF file, logical or not, a *compile error* results: the program stops and an error message appears. An example of using a not-yet-created file would be this command: COPY STRUCTURE TO TEMP.

This would generate a "File not Found" error during compilation unless an old TEMP file already existed.

To avoid this, use a macro to represent the filename of the database to be created, because macros are not compiled. For instance, to create the file TEMPABC, use the following sequence of commands:

```
TempFile="TEMPABC"
USE ABC
COPY TO &TempFile
USE ABC COMPILE
USE &TempFile
```

The references to macros prevent VP-Info from testing execution on the lines containing them. The USE ABC COMPILE command instructs the compiler to make its checks on fieldnames based on the ABC database.

3. The compiler tries every command line, including the conditional ones. This means that if a CASE structure opens a database or clears all the memory variables, then when the compiler reads that line, it checks execution of the line, and then when it arrives in the next CASE, where those new conditions are no longer relevant, it crashes because an irrelevant database is opened and the relevant one closed, a memory variable no longer exists, etc.

   To avoid this, avoid changing databases and indexes inside conditional structures, and avoid using RELEASE, CLEAR, or RESTORE inside them.

4. When you type DO *filename*, the environment is cleared — databases are closed, memory variables are discarded.

   This is only a problem if you mix interactive and command modes carelessly. Once you turn control over to a DO file, databases, indexes, and memory variables are retained and passed along to the next DO file, subject to the limitations on conditional structures.

5. You should always clear any existing GETS (Module 34) before a DO or a RETURN (Module 9).

APPLICATIONS

By now, if you are following the learning sequence, you can see that there are many applications for the DO command. It allows you to program an elaborate operation, save the program, and reuse it, avoiding the need to retype every command in the operation. It can also be used from within command files to cause subsequent command files to run. An example of this use of the DO command is illustrated in the Typical Operation below. It allows you to create a work environment in which an operator with no knowledge of VP-Info's workings can enter data, write reports, perform transactions. By including the startup command VPI *filename* in a DOS AUTOEXEC file, you can even have the computer itself create the necessary environment upon startup.

TYPICAL OPERATION

In this illustration a pair of small command files is prepared and the DO command is used to run them. Then a third command file is used to select and command any existing database. Begin at the VP prompt.

1. Type **WRITE Level1** and press **Return** to use the VP-Info editor.
2. Type the following command file. (Do not type the explanatory remarks.)

```
                                               Remarks
* DLEVEL1.PRG  Demonstrates nested DO files.
CLS                                ; Clears the screen.
USE ABC                            ; Opens the ABC database.
Lvl1=" Level1"                     ; Stores a variable.
? Lvl1                             ; Prints it on the screen.
? " Press Return to read STATUS (PICNIC [File 2] was closed)."
WAIT                               ; Waiting for a keystroke before going on.
STAT                               ; Display list of open files.
?" Going to Level2"                ; Print warning message.
DO DLevel2                         ; Open second command file.
?
? " Back from Level2. PICNIC is open."   ; After the RETURN in Level2.
DISP                               ; Display the current record in the open file.
? " Next, a list of the memory variables in Level1."
WAIT                               ; Pause for keystroke.
LIST MEMORY                        ; List current variables.
CANCEL                             ; Return to VP prompt.
```

3. Press **End** and then **Return** to write the command file to disk.
4. Type **WRITE DLEVEL2** to return to the editor.
5. Type the following command file. (Do not type the explanatory remarks.)

```
                                               Remarks
* DLEVEL2.PRG
Lvl2="      Level2"                ; Create a new variable.
? Lvl2                             ; Print it.
? "      ABC still open."          ; Message to accompany display of the first
DISP                               ; record in ABC.
USE PICNIC                         ; Close ABC; open PICNIC.
? "       Going back to Level1 when you press Return."
RETURN                             ; Back to Level1
```

6. Press **End** and then **Return** to save this file.
7. Before using the files, type **USE#2 PICNIC** and press **Return**. This opens the database as File 2 in the STATUS list.
8. Type **Lvl0 = 'Level0'** and press **Return**. This creates a current memory variable, which the call to DO DLEVEL1 is going to erase.
9. Type **DO DLevel1** and press **Return**. Compare your screen to the following:

```
 Level1
 Press Return to read STATUS (PICNIC [File 2] was closed).
WAITING
```

10. Press **Return**. Notice that the STATUS screen does not list PICNIC as File 2. Calling DLEVEL1 has cleared the environment of open files and memory variables.
11. Press **Return**. Notice that LVL0 is gone from the list of variables, and LVL2 is listed, but it is of unknown type. The compiler stores space for it, but it has not been used yet.
12. Press **Return**. Compare the bottom of your screen to the following:

```
Press <Enter> to continue
  Going to Level2
    Level2
    ABC still open.
00001  Sergio, Vincent      3596 2084 19821021 29
     Going back to Level1 when you press Return.

  Back from Level2. PICNIC is open.
00001  Johns, Bill             3 Chips           5 Bags
 Next, a list of the memory variables in Level1.
WAITING
```

Notice that going to level 2 did not close ABC, and returning to level 1 did not close the PICNIC file opened in level 2.

13. Press **Return** once more, and notice that LVL2 now is a character variable, and LVL1 is still in existence.
14. Type **CLEAR ALL** and press **Return** to clear the files and variables.
15. Save these files for use in the next module in the learning sequence.
16. To observe macro use in opening datafiles, type **WRITE MACRON** and press **Return**.

17. Type the following command file. (Do not type the explanatory comments.)

```
                                                  Remarks
* MACRON.PRG  Demonstrates using macros as datafile names
TempFile='TEMPX'               ; Create a temporary file name.
TrueFile='        '            ; Initialize variable for existing file's name.
ACCEPT "Datafile: " TO TrueFile ; Get name of existing file.
USE &TrueFile                  ; Use that file.
COPY TO &TempFile              ; Copy it, records and all, to TEMPX.
USE#2 &TrueFile COMPILE        ; Use TrueFile as a compiler model.
USE#2 &TempFile                ; Use &TempFile.
USE PICNIC                     ; Close TrueFile, open PICNIC.
*   In the next command, the first two fields of the open file are referred to
*   by their vectors or locations.
LIST#2 &TempFile[1], &TempFile[2] ; List the first and second fields.
RETURN                          ; Leave the command file.
```

18. Press **End** and then **Return** to save this file.
19. Type **DO MACRON** and press **Return**. When the prompt "Datafile: " appears, type the name of any existing file (ABC or PICNIC should do).
20. Notice that the vector reference allows you to list the first two fields, regardless of their field names.
21. Turn to Module 10 to continue the learning sequence.

Module 26

DO CASE, CASE, OTHERWISE, ENDCASE

DESCRIPTION

The family of CASE commands is used to check for a specified condition. If the condition is detected — that is, "in case it's true" — the appropriate CASE statement is used. The following paragraphs describe each element of the CASE statement, beginning with DO CASE.

DO CASE The DO CASE command is the first statement used. This statement tells VP-Info that a DO CASE . . . ENDCASE structure follows, with one or more CASE statements.

```
DO CASE
  CASE X = 1
    command line(s)
  CASE X = 2
    command line(s)
  CASE ...
    :
ENDCASE
```

CASE Each CASE statement is followed by one or more command lines. If a CASE expression is true, the command lines associated with that CASE statement are used. Once a true CASE has been found and its commands executed, control passes to the command line following the ENDCASE statement. All remaining CASE statements are ignored once a case statement is satisfied.

The CASE statements are evaluated one at a time, from top to bottom. If a CASE statement is false, associated command lines are ignored and control passes to the next CASE statement. This process continues until either a true CASE is found, or the ENDCASE statement is reached.

ENDCASE As you have probably noticed, the CASE structure starts with DO CASE and ends with ENDCASE. ENDCASE is necessary to complete the CASE statement. When ENDCASE is encountered in the command file, control passes to the command line following the ENDCASE statement.

OTHERWISE OTHERWISE is an optional statement that is used as an alternative case. If none of the CASE expressions are true, the OTHERWISE statement comes into play, and the command lines associated with the OTHERWISE statement are used. Look at the following example:

```
DO CASE
  CASE X = 1
    command line(s)
  CASE X = 2
    command line(s)
        :
  OTHERWISE
    command line(s)
ENDCASE
```

Since the Case statements are read in order, OTHERWISE must be the last one. A sample DO CASE . . . ENDCASE structure is diagrammed in the following illustration. The path line on the left illustrates execution if the variable ZIP currently equals 84107, and that on the right is for ZIP equals 75275.

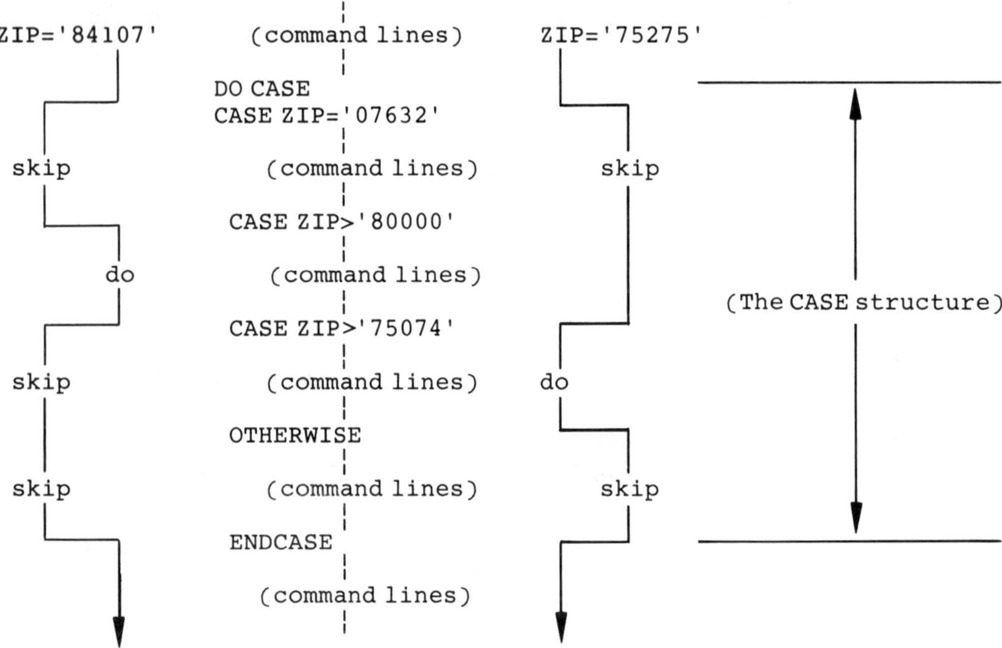

APPLICATIONS

You can apply the DO CASE series of commands any time you are confronted with a "multiple choice" situation. You can test as many alternatives (or CASES) as you like, since there is no limit to the number of CASE expressions within the CASE statement. For example, if you are checking property descriptions in a real estate database or options and colors in an automobile dealership database, you can use CASE after CASE to find those records that match your customer's needs.

TYPICAL OPERATION

In this illustration the CASE statement is used in a command file to check for a keyboard entry. Begin at the VP prompt.

1. Type **WRITE TRYCASE** and press **Return** to use the VP-Info editor.
2. Type the following command file. (Do not type the explanatory remarks.)

```
                                                    Remarks
* TRYCASE.PRG - Uses the CASE commands.
CLS                                   ; Clears screen.
TEXT                                  ; Displays text until ENDTEXT is encountered.
          Type 1 to display fruit.
          Type 2 to display sports.
          Type 3 to display colors.
ENDTEXT
ACCEPT 'Type 1, 2, or 3 ' to Key ; Pauses operation, displays prompt, stores
*                                      key typed to memory variable Key.
CLS
DO CASE                               ; Begins CASE structure.
  CASE Key='1'                        ; Checks for Key = '1.'
    ? 'Apples, Bananas, Cherries, Oranges, Peaches'
  CASE Key='2'                        ; Checks for Key = '2.'
    ? 'Baseball, Basketball, Football, Golf, Tennis'
  CASE Key='3'                        ; Checks for Key = '3.'
    ? 'Blue, Green, Orange, Red, Yellow'
  OTHERWISE                           ; Operates on any other Key response.
    ? "You didn't type 1 through 3."
ENDCASE                               ; Ends CASE statement.
WAIT                                  ; Pauses operation; displays "WAITING" prompt.
CLS
RETURN                                ; Returns control to VP prompt.
```

3. Press **Alt-F**. Notice how the automatic indentation resets the CASE statements.
4. Proofread the file and then press **End** and **Return** to save it.
5. Type **DO TRYCASE** and press **Return**.
6. Try selections 1, 2, 3, and any other key to see how the CASE commands work.
7. When you are finished experimenting with the CASE commands, type **DELE FILE TRYCASE.PRG** and press **Return** to delete the file from your disk.
8. Turn to Module 37 to continue the learning sequence.

Module 27

DO WHILE, BREAK, LOOP, ENDDO, EOF

DESCRIPTION

The DO WHILE command is a *looping* command that sustains operation "while" some condition is true. The first line of the DO WHILE structure has the form:

```
DO WHILE expression
```

Continuous operation is sustained as long as the *expression* is true or until an exit command (BREAK, CANCEL, RETURN, or QUIT) is encountered. The complete DO WHILE structure has the form:

```
DO WHILE expression
   :
   (command lines)
   :
ENDDO
```

The BREAK command transfers control from within the DO WHILE loop to the command line following the ENDDO statement, which is always the last line in a DO WHILE structure.

The LOOP command, on the other hand, transfers control back to the command line following (immediately below) the DO WHILE command line. The series of commands beginning with DO WHILE *expression* and ending with ENDDO is considered the complete structure. You can think of DO WHILE and ENDDO as bookends with the books in between representing command statements. So for every DO WHILE there is always a corresponding ENDDO.

You can "nest" DO WHILE . . . ENDDO structures as well as IF . . . ENDIFs and DO CASE . . . ENDCASEs within a DO WHILE statement. The following example contains an IF . . . ENDIF structure. Notice how each DO WHILE and IF has a corresponding ENDDO and ENDIF. Interior (nested) DO WHILE . . . ENDDO structures (and IF . . . ENDIF structures) must reside within the statement in complete paired sets. Notice also how indentation is used to signal the structural relationships of the END terms.

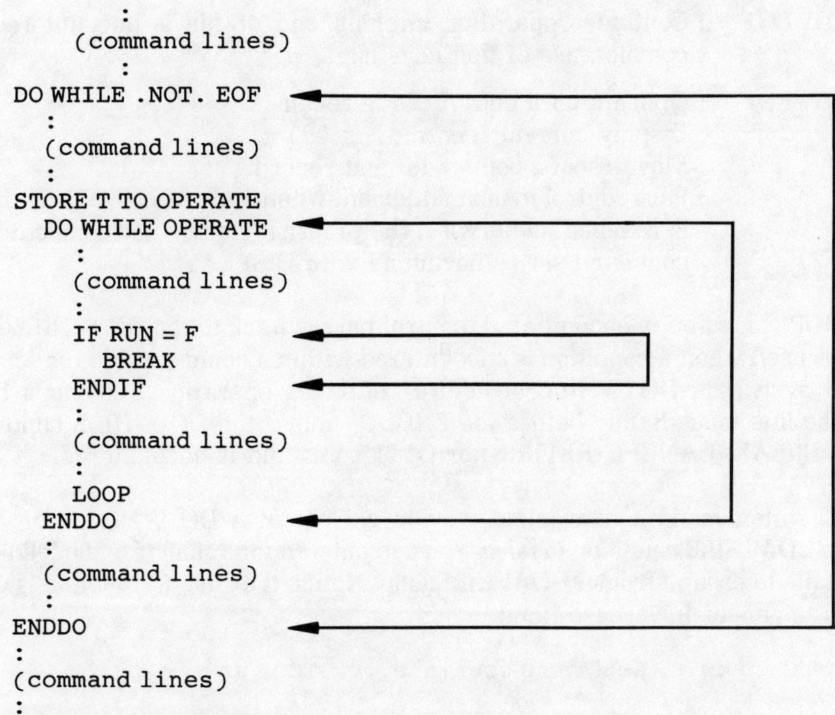

If an ENDDO or ENDIF statement is missing or misplaced, command file operation stops, sometimes locking up the computer in the process. If this happens, carefully count your ENDIF and ENDDO statements. If you always conclude your WRITE tasks by pressing Alt-F, VP-Info automatically indents all structures to provide a visual check for complete sets.

Here are some examples of DO WHILE statements:

DO WHILE T ; Continues operation until an EXIT, CANCEL, RETURN, or QUIT command is encountered.

STORE T TO Run ; Stores a true value to the memory variable Run.

DO WHILE Run ; Continues operation until an ENDDO or the command STORE F TO Run changes the value of Run.

STORE ' ' TO Okay ; Stores a blank space to the memory variable Okay.

DO WHILE .NOT. Okay = 'X' ; Continues operation until an exit command occurs or the value of Okay is changed to X. This value is changed by one of the following commands.

Okay = "X"
STORE 'X' TO Okay

ACCEPT 'Type a key ' TO Okay ; Displays "Type a key " prompt and stores keyboard entry to the memory variable Okay.

DO WHILE .NOT. EOF ; Continues operation until an end of file is encountered. A common use of this form is:

```
DO WHILE .NOT. EOF    ; Operate until end of file is reached.
    DISPLAY           ; Display current record.
      SKIP            ; Move record pointer to next record.
ENDDO                 ; Pass control to next statement when end-of-file (EOF) condition
                        is reached. Otherwise, the program returns to re-execute the
                        command series beginning with DISPLAY.
```

LOOP When the LOOP command is encountered, control passes back to the DO WHILE line. The LOOP command is used when a condition is encountered within a command file that makes it necessary to start over. The DO WHILE structure continues operation and loops back automatically after the line immediately before the ENDDO, unless the DO WHILE condition becomes false or the BREAK, CANCEL, RETURN, or QUIT command is encountered.

BREAK The BREAK statement is a convenient way to get out of a DO WHILE loop. The alternative is to set the DO WHILE condition to false. You can put a routine similar to the following one in your command file to escape from a DO WHILE loop. Notice that the !( ) function is used to interpret either an upper- or lowercase input.

```
ACCEPT 'Press "X" to exit, Return to continue... ' TO MVar
IF !(MVar) = 'X'
  EXIT
ENDIF
```

EOF The EOF function, which stands for *end-of-file*, is used with several commands including DO WHILE, DO CASE, and IF. When an end-of-file condition exists, EOF returns a true value. Going to the bottom of a file with GO BOTTOM doesn't position the record pointer to the end of the file; it positions the record pointer to the last record in the file. There's a distinct difference. To prove this to yourself, try the following commands from the VP prompt.

```
                        Remarks
1>USE PICNIC         ; Put the PICNIC database file in use.
1>GO BOTTOM          ; Go to the last record in the file.
1>? EOF              ; Check for end-of-file status.
F                    ; VP-Info says False.
1>SKIP               ; Move record pointer down. (hits end-of-file).
1>? EOF              ; Check for end-of-file status.
T                    ; VP-Info says True, you've reached end-of-file.
```

You can go to the end of the file with the LIST or DISP ALL commands, or with an unsuccessful LOCATE command. (However, an unsuccessful FIND command positions the record pointer at the "zeroth" record, an unusable record stored before the first and always a blank.) You can also go to the end-of-file with the COUNT command. If COUNT had been used in place of GO BOTTOM in the last example, the first ? EOF check would have returned a True value. Finally, if you set a SCOPE on an indexed file (see Module 55), an EOF condition exists when you reach a record that does not match the scope.

APPLICATIONS

You use the DO WHILE structure any time sustained operation is required. A delay loop was illustrated in the DO WHILE and LOOP description early in this module. But the DO WHILE structure is also useful for repetitive operation, such as displaying every record in a database until the end of file is reached (DO WHILE .NOT. EOF). You can also use DO WHILE, STORE, and LOOP as an incrementor or decrementor, as shown in the following delay loop example (although the REPEAT structure, covered in Module 50, is tailor-made for incrementing). You can apply this principle to count displayed lines and cause a line feed (EJECT) when the bottom of a page is reached. The command file in Module 29 illustrates this application.

As mentioned, a practical use for the DO WHILE statement is to install time delays. For example, you may wish to display a message for several seconds, and then move on to another activity. The following illustration demonstrates this process. First, the message is displayed. Then a time delay is established using a DO WHILE loop. Once the delay loop is exhausted, the screen is erased and following commands are processed.

```
                                          Remarks
* DELAY.PRG – Displays a message for approximately 5 to 10 seconds.
CLS                                  ; Clears the screen.
? '       THIS MESSAGE WILL DISAPPEAR IN A FEW SECONDS'
X = 370                              ; Store 370 to the memory variable X.
DO WHILE X >- 1                      ; Continue operation until X equals 0.
  X = X-1                            ; Subtract 1 from X for every pass of the loop.
ENDDO                                ; When the DO WHILE expression becomes false
*                                      (X = 0), control passes to the next line.
CLS                                  ; Clears the screen.
RETURN                               ; Returns control to VP prompt.
```

In this example, the DO WHILE X > – 1 statement sustains operation while X is 0 or more. By counting down, you can reduce the amount of modification needed to change the time delay. To triple the delay, simply use 1000 rather than 370. Also, beware of using equality as your cutoff point. By specifying X > – 1, you avoid the danger of missing your target through miscalculation. For example, DO WHILE .NOT. X = 0 would go on forever if you counted down from 20 by threes. The command STORE X – 1 TO X reduces the value of X by one each time the LOOP command sends you through the DO WHILE . . . ENDDO set. When the value of X reaches – 1, the DO WHILE loop terminates without executing.

Finally, the EOF function is often used to display or print a complete set of records. The ability to return a True condition when the end of file is reached makes the EOF function a useful tool.

TYPICAL OPERATION

In this illustration DO WHILE, DO CASE, and EOF are used in a command file to demonstrate their use. The PICNIC database created in Module 64 is used by the command file. Begin at the VP prompt.

1. Type **WRITE DOCMDS** and press **Return** to use the editor.

2. Type the following command file. (Do not type the explanatory remarks or the indentations.)

```
                                        Remarks
* DOCMDS.PRG – Illustrates the use of various DO structures.
USE PICNIC
DispList='NAME,AMOUNT,MEASURE,BRING'   ; Create macro to save space and
*                            lessen danger of typos on DISPLAY command line.
DO WHILE T                  ; Continue operation while true.
    CLS                     ; Clears the screen.
    TEXT                    ; Displays following text.

    SELECT A NUMBER TO DISPLAY WHAT'S BEING BROUGHT
                                             PRESS
              POTATO CHIPS                     1
              DIP                              2
              HOT DOGS                         3
              BUNS                             4
              BEANS                            5
              MUSTARD                          6
              RELISH                           7
              PICKLES                          8
              EVERYTHING                       9
              EXIT TO VP                 Press 0

    ENDTEXT
    CURSOR 4,15             ; Position cursor on first choice.
    Mselect=MENU(9,30)      ; Make 30-column lightbar to select choice.
    CLS                     ; Clear the screen.
    ? " Name                  Bringing"
    DO CASE                 ; Start DO CASE; look for Mselect value.
    CASE Mselect=1          ; If user selected = '1.'
        DISP ALL &DispList FOR BRING='Chips' OFF    ; Macro DispList used.
*     Display name, amount, measure, and bring in all records with 'Chips'
*       in the BRING field, with record numbers off.
    CASE Mselect=2          ; If Mselect = '2.'
        DISP ALL &DispList FOR BRING='Dip' OFF
*     Display records with 'Dip' in BRING field.
    CASE Mselect=3
        DISP ALL &DispList FOR BRING='Hot Dogs' OFF
*     Display for 'Hot Dogs' in BRING field.
    CASE Mselect=4
        DISP ALL &DispList FOR BRING='Buns' OFF
    CASE Mselect=5
        DISP ALL &DispList FOR BRING='Beans' OFF
    CASE Mselect=6
        DISP ALL &DispList FOR BRING='Mustard' OFF
    CASE Mselect=7
        DISP ALL &DispList FOR BRING='Relish' OFF
    CASE Mselect=8
        DISP ALL &DispList FOR BRING='Pickles' OFF
    CASE Mselect=9             ; If Mselect = 9, then
        DISP ALL &DispList OFF ; Display all records in database.
    CASE Mselect=0             ; If Mselect is "EXIT to VP,"
        CLS
```

```
        CLEAR ALL               ; Close database and erase variables.
        BREAK                   ; Exit from the DO WHILE loop.
    OTHERWISE                   ; If error occurred, execute following command.
        LOOP                    ; Return to first line in DO WHILE structure.
    ENDCASE                     ; Completes DO CASE structure.
    WAIT                        ; Pause operation, display "WAITING" prompt.
ENDDO                           ; Completes DO WHILE structure.
USE                             ; Close database file.
CLEAR                           ; Clear the screen and memory.
RETURN                          ; Return control to VP prompt.
```

3. Notice the use of the memory variable DispList to shorten the DISPLAY command and lessen the chance of a typing error in the repeated list of fields. Notice also the bar down the side of the TEXT, which is necessary to maintain the column spacing when you reformat with Alt-F. (Avoid this problem by making the TEXT . . . ENDTEXT a TXT file.)
4. Press **Alt-F** to reformat the file, then proofread, checking for uniform indentation of structures.
5. Press **End** and then **Return** to write the command file to disk.
6. Run the command file by typing **DO DOCMDS** and pressing **Return**. Compare your screen to the following:

```
SELECT A NUMBER TO DISPLAY WHAT'S BEING BROUGHT
+-                                        PRESS
|           POTATO CHIPS                      1
|           DIP                               2
|           HOT DOGS                          3
|           BUNS                              4
|           BEANS                             5
|           MUSTARD                           6
|           RELISH                            7
|           PICKLES                           8
|           EVERYTHING                        9
|           EXIT TO VP                  Press 0
+_
```

7. Type **2** and compare your screen to the following:

```
 Name                      Bringing
Collins, Ric            3 Cartons    Dip
Jasper, Dave            2 Cartons    Dip
WAITING
```

8. Press any key to redisplay the menu. Try other selections, using either a number key or the cursor key movement of the lightbar to make your selections. When you finish experimenting with the program, type **0** to exit. Notice that the lightbar does not go to the 0 selection.
9. Turn to Module 50 to continue the learning sequence.

Module 28

EDIT

DESCRIPTION

The EDIT command is used to change the contents of one or more records in a database. The BROWSE command (Module 8) is also used for editing. Before the EDIT command is used, a database must be opened with the USE command. Forms of the EDIT command are presented in the following list. As with all commands, you must press Return at the end of the command line.

1. EDIT — Displays the contents of the current record in an "editing mask" or template. Editing is achieved by typing in new information, deleting old information, or both. When a record is displayed, you can delete the entire record by pressing Ctrl-U. When you are back at the prompt, typing PACK and pressing Return eliminates such records from the database.
2. EDIT *n* — Edits the specified record number.
3. EDIT FIELDS *field1,field2* — Restricts editing to the named field or fields.

For example, to edit record number 2 of the MEMBERS database modified in Module 42, type the following command lines:

```
1>USE MEMBERS
1>EDIT 2
```

Record number 2 is displayed in an editing mask, as in the following screen.

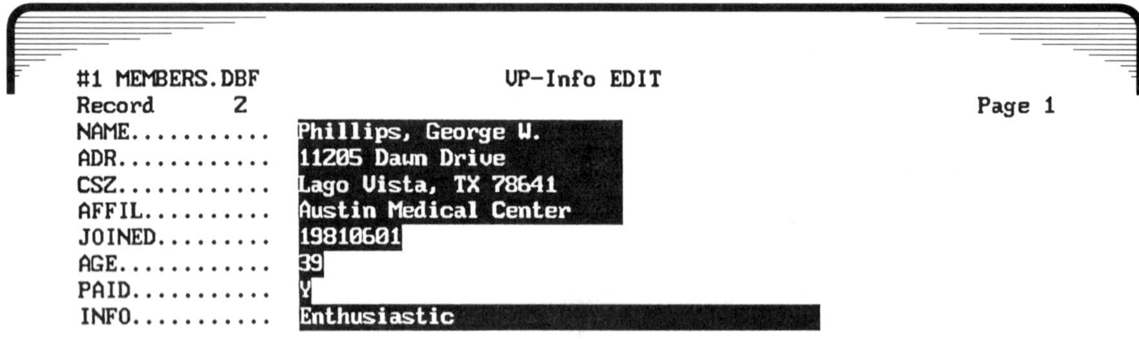

The cursor is positioned at the beginning of the NAME field, ready for use. You can move the cursor within the record with the cursor control keys to make changes. You can strike over text or erase text with the Spacebar. You can delete text and turn on insert mode using Del and

Ins. You can jump to the previous record with PgUp and jump to the following record with PgDn. Attempting to move beyond the last record within the database takes you back to the VP prompt.

Once you have made your changes, you can save them and return to the VP prompt by pressing End. If you decide not to save a change in the current record, you can press Ctrl-Q (for "quit"). This abandons the displayed record without saving changes in it and takes you back to the VP prompt. However, you should know that if you edit the contents of a record and move to another record, the edited record is automatically saved when you move to the next record. This automatic save can be disabled by typing SET SAVE OFF at the VP prompt.

APPLICATIONS

The EDIT command lets you update or correct the contents of a database. It is also used to display the contents of a record for review purposes. Once you review the record contents, you can return to the prompt with Ctrl-Q.

TYPICAL OPERATION

In this illustration the EDIT command is used to change the PAID status in record number 1 of the MEMBERS database last modified in Module 42. Begin at the VP prompt.

1. Type **USE MEMBERS** and press **Return.**
2. Type **EDIT 1**, press **Return**, and notice the following display:

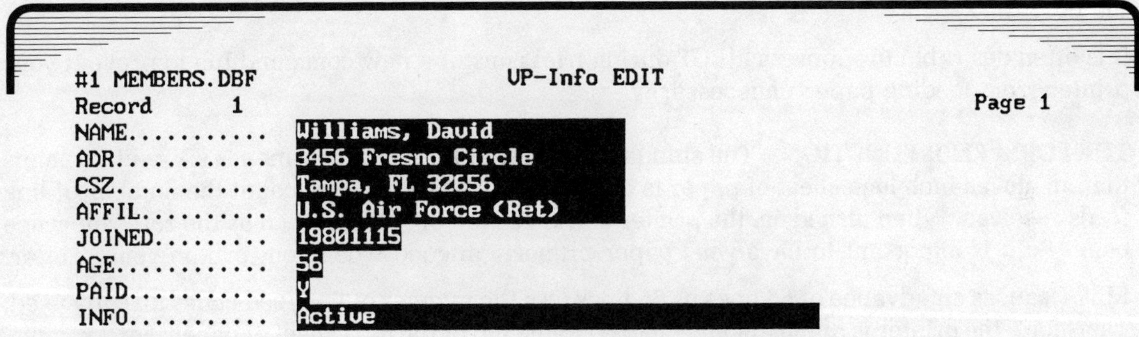

3. Move the cursor to the PAID field with the **Down Arrow** key and type **F.**
4. Press **PgDn** and notice that record number 2 is displayed.
5. Press **End** to finish saving your changes and to return to the VP prompt.
6. Type **USE** and press **Return** to close the database.
7. Turn to Module 8 to continue the learning sequence.

Module 29

EJECT

DESCRIPTION

The EJECT command causes a printer form feed. Most computer printers use continuous-form paper, although some are sheet fed. If the printer uses a form tractor or a cut-sheet feeder, EJECT causes the printer to advance the present sheet up and out of the way and the next sheet is rolled into position, ready for printing. The EJECT command operates independently of the SET PRINT ON command, which echoes, or simultaneously prints, displayed text.

The form of the EJECT command is:

```
1>EJECT
```

The EJECT command is entered either from the prompt or from a line within a command file.

DEBUGGING A COMMAND FILE CONTAINING THE EJECT COMMAND To suppress form feeds caused by the EJECT command, you can place an asterisk in front of the line that contains the EJECT command. This converts the line into a comment, which is ignored during command file operation.

It is often desirable to suppress EJECT during trial runs of a new command file to prevent your printer from feeding paper unnecessarily.

THE FORM FEED FUNCTION The standard number of line feeds per inch is six, which means that an eleven-inch-long sheet of paper is 66 lines long. Most printers count the number of line feeds received. When turned on, the printer marks the top-of-form position as the zero reference point. So it is important to have your paper properly aligned when you turn on your printer.

EJECT causes an advance of 66 lines or 66 lines less the number of line feed codes already used. Therefore, the printer is automatically indexed to the top of the next sheet of paper. For example, if your printer has received 30 line feed codes and then receives an EJECT command, it will issue 36 additional line feed codes (30 + 36 = 66) to advance to the top of the next sheet of paper. In summary, your printer counts the number of line feed codes received to "know" how many additional line feeds are required to reach the top of the next sheet of paper.

APPLICATIONS

The EJECT command is applied in a number of ways. First, it is often placed at the beginning of a print run to ensure that a clean sheet of paper is in position before printing begins. It is sometimes used to cause a form feed after each full-page is printed to start the next report at the top of a clean sheet.

The EJECT command is often used in command files designed to print custom reports. The following command lines, or ones like them, are used to control form feeds when the page reaches a certain number of lines. You may wish to adopt this technique in command files of your own.

```
                                          Remarks
* EJECT.PRG                      ; Demonstrates use of the EJECT command.
CLS                              ; Clears the screen.
SET PRINT ON                     ; Causes displayed text to be printed.
EJECT                            ; Causes a form feed to the top of the next sheet.
USE MEMBERS                      ; Puts MEMBERS database in use.
X = 0                            ; Stores 0 to the memory variable X.
? '----------------------------------------' ; Draws a line.
DO WHILE .NOT. EOF( )            ; Causes continuous operation until the end of
*                                  the file is encountered.
   IF X = 50                     ; Checks for a condition where X equals 50.
      ? '----------------------------------------' ; Draws a line.
      EJECT                      ; Causes a form feed (if X = 50).
      ? '----------------------------------------' ; Draws a line.
      X = 0                      ; Resets memory variable X to 0 (if X = 50).
   ENDIF                         ; Passes control to next command line.
   DISPLAY Name, Affil           ; Displays the Name and Affil fields.
   X = X + 1                     ; Adds 1 to the present value of X.
   SKIP                          ; Moves record pointer to the next record in line.
ENDDO                            ; Passes control when EOF is encountered.
? '----------------------------------------' ; Draws a line.
EJECT                            ; Causes form feed.
SET PRINT OFF                    ; Turns off printing.
ERASE                            ; Clears screen.
CLEAR                            ; Closes files.
CANCEL                           ; Returns to prompt.
```

TYPICAL OPERATION

In this illustration the EJECT command is used in conjunction with the MEMBERS database modified in Module 42. Selected fields are listed to your printer and then the EJECT command is used to feed the next clean sheet into position. Begin at the VP prompt. Be sure your printer is turned on and loaded with paper.

1. Type **USE PHONE** and press **Return.**
2. Type **LIST NAME, CSZ** and press **Return**. Notice that the LIST command's output is sent to the printer as well as to the screen. Compare your screen to the following:

```
1>USE PHONE
1>SET PRINT ON
1>LIST PARTY, NUMBER
00001  Smith, John              (408) 232-1210
00002  Hood, J.T.               (408) 343-1090
00003  Maxwell, Mary            (214) 232-4545
00004  Jackson, Lois            (201) 599-6111
00005  Acme Brick Company       (512) 960-1415
1>
```

Notice that the final record has not yet printed, however. To print this line, you must either send an empty PRINT command (by typing ? and pressing Return at the VP prompt or in your command file) or use the EJECT command.

3. Type **EJECT** and press **Return**; notice that the last record prints and a printer form feed advances the paper.
4. Type **USE** and press **Return** to close the database.
5. Turn to Module 39 to continue the learning sequence.

Module 30
ERASE, CLS

DESCRIPTION

The ERASE command is used to erase all or part of the screen. Alternatively, CLS can be used as a synonym for ERASE. The form of the ERASE command is:

```
ERASE row number , row number
CLS row number , row number
```

Row numbers begin with 0 and go to 24. You may use ERASE or CLS with no row numbers to erase the entire screen; if you specify a row number, however, you must specify both numbers. For example, if you wish to erase only the top row on the screen, type: ERASE 0,0.

Row 0 (the first row) is blanked and the prompt appears immediately below it.

When used without row numbers, ERASE clears the screen, placing the cursor in the second row, after the prompt. You may specify any numbers between 0 and 24, as long as the second number is greater than the first. The prompt always appears immediately below the first erased row, so that ERASE 10,13 places the cursor on row 11.

APPLICATIONS

The ERASE command is generally used in Interactive mode to unclutter the screen. In a command file, it is used to clear the screen prior to sending messages.

TYPICAL OPERATION

In this illustration the screen is deliberately filled with information, and then the ERASE command is used to clear the screen.

1. Type **HELP** and press **Return**. In a moment, the main Help menu appears.
2. Press **Esc** to exit from the menu. Notice that the VP prompt appears at the bottom of the screen.

3. Type **ERASE 7,8** and press **Return**. Compare your screen to the following:

```
                              UP-Info Help

Use the arrow keys to move the lightbar and select a topic from the list
below, then press the <ENTER> key.  You may also move the lightbar to the
bottom of the screen and type the name of a specific command or function.

                              1. Commands List

1>
                              4. Command and Field Redirection
                              5. Date Input Formats
                              6. Date Output Formats
                              7. Editing Keys
                              8. Format Strings
                              9. Get Tables
                             10. REPORT Command
                             11. TEXT
                             12. Variables

Selection Bar ↑↓  Select - ↵. Exit with <Esc> or Enter command.
1>ERASE 7,8
```

4. Notice that the command erases only the 8th and 9th row, and the prompt appears on the row immediately below the first erased row.
5. Type **ERASE** and press **Return** again. Note that the entire screen is erased and the prompt appears at the top of the screen.
6. Press **F1** and then **Return** to call the main Help screen, then press **Esc** to exit from Help.
7. Type **CLS** and press **Return**. Notice that CLS clears the screen, just as ERASE did.
8. Turn to Module 62 to continue the learning sequence.

Module 31

FILES, SET DEFAULT TO

DESCRIPTION

The FILES . . . ENDFILES structure, the FILES command, and the SET DEFAULT TO command are used to specify locations of types of files. The FILES structure is most useful in the VPI.CNF configuration file. It allows you to specify that certain files are to be found on specific disks. For example, if you prefer to keep all your .PRG files on the B drive, your databases and indexes in a \DATA subdirectory of your C hard disk, your VPI program and overlays in a \VPIPRG subdirectory, and your TEMP files on a RAMDisk D, you need the following command in your VPI.CNF file:

```
FILES
   TEMP*.*, D:\
   *.PRG, B:\
   *.DBF, C:\DATA\
   *.NDX, C:\DATA\
ENDFILES
```

The FILES command may be used from the prompt (not in programs) to change the FILES . . . ENDFILES structure. If you type FILES LIST, your current structure is listed on screen. To change a FILES setting, type FILES followed by the file type and the new location separated with a comma, like this:

```
FILES *.DBF, D:\DATA\
```

If you then type FILES LIST again, your new specification for data files appears in the structure.

You can also use the FILES command to delete FILES structures. If you type the command with no specifications, the entire structure is deleted; if you specify a file type—*.DBF, for example—then that file type's location is deleted.

The SET DEFAULT TO command may be used to change the default, or assumed locations of .DBF and .NDX files (but only those file types). It does not affect any other specifications in a FILES directive, nor does a FILES directive change a SET DEFAULT TO command. To undo a SET DEFAULT TO command, you must either restart or issue the command again with no drive specified. This procedure returns the defaults to the active FILES directive.

Two errors are easy to make when using the FILES structure. Remember that only one FILES directive is active at a time. In other words, if you issue a FILES directive while in VP-Info, the VPI.CNF FILES structure is discarded. If you mean your new FILES directive to supplement, rather than replace the old one, then you must include all the specifications of the old one in the new one. Secondly, keep in mind that the specifications in the FILES structure are read in the order they appear. Compare these two FILES structures:

```
 A.                     B.
FILES                  FILES
 *.DBF,B:\              TEMP*.*,D:\
 *.NDX,B:\              *.DBF,B:\
 *.PRG,C:\              *.NDX,B:\
 TEMP*.*,D:\            *.PRG,C:\
ENDFILES               ENDFILES
```

The intended effect is to use B for data, C for command files, and D to hold temporary files of any kind. If you type USE TEMP, for example, the computer should seek TEMP.DBF on the D drive. However, this only happens with the second FILES structure, because the lines are stored in order, and the first instruction for handling any .DBF file in the first structure is to look on B for it. Only TEMP*.* files that are not .DBF, .NDX, or .PRG files are assumed to be on the D drive. By specifying the TEMP locations first, the second FILES structure warns the computer that only .DBF, .NDX, and .PRG files which do not have filenames beginning with "TEMP" are in the default locations.

APPLICATIONS

The SET DEFAULT TO command and the FILES structure allow you to organize your files throughout your drives and subdirectories in a logical, consistent manner. When writing an application, a carefully thought-out FILES structure invoked at the beginning of the application can save a great deal of time for the user.

TYPICAL OPERATION

This operation demonstrates the changes that occur when you use SET DEFAULT TO or a new FILES structure. Then you create an A:RESET.PRG to restore the VPI.CNF FILES structure after other structures have been invoked. The instructions are based on the assumption that you are using the VPI.CNF file recommended in Module 2. If you are not, some drive specifications may vary. Begin at the VP prompt.

1. Type **USE ABC** to open a database. Notice that the B drive's light comes on, signalling a search there.
2. Type **COPY TO A:TEMP** to create a copy on the A drive. Notice the A drive light.
3. Type **WRITE FILIT** and use the editor to create this FILIT.PRG on the default B drive:

```
FILES
  N*.PRG,B:
ENDFILES
```

4. Press **End** and **Return** to save the command file. Notice the B drive light.
5. Type **DO FILIT**. Notice the B drive light.

6. Type **USE ABC**. Notice that the B drive light did not come on (and the ABC database is reported missing). The FILES directive in FILIT has erased all FILES specifications except the one it contains.
7. Type **SET DEFAULT TO B** and press **Return**. Then type **USE ABC** again. Notice the B drive light, indicating that the DBF files are being sought on the B drive.
8. Type **DO FILIT**. Notice that only the A drive light comes on, and the file is not found.
9. Type **WRITE NEWFILE** and press **Return**.
10. Type this line into the Editor, then save the file:

```
This is NEWFILE.
```

Notice that when you press End and Return to save it, the B drive light signals that the file is being saved on the B drive, as specified by FILIT.PRG.

NOTE

If this procedure doesn't seem to work, try typing COMPILE B:FILIT. If a FILIT.CPL program exists, VP-Info uses it rather than the FILIT.PRG.

11. Type **SET DEFAULT TO A**.
12. Now type **WRITE RESET** and press **Return**. Create the following command file to restore the recommended VPI.CNF FILE structure.

```
FILES
 TEMP•.•,C:\
 •.DBF,B:\
 •.NDX,B:\
 •.PRG,B:\
 •.TXT,B:\
 •.LIB,B:\
 •.CPL,B:\
 •.FRM,B:\
 VPI.HLP,B:\
ENDFILES
```

13. Press **End** and **Return** to save the file, and then type **DO RESET** to invoke the files configuration program.
14. Type **WRITE FILIT** and press **Return**. Notice that the file is searched for on the B drive.
15. Press **Ctrl-Q** and type **Y** to exit from the Editor.
16. Type **USE ABC**. Notice that the FILES structure in RESET.PRG did not cancel the SET DEFAULT TO A command.
17. Type **SET DEFAULT TO** and press **Return**, then type **USE ABC** again to confirm that the DBF default is back to normal.
18. Turn to Module 53 to continue the learning sequence.

Module 32

FIND

DESCRIPTION

The FIND command lets you find the first record within an indexed database that matches a specified expression.

The FIND command is similar to LOCATE. However, FIND only operates with key fields of the active index. (See Module 38.) Also, FIND always resets the record pointer to the top of the database, so it only finds the first match within a database. LOCATE uses CONTINUE to search through records beyond the first matching record. Also, the FOR expression, as in LOCATE FOR AGE > = 35, is unavailable with FIND. LOCATE can be used with logical values (T or F), while FIND requires a string match even if the index is keyed to a logical value. If you specify "FIND Y" for a database indexed on a logical value, the FIND command skips any records whose logical value is recorded as the synonym "T."

Some forms of the FIND command are shown in the following list.

1. FIND *expression* Positions the record pointer to the first record containing the expression in a key field.

`1>FIND JO` ; Finds the first record containing "JO" as the first two characters of a key field. "JO" matches strings such as "JONES" or "JOHNSON." FIND automatically converts the specified string to uppercase. Indexing on the uppercase rendering of your key eliminates potential variations in, for example, the capitalization of names, and it speeds up the FIND process slightly.

`1>DISPLAY NAME, ZIP` ; Displays the NAME and ZIP fields for the found record.

2. FIND & "*expression*" Adding the ampersand and quotation marks allows FIND to search for case-sensitive matches in those cases where the index is not uppercase.

`1>FIND # "Jo"` ; Finds the first record containing that exact string in the indexed field.

3. FIND &Mname Finds the first record containing the character string stored as the variable Mname.

`1>STORE 'Joh' TO MNAME` ; Stores the string "Joh" to MNAME.

`1>FIND #MNAME` ; Finds the first record containing "Joh" as the starting string of the key field. This use of the macro function also makes FIND case-sensitive (but if the index was made with the uppercase function, !( ), then you must change the variable to uppercase by typing FIND &!(MNAME).

If you want to FIND only those records with an exact match for the FIND string, you can enter the statement SET EXACT ON. When EXACT is on, the statement "FIND Smith" ignores Smithe, Smithville, or Smithsonian.

FIND also works with numeric fields because what it actually searches is the index file, and the INDEX command automatically creates a string from the keys it uses. However, the numeric expression must contain exactly the correct number of leading blanks for the FIND to work. If Mcost is "   2.76" then FIND can locate it if the index was made using STR(cost,7,2) as the index key.

APPLICATIONS

FIND is fast and simple to use. Once a file is indexed, the first matching record is easy to find. The major advantage to FIND is speed. The search is practically instantaneous, while LOCATE may take some seconds to find a matching record in a database with even a fairly small number of records. Disadvantages include the fact that only the first record is found, that FIND demands uppercase indexes, and that FIND cannot use a FOR expression. FIND can be used both in the immediate mode (from the VP prompt) and in command files.

TYPICAL OPERATION

In this illustration the FIND command is used to locate selected records within the ABC database last modified in Module 38. Begin at the VP prompt.

1. Type **USE ABC** and press **Return**.
2. Index the ABC database file by typing **INDEX ON !(NAME) TO ANAMES** and pressing **Return**.
3. Find the record containing "Bishop" by typing **FIND bish** and pressing **Return**. Remember that FIND always searches in uppercase, unless the macro symbol and quotation marks are used to make the search literal.
4. Check the position of the record pointer by typing **DISPLAY** and pressing **Return**. Notice that the record containing Bishop was found.
5. Store the string "SER" to the memory variable MNAME by typing the following (pressing **Return** at the end of the command line):

```
1>STORE 'SER' TO MNAME
```

Notice that because we are using a macro, we must use all caps so that the variable will match the index.

6. Find the record containing Sergio by typing **FIND &MNAME** and pressing **Return**.
7. Check the position of the record pointer by typing **DISPLAY** and pressing **Return**. Notice that the record containing Sergio was found.
8. Type **STORE 'Sergio' TO MNAME** and press **Return**.
9. Type **FIND &MNAME**.

Notice that the message "NO FIND" reports a failed search, because the index is in uppercase and the variable string is not.

10. Type **FIND &!(MNAME)** and press **Return**. Type **DISP** to verify success.
11. Type **SET EXACT ON** and press **Return.**
12. Type **FIND &!(MNAME)** and press **Return**. Notice that the find fails. With EXACT ON, only MNAME = 'SERGIO, VINCENT' can find record 1.
13. Type **CLEAR ALL** to close all files and remove all memory variables.
14. Delete the index file by typing **DELETE FILE ANAMES.NDX** and pressing **Return.**
15. Turn to Module 55 to continue the learning sequence.

Module 33

FLUSH

DESCRIPTION

The FLUSH command is used to "save and continue." It saves data changes to the disk without closing the database or its indexes and without moving the record pointer.

There are five common ways to update a database to disk. FLUSH is the only one which allows you to continue working where you left off. Here are the five common methods and their effects:

1. QUIT — Closes and updates all files and exits from VP-Info to the DOS prompt.
2. CLEAR — Closes files and releases memory variables, but remains in VP-Info at the prompt.
3. USE — Closes and updates files but retains variables. IF you are using DATA1.DBF and you type USE DATA2, DATA1 is closed and DATA2 is opened.
4. CLOSE — Closes the selected file but retains the variables. The CLOSE command is functionally identical to USE without a filename.
5. FLUSH — Updates the database and its indexes to the disk without closing the files and without closing the files and without moving the file pointer.

APPLICATIONS

The FLUSH command saves changes to the database and indexes. It may be used from the VP prompt or from within a command file. You can use it, as you would the Save and Continue function of a word processor, as insurance against loss of data during power surges or other electrical accidents. It can also be used to monitor and confirm changes.

TYPICAL OPERATION

In this illustration the ABC database, created in Module 5, is used and indexed. Then one record is edited and FLUSH is used to write the changes to disk.

NOTE

Index files are created with the INDEX command described in Module 38. If you are not familiar with index files yet, just follow the procedure to observe the FLUSH command.

1. Type **USE ABC** and press **Return**.
2. Create your index file by typing **INDEX ON NAME TO ANAMES** and pressing **Return**. Notice the messages "6 RECORDS READ" and "6 RECORDS INDEXED."
3. Display the open files by typing **STATUS** and pressing **Return**. Notice the top of the display, reporting that ABC is indexed by the NAME field. (Disregard the rest of the screen display for now.)

```
Thursday, June 25, 1987              VP-Info STATUS

Rec #              File name         Indexed by
00001 *File 1 ... ABC.DBF            NAME
00000  File 2 ...
```

4. Press **Esc** to return to the prompt.
5. Type **LIST** and press **Return** to see the indexed order of the names. Notice the record number for Robert Harris. (The alphabetizing of the record you added in Module 5 makes it impossible to predict record numbers at this point.)
6. Using Harris' record number, type **EDIT** # and press **Return** (for example, if Harris is number 4, type **EDIT 4**). Change "Harris" to "Barris" by typing a capital **B**, then press **End** to record the change. Notice that the disk drive does not respond. The change is recorded in the memory of the computer.
7. Type **FLUSH** and press **Return**. Notice that the drive light signals a write operation.
8. Type **DISP** and press **Return**. Notice that the current record is still the number for Robert Barris.
9. Repeat steps 6 through 8 to change "Barris" back to "Harris."
10. Type **CLOSE** and press **Return** to close the file.
11. Turn to Module 28 to continue the learning sequence.

Module 34

GET, GET PICTURE, CLEAR GETS, READ, ON FIELD

DESCRIPTION

This module deals with a set of VP-Info statements used in command files to display and change the contents of database fields and memory variables. The GET, CLEAR GETS, and READ statement were briefly introduced in Module 54 with the SAY statement. Because the GET statement is often used in combination with @ *row,col* and SAY, these statements are also presented to show the roles they play with forms of the GET statement. For more information about @ *row,col* and SAY, see Modules 6 and 54.

Some forms of GET are presented in the following list.

1. @ *row,col* GET *field name* The statement specifies the row and column coordinates and the effected field name of the database in use. Information is either displayed or can be entered into the field from the keyboard, depending upon following READ or CLEAR GETS command. READ and CLEAR GETS are described later in this module.

   For example:

   ```
   @ 12,10 GET NAME          ; This command displays the NAME field of the active
                               database at row 12 column 10.
   ```

2. @ *row,col* SAY "*text*" GET *field name* Here, the GET statement is preceded with a SAY statement to display a user prompt on the screen. This form of the statement lets you guide a user through the data entry process by displaying helpful information.

   For example:

   ```
   @ 12,10 SAY "Name: " GET NAME     ; Presents the current value of the field NAME for
                                       modification.
   ```

3. @ *row,col GET fieldname* PICTURE *expression* The PICTURE clause allows you to control the format of displayed or printed field contents. Function and template characters used within the PICTURE clause are contained in Module 54, Table 54-1.

   For example:

   ```
   @ 12,10 GET UNIT PICTURE '!!!!!!'    ; Displays the field in all uppercase letters.
   ```

ORGANIZING GET STATEMENTS When the GET statement is used, organize row and column positions sequentially. That is, row numbers should start at the top and move down. Likewise, column positions should begin at the left and move to the right. This is essential when information is printed, because the printer operates from left-to-right, top-to-bottom, and can't back up if a row-column position is out of order.

CLEAR GETS and READ If one or more GET statements are followed by a command line containing the CLEAR GETS command, the field contents are restricted to display only. CLEAR GETS prevents the displayed field information from being modified, because you cannot place the cursor in the field to make alterations. However, if GETs are followed by READ instead of CLEAR GETS, you can move the cursor to the field, and you can enter changes from the keyboard. Therefore, the READ statement lets you enter information that is read into the database. An example of the GET statement used with CLEAR GETS and READ follows for clarification.

```
USE INVTORY
@ 10,55 GET DES
@ 11,55 GET PN
CLEAR GETS
@ 12,55 GET QTY
@ 13,55 GET COST
READ
```

Here, the values of DES and PN are displayed but cannot be changed. The values of QTY and COST, however, can be modified. The cursor appears in the field QTY. Pressing Return leaves the field unchanged, pressing the cursor keys allows movement among the active fields.

The fields QTY and COST and internal data on their screen locations, formats, etc., constitute the GET TABLE, a memory table of the active GET fields.

COMBINING GET WITH SAY When the SAY . . . GET combination is used, as in the next example, the field contents are displayed immediately to the right of the SAY text. An example of this form of the GET statement follows.

```
USE MEMBERS
@ 5,15 SAY "                    Member's Name " GET NAME
@ 6,15 SAY 'Street Address ' GET ADR
@ 7,15 SAY '          City, State, and Zip Code' GET CSZ
CLEAR GETS
@ 8,15 SAY "Are this member's dues paid (Y/N)?" GET PAID
READ
```

The NAME, ADR, and CSZ fields are restricted to display in rows 5, 6, and 7; the CLEAR GETS command prevents field contents from being modified. However, the cursor is positioned at the PAID field to allow modification. This is accomplished with the READ command on the line following the last GET statement.

USING GET WITH MEMORY VARIABLES You can also get memory variables with the GET statement. This small command file demonstrates the use of the GET statement with memory variables. You may wish to type it and try it out on your computer.

```
* GETEST.PRG
X = 0
Y = 0
C = 5
CLS
@ 5,5 SAY 'Enter a new value for X ' GET X
@ ROW()+1,C SAY 'Enter a new value for Y ' GET Y PICT '99'
READ
SET INTENSITY OFF
CLS
@ 5,C SAY 'The values for X and Y are ' GET X PICTURE '99'
@ ROW()+1,C+23 SAY 'and ' GET Y PICTURE '99'
CLEAR GETS
WAIT
SET INTENSITY ON
CLS
CANCEL
```

If you try this program, notice that the input GET for X uses the default number format ('9999999.99') and the input GET for Y sets its own default. As a result, you can enter a wide range of numbers for X but only one- or two-digit numbers as Y. However, if you enter anything except a one- or two-digit number as the X value, it cannot be displayed, because the display GET specifies a '99' format. If you enter "100" as the value of X, the screen displays "**" to indicate a number too large for the format.

CONTROLLING INPUT WITH THE ON FIELD . . . ENDON STRUCTURE By inserting an ON FIELD structure between the GET commands and the READ command, you can impose a number of controls on the READ command. ON FIELDS allows you to include commands that are executed when a specified field is altered for error checking or display purposes. Using the :FIELD system variable, you can even affect the order in which fields are read.

VP-Info provides a separate command, NOUPDATE, which can be included in an ON FIELDS structure to prevent updating of data during a READ operation. Unless you have SET SAVE OFF, changes to data are recorded as the record pointer moves. However, if you wish to include some error-checking mechanism inside a routine that allows the operator to edit existing records, you must prevent the updating of data until checking is completed. By including NOUPDATE options in the ON FIELDS routines in CASE or IF structures, pairing the NOUPDATEs with FLUSH commands (Module 33), you can control the moment of updating. The FLUSH/NOUPDATE sequence is used in the program for the Typical Operation section of Module 44.

ON FIELD is followed by numbered references to the active fields in the Get Table, with instructions for execution after that field is read. These commands are normally executed twice, once when the field is read and again as the computer exits from the structure through the ENDON command. To suppress the second execution, include the directive, SET EXECUTE OFF before the ON FIELD command. While the fields are being read, VP-Info keeps track of the current field's Get Table number in the system variable :FIELD. By changing that variable, you can change the order of the Reads. Here is the ON FIELD structure from the program in the Typical Operation for this module. The program adds records to the ABC database.

```
                                     Remarks
ON FIELD                             ; Include the field names in your comments.
FIELD 1                              ; NAME. Check for duplicate name.
   LOCATE for NAME = MName
   IF .NOT. EOF                      ; A record number was located.
     @ 10,10 SAY MName+" is in the database. Use EDIT to change record."
     WAIT                            ; Let the user read the message.
     @ 10, 0                         ; Erase message.
       :FIELD = 1                    ; Go back to MName input for correction.
   ELSE
       :FIELD = 3                    ; MName is new, so accept it and go to Extn.
   ENDIF
FIELD 2           ; YEAR. Since YEAR is on the same line as NAME, normally it would be read second.
   MAge = VAL($(DATE,1,4)) - VAL(Year)      ; Figure AGE by subtracting the birth year
*                                             from the current year.
   :FIELD = 5                        ; Go to Memo (Last field).
FIELD 3           ; EXTN               Accept Extn.
FIELD 4           ; MAIL               Accept Mail.
   :FIELD = 2                        ; Go back to Year.
FIELD 5           ; MEMO               The last field.
   IF !(Memo) = "Y"                  ; Create a memo.
      MInfo= :AVAIL                  ; Give it the next available volume number.
      WINDOW 15,23                   ; Open an Editor window.
      WRITE .MInfo                   ; Write the memo volume.
      WINDOW                         ; Close the window.
   ELSE                              ; DON'T write a memo.
      MInfo= 1                       ; Link Info to the "No Memo" message.
   ENDIF
ENDON                                ; End of Field structure.
```

Ordinarily, the @YEAR field is read second, but this ON FIELDS structure forces column-wise reading, while saving the @Memo field for last because the WINDOW and WRITE commands make complex demands on the screen. If the last field read is not the field in the Get Table with the highest number, then you must include the command :FIELD = 65 in the instructions for the field that is being read last. Otherwise, the :FIELD system variable is incremented to the next field in numerical order and your Get Table is trapped in a loop that forces restarting the computer. Here is an example where Memo is read before Year:

```
FIELD 2         ; YEAR              Normally would be read second.
   MAGE = val($(DATE,1,4)) - val(Year)
   :FIELD = 65                    ; Exit Get Table.
FIELD 3         ; EXTN              Accept Extn.
FIELD 4         ; MAIL              Accept Mail.
FIELD 5         ; MEMO              The last field.
   IF !(Memo) = "Y"               ; Create a memo.
      MInfo= :AVAIL               ; Give it the next available volume number.
      WINDOW 10,20                ; Open an Editor window.
      WRITE .MInfo                ; Write the memo volume.
      WINDOW                      ; Close the window.
   ELSE                           ; DON'T write a memo.
      MInfo= 1                    ; Link Info to the "No Memo" message.
   ENDIF
   :FIELD = 2                     ; Go back to Year.
ENDON                             ; End of Field structure.
```

APPLICATIONS

The GET statement has many applications. With @ *row,col* designator, GET is used to display and modify the contents of fields and memory variables at specific screen positions. The ability to use SAY with GET lets you display or print field contents at any row and column position with corresponding text. If the GET statement is followed by the CLEAR GETS command, then the contents cannot be edited. They can be edited if followed by the READ command.

The PICTURE clause is used to format field contents with dollar signs, commas, slash signs or other desired characters or symbols. It controls the format of data entry. For example, you can force uppercase entry by using a statement like:

```
@ 12,15 GET NAME PICTURE '!!!!!!!!!!'
```

The ON FIELDS . . . ENDON structure allows you to insert error-checking in a Get Table, control the order of Field reading, include HELP screens with Fields, and generally modify and customize data entry on a field-by-field basis.

TYPICAL OPERATION

In this illustration several variations of GET are used in a command file named GET.PRG. The command file uses the ABC database last used in Module 58. Begin at the VP prompt.

1. Type **WRITE GET** and press **Return** to use the VP-Info editor.

2. Type the following command file. (Do not type the explanatory remarks or indentation.)

```
                                        Remarks
* GET.PRG    Uses ON FIELDS structure to add records to ABC.
CLS
USE ABC
SET LIBR to ABCMEMO                     ; Volume 1 contains "No memo for this record."
MNAME= "                                "
YEAR = "1900"
MEMO = "N"                              ; Initialize variables.
APPEND BLANK                            ; Create empty record.
REPLACE DATE with DATE(8)               ; Store today's date to new record.
SET EXECUTE OFF                         ; Suppress second run through FIELDS
TEXT                                    ; Display the following:
          Name: @MName                           Birth Yr: @Year
     Extension: @Extn
     Mail Drop: @Mail
     Memo Y/N : @Memo
ENDTEXT
ON FIELD
FIELD 1           ; NAME                  Check for duplicate name.
   LOCATE FOR NAME = MName
   IF .NOT. EOF                         ; A record number was found.
      @ 10,10 SAY MName+" is in the database. Use EDIT to change record."
      WAIT                              ; Let the user read the message.
      @ 10, 0                           ; Erase message.
      :FIELD = 1                        ; Go back to MName input for correction.
   ELSE
      :FIELD = 3                        ; MName is new, so accept it and go to Extn.
   ENDIF
FIELD 2           ; YEAR                  Normally would be read second.
   MAge = VAL($(DATE,1,4)) - VAL(Year)
   :FIELD = 5                           ; Go to Memo (Last field).
FIELD 3           ; EXTN                  Accept Extn.
FIELD 4           ; MAIL                  Accept Mail.
   :FIELD = 2                           ; Go back to Year.
FIELD 5           ; MEMO                  The last field.
   IF !(Memo) = "Y"                     ; Create a memo.
      MInfo= :AVAIL                     ; Give it the next available volume number.
      WINDOW 10,20                      ; Open an Editor window.
      WRITE .MInfo                      ; Write the memo volume.
      WINDOW                            ; Close the window.
   ELSE                                 ; DON'T write a memo.
      MInfo= 1                          ; Link INFO to the "No Memo" message.
   ENDIF
ENDON                                   ; End of Field structure.
READ                                    ; Read active fields, using Field structure.
*   The REPLACE command stores the three memory variables as data fields.
REPLACE NAME WITH MNAME, INFO WITH Minfo, AGE WITH Mage
  RETURN                                ; Exit from program.
```

3. Press **Alt-F** to format the file, then proofread it carefully.
4. Press **End** and then **Return** to write the command file to disk.
5. Before you run the command file, ABCMEMO.LIB must be available, and it must contain the "No memo" message. If you have not created this file, go to Module 18 for instructions.
6. For consistency, adjust all the current records without memos to key them to volume 1 by typing **REPLACE ALL INFO WITH 1 FOR INFO <1**.
7. Type **DO GET** to invoke the program.
8. When the input screen appears, type **Johns, Bill T.** and press **Return**. Compare your screen to the following:

```
            Johns, Bill T.        is in the database. Use EDIT to change record.
WAITING
```

9. Press **Return**. Notice that the cursor jumps back into the Name field.
10. Type **Sergio, Alice** and press **Return**. Notice that the cursor now moves to the Extn field.
11. Type **1234** as the Extn field, then **5432** as the Mail field. Notice that the cursor jumps from field to field as you fill them, and finally jumps up to the Year field.
12. Type **1947** as the Year field.
13. Type **y** as the Memo field.
14. When the WRITE window opens, type **Alice's memo.** and then press **End** and press **Return** to save the memo. This program returns to the VP prompt after each record entry.

15. Type **LIST** and press **Return** to view the new data. Compare your screen to the following:

```
         Name: Sergio, Alice                               Birth Yr: 1947
    Extension: 1234
    Mail Drop: 5432
    Memo Y/N : Y



1>list
00001  Sergio, Vincent       3596 2084 19821021 29    2
00002  Bishop, Sam           2234 430  19811110 34    1
00003  Collins, Arthur       4554 323  19830612 43    1
00004  Harris, Robert        3353 2230 19850131 38    1
00005  Alexander, T.G.       1104 2084 19820202 26    1
00006  McAllister, Mick      9857 5267 19830625 41    1
00007  Johns, Bill T.        2332 4544 19850915 24    1
00008  Sergio, Alice         1234 5432 19870702 40    3
1>
```

Notice that Alice's age has been computed, and her memo is listed by volume number.

16. After experimenting with the command file, close the library and database by typing the following commands:

    1>**SET LIBRARY TO**
    1>**CLEAR ALL**

17. Delete the command file by typing **DELE FILE GET.PRG** and pressing **Return**.
18. Turn to Module 26 to continue the learning sequence.

Module 35

GO, GOTO, GO BOTTOM, GO TOP, SKIP

DESCRIPTION

This module describes commands used to move the record pointer to a specific record within a database file. As with any command, you must place a database in use before a record positioning command operates. Once the database is open, you can position the record pointer to records within the database using the GO and SKIP commands. A summary of each of these commands is included in the following list.

1. GO *n*, GOTO *n*, or *n* Moves the record pointer to record n. Notice that GO, GOTO, and simply typing a number all position the pointer to the specified record number (n). To save keystrokes, you may prefer to use n or GO n.
2. GO BOTTOM Positions the record pointer to the last record of the database in use.
3. GO TOP Positions the record pointer to the first record of the database in use.
4. SKIP Moves the record pointer to the next record.
5. SKIP *n* Moves the record pointer n records below the present record position.
6. SKIP –*n* Moves the record pointer n records above the present record position.

Most of the entries in this list are self-explanatory. Here is an example of each, provided to ensure that you understand their use. To follow the example, assume you are using a database file named INVTORY that contains 10 records.

```
1>USE INVTORY          ; Puts INVTORY database in use.
1>GO BOTTOM            ; Moves record pointer to last record in database.
1>? #                  ; Displays record number.
     10.00             ; VP-Info conversation displays last record number.
1>3                    ; Moves record pointer to record 3.
1>SKIP 3               ; Moves record pointer to record 6.
1>SKIP -2              ; Moves record pointer to record 4.
1>GOTO 7               ; Moves record pointer to record 7.
1>STORE # TO X         ; Stores record number to memory variable X.
1>GO TOP               ; Moves record pointer to record 1.
1>GO X                 ; Moves record pointer to record 7, the value of X.
1>3                    ; Moves record pointer to record 3.
1>CLEAR                ; Closes database and frees variables.
```

APPLICATIONS

As you can see, moving the record pointer to any record within a database is easy. The GO TOP and GO BOTTOM commands are often used in command files. A popular combination is to APPEND BLANK, which adds a blank record to the bottom of a database (see Module 5), and then move the record pointer to the bottom of the database with GO BOTTOM to enter field contents from the keyboard in response to displayed prompts.

The GO TOP and SKIP commands are also commonly used both from the prompt and within command files. By using the DO WHILE command (Module 27), you can go to the top of a database file, display the current record, SKIP to the next record, display it, and so on until the end of the file is reached. The records can be printed simultaneously using SET PRINT ON. These commands are demonstrated in the Typical Operation section of this module.

TYPICAL OPERATION

In this illustration the GO TOP and SKIP commands are used to display certain fields of each record in the MEMBERS database, modified in Module 42. Begin at the VP prompt.

1. Type **WRITE SHOW** and press **Return** to use the VP-Info editor.
2. Type the following command file. (Do not type the explanatory remarks or indentation.)

```
                                        Remarks
* SHOW.PRG   Lists names and membership dates
ERASE                        ; Clears screen.
USE MEMBERS                  ; Puts MEMBERS database in use.
GO TOP                       ; Positions record pointer to top of database.
IF PRINTER()                 ; Checks for printer. Next 5 lines (an IF. . .ENDIF structure) only
* execute if a printer is present and ready.
    SET PRINT ON             ; Prints and displays data simultaneously.
ENDIF                        ; Ends conditional structure.
DO WHILE .NOT. EOF           ; Causes operation until end-of-file encountered.
    DISPLAY NAME, JOINED OFF    ; Displays NAME and JOINED, no record numbers.
    SKIP                     ; Position record pointer to next record.
ENDDO                        ; Ends DO loop; passes control to next statement.
?
SET PRINT OFF                ; Turns simultaneous printing off.
WAIT                         ; Pauses operation; displays "WAITING" prompt.
USE                          ; Closes database.
ERASE                        ; Clears screen.
CANCEL                       ; Returns control to VP prompt.
```

3. Press **Alt-F** to reformat the program. Notice that the lines inside the IF . . . ENDIF and DO WHILE . . . ENDDO are indented. This indentation provides a quick review of whether structures have been ended properly.
4. Press **End** and then **Return** to write the command file to disk.
5. Prepare your printer for operation. When ready, type **DO SHOW** and press **Return**. Notice that the following information is displayed and printed simultaneously.

```
Williams, David          19801115
Phillips, George W.      19810601
Galvin, Theodore A.      19830215

WAITING
```

6. Press any key to return to the VP prompt when printing is finished.
7. Turn to Module 21 to continue the learning sequence.

Module 36

HELP

DESCRIPTION

The HELP command is used to display on-screen help information about the various VP-Info commands. The HELP command is entered at the VP prompt by pressing the F1 key and Return or by typing:

```
1>HELP
```

and pressing Return. The following HELP menu is displayed.

```
                         VP-Info Help

  Use the arrow keys to move the lightbar and select a topic from the list
  below, then press the <ENTER> key.  You may also move the lightbar to the
  bottom of the screen and type the name of a specific command or function.

                     1. Commands List
                     2. Functions List
                     3. Color Attribute Table
                     4. Command and Field Redirection
                     5. Date Input Formats
                     6. Date Output Formats
                     7. Editing Keys
                     8. Format Strings
                     9. Get Tables
                    10. REPORT Command
                    11. TEXT
                    12. Variables

  ________________________________________________________________________
  Selection Bar ↑↓  Select - ↵. Exit with <Esc> or Enter command.
              Enter topic
```

At this point you can make a selection by moving your cursor down or up with your arrow keys to highlight the selection of your choice. Once the selection is highlighted, press Return. The selected HELP screen is displayed. For example, if you wish to see the "7. Editing Keys" screen, press the Down Arrow six times and then press Return. The following screen is displayed.

```
EDITING KEYS

Use these editing keys to edit field contents during APPEND, EDIT, and BROWSE.
Except as noted, these commands work identically with the above commands:

Moving the Cursor

    Within a field:  Left arrow or Ctrl-S    (one character left)
                     Right arrow or Ctrl-D   (one character right)
                     Ctrl-Left arrow         (to beginning of field)
                     Ctrl-Right arrow        (to end of field)

    Between Fields:  Up arrow or Ctrl-E      (to previous field)
                     Down arrow or Ctrl-X    (to next field)
                     ENTER                   (to next field)

    Between pages:   Ctrl-K                  (to previous page)
                     Ctrl-L                  (to next page)

    Between records: PgUp or Ctrl-R          (to previous record-EDIT/BROWSE)
                     PgDn or Ctrl-C          (to next record)

Next screen - <PgDn>  Previous Screen - <PgUp>   Exit with <Esc>.
             Enter topic
```

Now you can request information on another topic (APPEND, for example), or press PgDn to see the second screen on Editing Keys, or press PgUp to return to the previous screen, the Help Main Menu. Moving around in VP-Info's HELP facility is easy. To leave the HELP facility, press Esc.

You can also display HELP information about a specific command by typing HELP command from the VP prompt, where command is any legitimate VP-Info command. For example, typing HELP USE displays:

```
USE

Opens or selects a data file, optionally with index files. Up to 6 data
files can be open at one time (only one file at a time can be selected).

Form: USE <filename> [INDEX <file list>] [COMPILE] [LOCK/SHARE/READ]

<filename> - The name of the selected data file.

Options: INDEX <file list> - Opens index files and maintains them while the
         data file is open. The first file listed is the active index; it
         determines the record order for all commands.
```

COMPILE - Directs the compiler to open and select a data file and use its fieldnames in place of another data file (see Appendix A).

LOCK/SHARE/READ - Establishes the data file's status on a network.

APPLICATIONS

The ability to display quick reference information on the screen is convenient if you forget which command performs a certain task. You can start by displaying HELP information, rather than referring to printed matter every time you get stuck or want to refresh your memory.

TYPICAL OPERATION

In this illustration the HELP command is used to display information about VP-Info's CREATE command. Begin at the VP prompt.

1. Press **F1** and **Return**. The following information is displayed.

```
                              VP-Info Help

Use the arrow keys to move the lightbar and select a topic from the list
below, then press the <ENTER> key.  You may also move the lightbar to the
bottom of the screen and type the name of a specific command or function.

                         1. Commands List
                         2. Functions List
                         3. Color Attribute Table
                         4. Command and Field Redirection
                         5. Date Input Formats
                         6. Date Output Formats
                         7. Editing Keys
                         8. Format Strings
                         9. Get Tables
                        10. REPORT Command
                        11. TEXT
                        12. Variables

Selection Bar ↑↓  Select - ←┘. Exit with <Esc> or Enter command.
           Enter topic
```

2. Press **Return** for "Commands List." Notice the following:

```
COMMANDS LIST

ASTERISK                  CONTINUE                  FILES
AT SYMBOL (@)             COPY                      FIND
EQUAL SIGN (=)            COPY STRUCTURE            FLUSH
```

```
QUESTION MARKS (? and ??)   COUNT            GLOBAL
ACCEPT                      CREATE           GO or GOTO
APPEND                      CURSOR           IF
APPEND FROM                 DEBUG            INDEX
APPEND TO                   DELETE           INPUT
AVERAGE                     DELETE FILE      LIST
BOX                         DIM              LIST FILES
BREAK                       DIR              LIST MEMORY
BROWSE                      DISPLAY          LOCATE
BROWSE OFF                  DISPLAY MEMORY   LOCK
CANCEL                      DO               LOOP
CASE                        DO CASE          MODIFY
CHAIN                       DO WHILE         NOTE
CLEAR                       EDIT             NOUPDATE
CLEAR GETS                  EJECT            ON ESCAPE
CLOSE                       ELSE             ON FIELD

Next screen - <PgDn>  Previous Screen - <PgUp>   Exit with <Esc>.
            Enter topic
```

3. Type **CREATE** and press **Return**. Compare your screen to the following:

```
CREATE

Displays a screen to create the structure of a new data file.  You may
choose from three types of data files.  Type 1 files allow up to 256 fields
per record.  Type 2 files are identical to those used by dBASE II, with a
maximum of 32 fields per record.  Type 3 files are identical to dBASE III
data files and allow up to 128 fields per record.  You must use the SET
FIELDS command before creating or using files with more than 32 fields.

To list editing keys, use SET MENU ON before entering CREATE.

Form: CREATE <filename> [<type>]

<filename> - The name of the new data file. If you do not specify a
file extension, VP-Info uses DBF.

Option: <type> - 1, 2, or 3: the type of data file to create.  The default
        is Type 2.  The value you specify for this option will be the
        used as the default value when you exit CREATE.

See also: SET FIELDS, MODIFY
```

4. Press **Esc** to exit the HELP facility.

Remember, you can go directly to the HELP CREATE screen by simply typing HELP CREATE from the VP prompt.

5. Turn to Module 17 to continue the learning sequence.

Module 37

IF, ELSE, ENDIF

DESCRIPTION

The IF, ELSE, and ENDIF commands form a complete branching structure. The entire set of commands is called the *IF structure*. It is similar in operation to the DO CASE, OTHERWISE, ENDCASE commands which form the CASE structure described in Module 26. However, the IF statement is better than CASE for checking the presence of a single condition. Look at the following IF statement.

```
IF expression
   :
 (command lines)
   :
ELSE
   :
 (command lines)
   :
ENDIF
```

The IF statement checks to see if the expression is true. If the expression is true, the command lines within the IF portion of the structure are used. If the expression is false, control passes to the ELSE portion or, if there is no ELSE portion, to the command line following the ENDIF statement.

The ELSE statement is an optional command that adds branching to the IF statement. For example, if you drink your coffee black unless real cream is available, you can use the following statements.

If real cream is available
    I'll take my coffee with cream.
Else
    I'll drink my coffee black.
End if (or the decision) process.

Here is the command form in "computerese:"

```
IF Cream
  Coffee+Cream
ELSE
  Coffee
ENDIF
```

When the IF statement is used within a DO WHILE statement, ENDIF must occur before ENDDO (see Module 27). This is illustrated in the following diagram, which also illustrates the indentation conventions for visually signalling the relationship of END terms in structures.

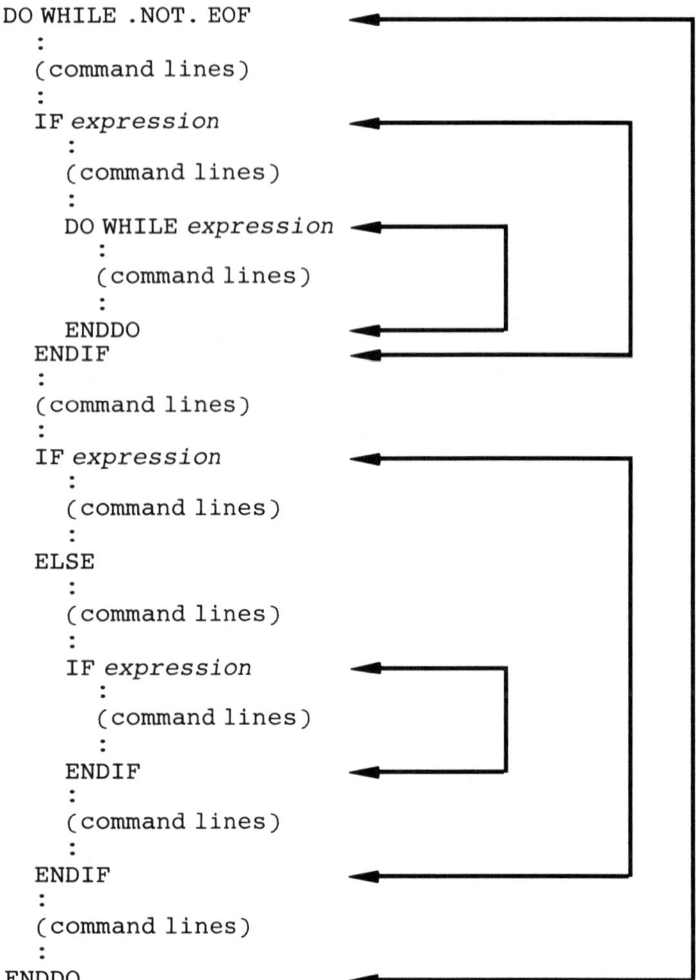

Notice how you can nest IF and DO WHILE statements within IF statements. Although it is not shown, you can also nest CASE statements within IF statements, so you have a large amount of flexibility in command file design. However, too many nested IF structures can cause a STACK OVERFLOW error, locking up the computer. Seven or eight is a reasonable limit, depending on your system configuration. Nesting IF structures also creates less readable programs than other command control structures. Compare the following example program segments, which both choose a command path correlated to a menu selection of 1 to 6:

```
IF Select=1
 (command set 1)
ELSE
 IF Select=2
  (command set 2)
```

```
DO CASE
 CASE Select=1
   (command set 1)
 CASE Select=2
  (command set 2)
```

```
ELSE
  IF Select=3
    (command set 3)
  ELSE
   IF Select=4
    (command set 4)
   ELSE
    IF Select=5
     (command set 5)
    ELSE
     IF Select=6
      (command set 6)
     ELSE
      ? "Invalid"
     ENDIF
   ENDIF
  ENDIF
 ENDIF
ENDIF
```

```
 CASE Select=3
   (command set 3)
 CASE Select=4
   (command set 4)
 CASE Select=5
   (command set 5)
 CASE Select=6
   (command set 6)
 OTHERWISE
   ? "Invalid"
ENDCASE
```

Not only is the IF . . . ENDIF structure longer, but even as straightforward as these selections are, it is hard to read. What is more, it contains one of the commonest of programming errors. (Hint: Each IF requires an ENDIF. Count them.)

APPLICATIONS

The IF command is a good tool to use for testing certain conditions. If the condition is true, the commands within the IF statement become operational. For example, you can use IF in conjunction with a set of commands that terminate operation of the current command file. The following three lines use IF to check the value of the memory variable "Choice." If Choice is equal to X, you can exit the current command file and return to the VP prompt with the CANCEL command.

```
IF Choice='X'
   CANCEL
ENDIF
```

You can exit the current command file to the operating system prompt with the QUIT command by including this structure:

```
IF Choice='X'
   QUIT
ENDIF
```

where QUIT terminates VP-Info operation and takes you back to DOS. If the current command file was called from another command file, you can return to the calling command file with the RETURN command in the form:

```
IF Choice='X'
   RETURN
ENDIF
```

In all three of these examples, IF is testing for an uppercase X. You can write the IF statement so that either an uppercase or lowercase X are accepted as true. Two forms that do this are:

```
IF Choice='X' .OR. Choice ='x'
```

or

```
IF !(Choice)='X'
```

The logical .OR. expression is used in the first example; the uppercase function, which converts lowercase characters to uppercase, is used in the second example, and preferred because it is shorter.

You can use IF to determine whether or not to print displayed text with the following command lines, which also use the PRINTER( ) function to make sure the printer is ready.

```
WAIT 'Type "P" to print, any other key to display ' TO Prt
IF !(Prt) = 'P'
  IF .NOT. PRINTER( )
    ? "Please check printer and type 'G' for Go when ready."
    ACCEPT " " TO Go
    IF !(Go) .AND. PRINTER( )
        SET PRINT ON
    ELSE
        ? "Printer has problem. PRINT abandoned."
    ENDIF
  ENDIF
SET PRINT ON
ENDIF
  :
(command lines)
  :
SET PRINT OFF
  :
RETURN
```

Notice that you can turn the printer "OFF" even if it isn't "ON," so there is no need to surround the SET PRINT OFF command with a second IF . . . ENDIF structure.

Some short and simple conditionals can be set up with the IFF function (See Appendix D). For example, if you have set a variable to logical False, then its value is 0 and you can do the following:

```
? IFF(PRINTER()=0,"No printer","OK")
```

Keep in mind that you cannot set up alternate command paths with this function, so it cannot substitute for the command text above.

TYPICAL OPERATION

In this illustration a small database is created that contains expense information. The IF statement is used in a command file that displays expense information according to the date. Begin at the VP prompt.

1. Type **CREATE EXPENSE** and press **Return**. Create the database structure as shown.

Name	Type	Width	Dec
ITEM	C	15	
DATE	C	8	
AMOUNT	N	6	2
TAX	N	5	2
TOTAL	N	6	2
<End>			

2. Type **APPEND** and press **Return**. Enter the following information into the database. Press **Return** in the TAX and TOTAL fields to leave them blank.

	ITEM	DATE	AMOUNT	TAX	TOTAL
00001	FILE CABINET	01/15/85	99.95	<cr>	<cr>
00002	FOLDERS	01/18/85	6.95	<cr>	<cr>
00003	DESK	02/14/85	350.00	<cr>	<cr>
00004	PAPER	04/02/85	22.50	<cr>	<cr>
00005	RIBBONS	06/16/85	59.00	<cr>	<cr>
00006	PRINTER CABLE	07/11/85	56.00	<cr>	<cr>
00007	FORMS TRACTOR	08/23/85	249.00	<cr>	<cr>
00008	SHEET FEEDER	10/21/85	899.95	<cr>	<cr>
00009	<End>				

3. VP-Info can calculate the TAX field for you. Type **REPLACE ALL TAX WITH AMOUNT * .05** and press **Return**.
4. Use the same method to calculate the TOTAL field: **REPLACE ALL TOTAL WITH AMOUNT + TAX**.
5. Now create your command file by typing **WRITE IFCMD** to use the VP-Info editor.
6. Type the following command file. (Do not type the explanatory remarks or indentation.)

```
                                        Remarks
* IFCMD.PRG — Demonstrates some uses of the IF command.
USE EXPENSE                           ; Put EXPENSE database in use.
Check = Y                             ; Create variables Check and Go
Go = ' '                              ; for Get Table.
DO WHILE T                            ; Continues operation until an exit command.
  CLS                                 ; Clears the screen.
  @  3, 5 SAY "About to print EXPENSES list."
  @  4, 5 SAY "Do you want to check it on the screen first? Y/N"
  @  4,60 GET Check                   ; Check keyboard for Yes/No response.
 READ                                 ; Read input.
  IF Check                            ; Want to check list on screen.
     WINDOW 10,5,23,74 DOUBLE         ; Create window for display.
     DISPLAY ALL                      ; Write display.
     WINDOW                           ; Return to main screen (window still visible).
  ENDIF Check                         ; You may type a note after ENDIF
  @  5, 5 SAY "Print Record Numbers? Y/N " GET Check  ; Using Check again.
  READ                                ; Read new value of logical variable.
```

```
@  6, 5 SAY "Ready to Print. Check printer and then press Return."
WAIT                              ; Allow user to check printer readiness.
IF PRINTER()                      ; System locks if told to set missing printer
   SET PRINT ON                   ; "ON," so this routine is a good safety
ELSE                              ; precaution. If the printer is not ready,
   @  7, 0                        ; the ELSE erases "WAITING" and signals error.
   @  7, 5 SAY "Printer problem. Please check printer"
   @  8, 5 SAY "type 'G' for Go when ready ==>" GET Go PICTURE '!'
   READ                           ; The PICTURE forces uppercase entry.
   IF Go='G' .AND. PRINTER()      ; The .AND. allows the computer to check
      SET PRINT ON                ; both conditions.
   ELSE                           ; When either condition is false, then
      IF .NOT. PRINTER()          ; if the false condition is PRINTER( )
         @ 23,10 SAY "Printer still has problem. PRINT abandoned."
         CANCEL                   ; Print message and return to VP prompt.
       ENDIF .NOT. PRINTER()      ; Notes help the reader keep track of
   ENDIF Go = 'G'                 ; the purpose of each ENDIF.
ENDIF PRINTER()                   ; Last IF . . . ENDIF structure here.
*  Now either the printer is ready or we have returned to the VP prompt.
CLS
SET FORMAT TO PRINT               ; Suppresses echo of printing on screen.
IF Check                          ; Check refers to printing record numbers.
   LIST                           ; If Yes, print them.
ELSE
   LIST OFF                       ; Otherwise, turn them off.
ENDIF Check
?                                 ; Sends last line to printer (always required).
SET PRINT OFF                     ; Stop sending to printer.
SET FORMAT TO SCREEN              ; Resume sending to screen.
RETURN                            ; Return to prompt.
ENDDO                             ; Completes DO WHILE statement.
RETURN                            ; Insurance. There is no path that should get here,
*                                   but always close command files.
```

7. Press **Alt-F** to format the file and then proofread it carefully. When ready, press **End** to write the command file to disk.
8. Run the command file by typing **DO IFCMD** and pressing **Return**. If you do not have a printer, you can still use the program, but you cannot test the PRINTER( ) = True portions.
9. Try all the various paths, including turning off the printer and then turning it on when the first "Printer problem" message appears.
10. Delete the command file by typing **DELE FILE IFCMD.PRG** and pressing **Return**.
11. Turn to Module 27 to continue the learning sequence.

Module 38

INDEX, REINDEX

DESCRIPTION

The INDEX command lets you resequence database records in alphanumeric order without actually organizing the records themselves. In this respect, INDEX is similar to SORT. The resulting index file has the extension .NDX, and is associated with the database from which it was created. Changes to records within a database file are reflected in the index file, because they maintain parallel records. The index file simply lets you look at a database in an indexed order. However, if you change the database file while the index file is not in use, you must use REINDEX to update the index file.

The INDEX command lets you use one or more *key* fields, where key fields are those used to control the indexing sequence. For example, you may want to index a customer database on the CITY and STATE fields. These fields, then, become your key fields. If you want to view the records within a database by state and cities within the state, your INDEX command would be:

```
1>INDEX ON !(STATE)+!(CITY) TO index name
```

where *index name* is a descriptive index filename of your choice. This command tells VP-Info to put states in alphabetical order and arrange the cities in alphabetical order within each state, using uppercase versions of the field values. Using uppercase to index simplifies the later use of the index. Indexing is done in ascending order, and you may use a portion of a field as your index, such as the Zip Code in a CSZ field containing data like "Tampa, FL 32111." If you index on numeric fields, you should convert them to strings with the STR( ) function, or you cannot use FIND (Module 32) with them.

USING AN INDEX FILE When you open a database, you can specify up to seven indexes for it. VP-Info automatically directs commands to the first index file specified, which is called the *active* index. If you have already opened the database file, you can still put the index file of your choice in use. For example, to use the index file SORTDEX, if the name of the database file from which the index file was created is STATS, open the SORTDEX index file with:

```
1>USE STATS INDEX SORTDEX
```

You can think of this statement as saying, "Use the STATS database with its index file named SORTDEX." If STATS is already open, open the index with:

```
1>SET INDEX TO SORTDEX
```

If you create a new index, VP-Info automatically sets all current indexes off and makes the new index the active one, unless you specify the current indexes as part of a new SET command. For instance, if you create COSTDEX while SORTDEX is already open, use this command to make COSTDEX active but keep SORTDEX open for updating:

```
1>SET INDEX TO COSTDEX, SORTDEX
```

INDEX COMMAND FORMS A few forms of the INDEX command were described in the preceding paragraphs. However, for your convenience they are collected in the following list with explanations of each.

1. INDEX ON *fieldname* TO *filename* Indexes database structure and contents, indexed on the named field in alphanumeric (ascending) order, to the named file.

   ```
   1>INDEX ON NAME TO TEMPFILE
   ```

2. INDEX ON *field1* + *field2*. . . TO *filename* Indexes database on the named fields to the named index file. The total number of characters in the fields selected may not exceed 60.

   ```
   1>INDEX ON ZIP+NAME TO TEMPFILE
   ```

3. INDEX ON STR(*numeric field,max length,dec*) TO *filename* Creates an index on a numeric field. Notice that because all index entries must be the same size, we must specify the maximum possible length of the numeric field. A FIND command requires that the leading blanks for the index key be included.

   ```
   1>INDEX ON STR(Cost,7,2) TO VALUE
   ```

4. INDEX ON *expression* TO *filename* The expression can be a portion of a fieldname, such as the Zip Code portion of a StateZip field using the pattern "CO 80120."

   ```
   1>INDEX ON $(StateZip,3,5) TO ZCODES
   ```

5. INDEX ON *key* TO *filename* FOR *expression* Creates an index consisting of only those records fitting the expression. This is useful when creating reports. Display limits imposed with INDEX are faster than those imposed by a FOR clause in a REPORT command. There is no way to tell after the fact what conditions were imposed on an index, so these indexes should be temporary.

   ```
   1>INDEX ON FNames TO TMFNMS FOR FNames >"Joe"
   ```

UPDATING INDEXES When changes are made to existing database records, the open index files are updated automatically. However, if you do not open an index before making changes to your database, that index is not automatically updated unless you open the indexes by typing: SET INDEX TO *filename1,filename2* . . . where *filename* is the name of one or more index files associated with the database in use. Once this command is in effect, type: REINDEX to bring the indexes up to date.

REINDEX The REINDEX command is available for updating existing index files. This is usually faster than using the SET INDEX TO command. Once you've made changes to a database, simply open the index file and type REINDEX. You'll see the message:

```
Re-index by field
    n RECORDS IN  TOTAL INDEXED
```

This process only takes a matter of seconds. Once done, the index file is ready for use, reflecting the latest database changes.

MOVING THE RECORD POINTER IN AN INDEXED FILE When you use an indexed file, you will notice that the record numbers are not in sequential order. When you GO BOTTOM or GO TOP, you do not arrive at the bottom or top of the database, you go to the bottom or top of the index file. You can still address records by record number, so if you store a record number in a memory variable, you can move to it in the indexed file. The following few command lines demonstrate the technique for storing a record number to a memory variable and then finding the record in an indexed file.

```
                                    Remarks
1>USE STATS                       ; Puts STATS database in use.
1>GO BOTTOM                       ; Positions record pointer to last record in database.
1>STORE # TO Nbr                  ; Store record number to memory variable NBR.
1>INDEX ON !(ST)+!(CITY) TO NEWDEX
*   Indexes on ST and CITY fields in uppercase to file called NEWDEX.
1>USE STATS INDEX NEWDEX          ; Puts NEWDEX index file in use.
1>GO Nbr                          ; Positions pointer to record number saved in NBR.
```

The FIND command, described in Module 32, is used to find the first record containing a specified expression. FIND locates character strings. Like several other VP-Info commands, FIND is only used with indexed database files.

APPLICATIONS

There are several major advantages offered by the INDEX command. First, it lets you work with a single database file that may be indexed in a variety of ways. Second, indexing is quick. It also lets you take advantage of the FIND command, which provides an extremely fast way to find a specified value within a database record. When you begin reorganizing information within a database on a regular basis, you will find yourself making frequent use of the INDEX command.

TYPICAL OPERATION

In this illustration the ABC database created in Module 5 is expanded with DATE and AGE fields. Next, the INDEX command is used to reorganize the database in date sequence. Finally, a new record is appended and the REINDEX command is used to update the index file. Begin at the VP prompt.

1. Type **USE ABC** and press **Return**.
2. Type **MODIFY** and press **Return**. Add the following fields:

```
DATE     Char      8
AGE      Numeric   2
```

3. Press **End** and then press **Return** to return to the VP prompt.

4. Type **BROWSE**, press **Return**, then press **Ctrl-Home** and update the database as shown, adding DATE and AGE values:

```
        NAME                 EXTN MAIL DATE     AGE
00001   Sergio, Vincent      4596 2084 19821021 29
00002   Bishop, Sam          2234 430  19811110 34
00003   Collins, Arthur      4554 323  19830612 43
00004   Harris, Robert       4353 2230 19850131 38
00005   Alexander, T. G.     1104 2084 19820202 26
00006   McAllister, Mick     8957 5267 19830625 41
```

5. When finished, press **End** to return to the VP prompt.
6. Type **INDEX ON DATE TO DSORT** and press **Return**.
7. Type **LIST** and press **Return**. Notice that the display is indexed in date order:

```
1>INDEX ON DATE TO DSORT
    6 RECORDS READ
    6 RECORDS INDEXED
1>LIST
00002  Bishop, Sam           2234 430  19811110 34
00005  Alexander, T.G.       1104 2084 19820202 26
00001  Sergio, Vincent       3596 2084 19821021 29
00003  Collins, Arthur       4554 323  19830612 43
00006  McAllister, Mick      9857 5267 19830625 41
00004  Harris, Robert        3353 2230 19850131 38
1>
```

8. Type **INDEX ON !(NAME) TO ANAMES** and press **Return**.
9. Type **LIST** and press **Return** to observe the new index order.
10. Type **APPEND** and press **Return**; then add the following record:

```
NAME     Johns, Bill T.
PHONE    2332
MAIL     4544
DATE     19850915
AGE      24
```

11. Press **End** to return to the VP prompt.

12. Type **LIST** and press **Return**. Observe that the new record has been inserted where it belongs alphabetically.

```
1>LIST
00005  Alexander, T.G.        1104 2084 19820202 26
00002  Bishop, Sam            2234 430  19811110 34
00003  Collins, Arthur        4554 323  19830612 43
00004  Harris, Robert         3353 2230 19850131 38
00007  Johns, Bill T.         2332 4544 19850915 24
00006  McAllister, Mick       9857 5267 19830625 41
00001  Sergio, Vincent        3596 2084 19821021 29
1>
```

13. Type **SET INDEX TO DSORT**, press **Return**; and then type **LIST** again. Notice that because DSORT was not open, the new record is missing.
14. Type **REINDEX** to update the index.
15. Type **LIST** and press **Return**. Notice that all the records are now in the proper indexed order.

```
1>LIST
00002  Bishop, Sam            2234 430  19811110 34
00005  Alexander, T.G.        1104 2084 19820202 26
00001  Sergio, Vincent        3596 2084 19821021 29
00003  Collins, Arthur        4554 323  19830612 43
00006  McAllister, Mick       9857 5267 19830625 41
00004  Harris, Robert         3353 2230 19850131 38
00007  Johns, Bill T.         2332 4544 19850915 24
1>
```

16. Type **CLEAR ALL** and press **Return** to close all files.
17. Type the following commands to recover disk space used by the practice index files:

```
1>DELETE FILE DSORT.NDX
1>DELETE FILE ANAMES.NDX
```

18. Turn to Module 41 to continue the learning sequence.

Module 39

INTERACTIVE MODE (?), # (RECORD NUMBER)

DESCRIPTION

You have already entered several commands at the VP prompt. Although you may not have realized it, you were operating in the interactive mode. The interactive mode, sometimes called "immediate" or "conversational" mode, lets you enter a command at the prompt to obtain an immediate response. To further your skills in interactive operations, this module describes the use of the question mark (?), which is a shorthand form of the DISPLAY OFF *field names* command.

This module also introduces the # function, where # stands for *record number*.

To begin, here is the # function. This series of commands is used to display the last record in a database.

```
1>USE WAREHOUS
1>GO BOTTOM
1>? #
     325.00
```

This list of commands puts a database named WAREHOUS in use, positions the record pointer to the last (or bottom) record, and displays the record number. VP-Info responds by displaying the record number, which appears as 325.00 in the numeric format.

The ? # combination displays a numeric value equivalent to the current record number (the record at which the record pointer is located). By converting the record number to a number, you can store the record number value to a memory variable for future use. Memory variables are discussed in detail in Module 63. Here, they are used for illustration purposes.

```
1>STORE # TO Nbr
```

At this point, you can check the contents of memory variable Nbr with the ? command. This is done as follows:

```
1>? Nbr
     325.00
```

What this command line really says is, "What is the value of memory variable Nbr?" The response is printed by VP-Info on the next line.

In addition to using the question mark as a DISPLAY command, you can also use it as a print statement. For example, a question mark by itself in a command file is the same as saying DISPLAY BLANK. This causes a blank line to be displayed. If you use SET PRINT ON to print a LIST or DISPLAY, following the LIST command with a ? command clears the printer of the last line of the list.

```
1>SET PRINT ON
1>LIST OFF
1>?

1>SET PRINT OFF
1>
```

A question mark followed by text within either single or double quotation marks or brackets displays the text. This is handy for user prompts. A more detailed explanation is provided in Module 47.

The interactive mode is used in many ways. The following list shows a few examples of interactive conversation.

1.
```
1>USE EMPLRECD          ; Put EMPLRECD database in use.
1>GO BOTTOM             ; Go to last record in database.
1>? #                   ; What's the number of the current record?
     325.00
```

2.
```
1>? 25 * 12             ; What's the product of 25 times 12?
     300.00
```

3.
```
1>? 5*(12 - 7)          ; Print 5 times quantity 12 minus 7.
      25.00
```

4.
```
1>X = 'CODE'            ; Store the string "CODE" to X.
1>? X                   ; What's the value of X?
CODE
```

5.
```
1>? DATE(2)             ; What's the system date in format 2?
11/04/87
```

6.
```
1>? CHR(7)              ; What's the value of CHR(7)?
<BEEP>                  ; CHR(7) causes a beep on the speaker.
```

7.
```
1>? '$10.00'+CHR(13)+'     __' ; CHR(13) is a carriage return without a Paper feed command
                               (ASCII 10); thus, when the printer is on, this command
                               underscores the '00' in '$10.00' on the printer.
```

8.
```
1>STORE 8 TO Y          ; Stores 8 to memory variable Y.

1>STORE 9 TO Z          ; Stores 9 to memory variable Z.

1>? Y * Z               ; What's the product of Y times Z?
     72.00
```

9.
```
1>USE WAREHOUS          ; Puts WAREHOUS database in use.
1>GO BOTTOM             ; Positions record pointer to last record.
1>? PART_NO             ; What's the content of the PART:NO field?
MT-0912
```

In the interactive mode, a double question mark (??) causes the display to appear on the same line. This is sometimes confusing, because the response is often run in with the command.

APPLICATIONS

There are many applications for using the question mark in the interactive mode. It lets you use VP-Info like a calculator. You can enter the question mark followed by mathematical expressions to get quick answers. If you need a "calculator tape," you can type the SET PRINT ON command before you start your calculations. This causes displayed information to be printed simultaneously. Once the printer is active, you can enter your calculations from the keyboard.

The question mark is also used to display the contents of memory variables and database fields. This application is shown in entries 1 and 9 in the previous list of examples.

The ability to convert a record number to an integer is also an extremely useful tool. Without this capability, it would be difficult to enter a command that stores a record number to a memory variable automatically. With the record number saved, the record pointer can be returned to the same record later in the command sequence.

TYPICAL OPERATION

In this illustration, the ? is used in the interactive mode to perform some calculations. Then you prepare a short command file that uses the record number function to save the record number value to a memory variable. Begin at the VP prompt.

1. Type the following commands and press **Return** after each.

```
1>STORE 7.50 TO RATE
1>STORE 40 TO HRS
1>? RATE*HRS
   300.00
1>? 52*(RATE*HRS)
  15600.00
1>? 156000/12
  13000.00
1>
```

2. Type **WRITE SHOWLAST** and press **Return** to use the VP-Info editor.
3. Type the following command file. (Do not type the explanatory remarks.)

```
                                  Remarks
* SHOWLAST.PRG              ; Saves and displays number of last record in database.
ERASE                       ; Clears screen.
File="        "             ; Initialize variable.
LIST FILES ON B:            ; Present list of available databases.
ACCEPT "Which DATABASE : " TO File        ; Accept input of filename.
?                           ; Displays a blank line.
? '      THIS PROGRAM SHOWS YOU THE LAST RECORD NUMBER'      ; Displays text.
?
? '       IN THE DATABASE CALLED '+File+'.'
```

```
?
USE &File
GO BOTTOM
Rec= STR(#,3,0)           ; Stores string of record number to memory variable REC.
?
? '          The Last Record in ',File,' is ',REC,'.'
WAIT                      ; Displays "WAITING" and waits for key press.
ERASE                     ; Clears screen.
CANCEL                    ; Returns to VP-Info prompt.
```

NOTE

The number-to-string function (STR) is described in Appendix D.

4. Press **End** and **Return** to write the command file to disk.
5. Type **DO SHOWLAST** and press **Return**.
6. The prompt "Which DATABASE : _" is displayed below a list of available files. Respond by typing a database file name, such as **MEMBERS**, and pressing **Return**.

```
PHONE.DBF       ALPHA.DBF       XYZ.DBF       PICNIC.DBF       MEMBERS.DBF

1063 bytes in 5 files.
3088966 bytes remaining.

which DATABASE :                                    ; Type MEMBERS and press Return
```

7. Compare the result to the following:

```
    THIS PROGRAM SHOWS YOU THE LAST RECORD NUMBER

    IN THE DATABASE CALLED MEMBERS.


     The Last Record in  MEMBERS  is    3 .
WAITING
```

8. Press any key to return to the VP prompt.
9. Turn to Module 35 to continue the learning sequence.

Module 40

LIBRARY, SET LIBRARY TO, REMLIB( )

DESCRIPTION

In addition to the TEXT structure, you can also use the LIBRARY facility for storing and retrieving texts. The SET LIBRARY TO *filename* command opens a file of text material called *filename*.LIB with volume numbers assigned to specific parts of the file. The next volume number available for storing new text is stored to the system variable :AVAIL. To add a text to the library, simply type WRITE .*number*, where the number is the contents of :AVAIL. You can also add previously created .TXT files to the library by opening the text file into the editor and then saving it with a volume number rather than a filename. For example, if you wished to add MENU.TXT to ADRBOOK.LIB, the following series of commands would do it:

```
1>SET LIBRARY TO ADRBOOK
1>WRITE MENU.TXT
```

In the editor, press End but instead of pressing Return to save the file, type .1 and press Del to erase the former filename. The contents of the editor are saved to the library without affecting the MENU.TXT file itself.

NOTE

This trick also allows you to make a copy of a TXT or PRG file.

A one-thousand-character text fills roughly four library volumes. A text can be edited by its volume number, but space in a library cannot be recovered when you edit a text. When creating a library, be sure to keep track of the starting volume numbers, because VP-Info does not provide a list of them. When using a library, be sure to close it afterwards with a second SET LIBRARY TO command, or you will have an open file on your disk.

The REMLIB function can remove an entry from a library. To use it, specify the volume number that you wish deleted from the current library. For example, REMLIB(1) would remove the first volume in the library.

APPLICATIONS

The LIBRARY file is a faster and more efficient way to store text data. Since all your texts are stored sequentially in one file, using a library file only consumes one of your twenty allowable open files. Speed is also gained by avoiding disk access for TXT files.

A LIBRARY can be created with its volume numbers keyed to the records of a database, allowing you to attach memos of indefinite length to individual records. For example, you could open a library called MEMBERS.LIB, and then modify the MEMBERS database by making the INFO field numeric with five places (the highest possible volume number is 65536). Thus, your database record would consume only 5 bytes for that field instead of 40. To add an informational memo to a record, store the available volume number to the INFO field, and then write the appropriate volume in the editor. This new text file would be stored sequentially in MEMBERS.LIB and could be retrieved by sorting the record's INFO field contents to a variable and then using that variable to select and display a volume.

TYPICAL OPERATION

This operation stores MENU.TXT as a portion of the ADRBOOK library file. Then it modifies the MENU program previously modified in Module 65 so it can use the library file.

1. Type **SET LIBRARY TO ADRBOOK** and press **Return**.
2. Type **? :AVAIL** and press **Return**. Notice that the first available volume number is 1, indicating that VP-Info has created the ADRBOOK.LIB file and the file is currently empty.
3. Type **WRITE MENU.TXT** and press **Return**.
4. Press **End** but do not press Return. Instead, respond to the prompt "Save this file as" by typing **.1** and then pressing **Del** until the original filename is gone.
5. Type **? :AVAIL** and press **Return**. Notice that MENU.TXT filled four volumes, leaving 5 as the next available volume.
6. Type **WRITE MENU** and press **Return**. Notice that since PRG is the assumed extension, it need not be specified.
7. Type the following as the second line of the file: **SET LIBRARY TO ADRBOOK**.
8. Modify the line reading "TEXT MENU" to read "TEXT .1" and then compare the top of your screen to the following:

```
MENU.PRG                              VP-Info WRITE                  INSERT

....+....1....+....2....+....3....+....4....+....5....+....6....+....7....+....8
* MENU.PRG◄
ERASE◄
SET LIBRARY TO ADRBOOK◄
SET TALK OFF◄
* Use a DO WHILE loop to sustain operation.◄
DO WHILE T◄
   store ' ' to Choice◄
   text .1◄
   read◄
* Use series of CASE statements to run the selected command file.◄
```

9. Press **End** and then press **Return** to save the modified file.
10. Type **DO MENU** to test the new file.
11. Type **7** to exit from the program.
12. When you are through experimenting with the program, do not delete the files created in this module; they are used in the following modules.
13. Turn to Module 70 to continue the learning sequence.

Module 41

LOCATE, CONTINUE

DESCRIPTION

The LOCATE command lets you find records within a database that match one or more specified string, numeric, or logical expressions. The location process begins with the first record in the active database and moves down in a top-to-bottom sequence. When a matching record is located, the record can be displayed, altered, or deleted, or you may want to extract information from one or more fields. If there are several records within the database that match the LOCATE parameters, you can move down to the next matching record using the CONTINUE command.

The general form of the LOCATE command is:

```
1>LOCATE FOR expression
```

Once a match is found, VP-Info displays the record number in the form, "Record *n*" where *n* is the record number. To find the next match, type CONTINUE and press Return. If the bottom of the file is encountered before another match is found, no "Record" message is displayed.

Examples of the LOCATE and CONTINUE commands are provided in the following list.

1. LOCATE FOR *expression* Positions the record pointer to the first record in which the named field satisfies the expression; reports the record's number.

   Examples:

```
1>LOCATE FOR NAME = 'Jo'        ; Locates first record whose name field begins
Record 27                       ; with 'Jo,' where NAME is a character-type
1>                              ; field that must match upper- and lowercase,
                                  such as Jones and Johnson. The located record's
                                  number is displayed.

1>LOCATE FOR ZIP = '07632'      ; Locates first record containing 07632 in
Record 288                      ; the ZIP field, where ZIP is a numeric-type
1>                              ; field.
1>DISPLAY ZIP,NAME OFF          ; Displays current record's ZIP and NAME
07632 Sergio, Vincent           ; fields.

1>LOCATE FOR PAID = T           ; Locates first record containing a logical true
Record 21                       ; value in the PAID field, where PAID is a
                                  logical-type field.

1>LOCATE FOR .NOT. PAID         ; Locates the first record containing a logical
Record 7                        ; false value in the PAID field.
```

2. CONTINUE Continues searching for next matching record beginning at the current record position. The CONTINUE command continues to find matching records until an end-of-file condition is encountered.

   Examples:

```
1>LOCATE FOR ZIP='80121'      ; Locate first record fitting
Record 251                    ; condition.
1>CONTINUE                    ; Locate next ZIP = '80121.'
Record 317
```

3. LOCATE FOR *expression* .AND. expression Positions the record pointer to the first record having fields that match the expressions. Two or more fields can be specified; the .OR. and .NOT. operators (as shown in previous examples) can also be used.

   Examples:

```
1>LOCATE FOR CSZ = "Tampa" .AND. AGE<40
Record 17
1>LOCATE FOR CSZ= "Culver City" .OR. NAME = 'Phillips'
```

4. LOCATE FOR @(*expression,fieldname*)>0 Locates the record containing a partial match within the named field. For example, if you're trying to find "Smithsonian" in the NAME field, you could locate it without paging through all the "Smith" entries by typing:

```
1>LOCATE FOR @['Smiths',NAME]>0
```

5. LOCATE FOR *fieldname* = *memory variable* Positions the record pointer to the first record wherein the field contents match the value of the named memory variable. The following example illustrates the use of a memory variable.

```
1>STORE 'Smith' TO MName
1>LOCATE FOR NAME = MName
```

6. LOCATE NEXT FOR *expression* The LOCATE command normally reads all of the database. CONTINUE allows you to continue searching for the same *expression* from the position where the first record was located. But if you change the expression, the record pointer returns to the top of the database to start over, unless you specify LOCATE NEXT for the new expression. This form of the 'NEXT' scope does not take a numeric argument, however; it simply avoids resetting the pointer.

```
1>LOCATE FOR ZIP = '75080'
Record 235
1>LOCATE NEXT FOR ZIP = '10010'
Record 293
```

The LOCATE command is a good way to identify records within a non-indexed database that match certain parameters. The operation speed of LOCATE is slightly slower when a database is indexed.

The FIND command is another VP-Info command that lets you search for specific records within a database. However, FIND only operates on key fields within an indexed database, and it only finds the first record in a database that matches the specified parameter. If you need to find a series of records, LOCATE is the preferable command. The FIND command is described in Module 32. INDEX is described in Module 38.

APPLICATIONS

Because of their ease of use, the LOCATE and CONTINUE commands are excellent for quickly finding all records within a database containing a specified expression within one or more fields. The LOCATE and CONTINUE commands are frequently used within DO WHILE loops in command files. Here, records in an active database can be found, displayed, or altered automatically. The Typical Operation section of this module illustrates such a procedure.

TYPICAL OPERATION

In this illustration the LOCATE and CONTINUE commands are used in a command file to display selected records within the ABC database last modified in Module 38. Begin at the VP prompt.

1. Type **WRITE SEARCH** and press **Return** to use the editor.
2. Type the following SEARCH.PRG command file. (Do not type the explanatory remarks or indentation.)

```
                                        Remarks
* SEARCH.PRG - A command file that locates a record for viewing.
USE ABC                              ; Puts ABC database in use.
STORE T TO Working                   ; Puts command file in DO WHILE loop as long as the
DO WHILE Working                     ; variable Working is True.
   ERASE                             ; Clears screen.
   ? '  ENTER THE NAME IN THE RECORD YOU WANT TO SEE'        ; Displays prompt.
   ?                                                         ; Displays blank line.
   ACCEPT '            OR PRESS RETURN TO QUIT  ' TO MNAME   ; Displays prompt.
   ERASE                             ; Clears screen.
   IF MNAME=' '                      ; Looks for condition where MNAME is blank.
*                                      The IF statement checks for the desire to quit.
*                                      The indented lines between IF and ENDIF are acted
*                                      upon only if Mname is blank.
      CLEAR ALL                      ; Closes files and memory variables.
      CANCEL                         ; Cancels command file operation.
   ENDIF                             ; Passes control to next command line.
   LOCATE FOR !(NAME) = !(MNAME)       ; Locates record with MNAME in NAME field.
*  Converts contents to uppercase to assure a match.
   IF EOF                            ; Looks for end-of-file condition.
      ? "CAN'T FIND That One."         ; Displays text.
      WAIT                           ; Pauses operation until a key is pressed.
      LOOP                           ; Returns to line below DO WHILE statement.
```

```
        ENDIF                              ; Passes control to next command line.
        DO WHILE .NOT. EOF                 ; Continues operation while not end of file.
            DISPLAY NAME,EXTN,MAIL OFF     ; Displays named fields.
            CONTINUE                       ; Locates next matching record.
        ENDDO                              ; Ends DO WHILE .NOT. EOF statement.
        WAIT                               ; Pauses operation until a key is pressed.
    ENDDO                                  ; Ends DO WHILE Working process.
    USE                                    ; Closes database file.
    ERASE                                  ; Clears screen.
    RETURN                                 ; Returns to display of VP prompt.
```

3. Press **Alt-F** to format the program, then proofread it carefully.
4. Press **End** and **Return** to save the command file.
5. Run the command file by typing **DO SEARCH** and pressing **Return**.
6. In response to the following screen prompt, type a name, **Bishop**, and press **Return**.

```
ENTER THE NAME IN THE RECORD YOU WANT TO SEE

      OR PRESS RETURN TO QUIT
```

Notice that the record containing the name you typed is displayed. If a match is not located, then the following prompt is displayed:

```
CAN'T FIND That One.
WAITING
```

If a match is found, then the match is displayed in a form similar to the following:

```
Bishop, Sam              2234 430
WAITING
```

7. Press any key, then enter another name to locate, and press **Return**, or press **Return** alone and return to the VP prompt.
8. Turn to Module 32 to continue the learning sequence.

Module 42

MODIFY

DESCRIPTION

There are times when you find that the structure of a database requires a change to fit an unexpected need. For example, you may need to add an additional field or change the length of a field. The MODIFY command lets you insert, delete, add, and change fields within your database structure.

To modify the structure of a database, put it in use with the USE *filename* command. Then type:

```
1>MODIFY
```

and press Return. The database creation mask is displayed showing field names, types, widths, and decimal places. You can move the cursor to the desired field and change the field information. You can also insert new fields at the cursor position by pressing Ctrl-N. Fields are deleted by pressing Ctrl-T.

Be careful not to modify field lengths or types that might affect important data. For example, if you make a field length shorter than the information contained within it, the data will be "trimmed" due to the shorter field length. If you change a character field that contains alpha text strings to a numeric field, you will lose the text, and the field will contain a value of zero.

BACKING UP FILES PRIOR TO MODIFICATION Always backup your files before modifying them, and always plan out the modifications beforehand, because the backup procedure of some modifications is different than that for others. Keep the following distinctions in mind:

1. If you wish to modify field names, make your backup with the command

   ```
   1>COPY TO B:TEMP SDF
   ```

   and do not add or delete fields or change field lengths, or your SDF data becomes scrambled when you append it to the new file.

2. If you wish to modify, add, or delete fields, or change field lengths, make your backup primarily for insurance purposes, because your data is appended automatically to the new structure, providing that

   a. you have not changed a field name (data for fields with changed names is lost), and

   b. you have not reduced the field size to less than the length of the data it contains. (Bits of character data past the new field length and numeric data that won't fit the new format are lost.)

APPLICATIONS

The MODIFY command is used to change field names, lengths, and types, and to change the number of decimal places in a numeric-type field. It is also used to insert and add new fields or to delete unnecessary fields.

You can also use the MODIFY command to intentionally delete the contents of one or more fields within a database. This is accomplished by first deleting the unwanted fields using Ctrl-T. Then return to the VP prompt. The data for the missing fields is discarded. Finally, use MODIFY again to insert the fields back into the database structure.

You can also use the REPLACE command to delete the contents of a single field. For example, if you wish to delete the contents of a character field named ZIP, use the command:

```
1>REPLACE ALL zip WITH ' '
```

The contents of the ZIP field of all records are replaced with a blank.

The contents of numeric fields are similarly replaced with:

1>REPLACE ALL *numeric field* WITH 0

TYPICAL OPERATION

In this illustration, you modify the structure of the MEMBERS database created in Module 17. The ST_ADR field is renamed to ADR, the C_S_Z field is renamed to CSZ, and the PAID_UP field is renamed to PAID. Then in a second session, the length of the INFO field is reduced to conserve space in the database. First our data is protected by copying it to a text-like data file with an SDF format. Begin at the VP prompt.

CAUTION

Always backup data and index files before using the MODIFY command. Use the SDF file format when changing field names and never mix field name changes with other changes in the same MODIFY procedure.

1. Type **USE MEMBERS** and press **Return**.
2. Type **COPY TO B:TEMP1 SDF** to create the backup file needed when you change field names.
3. Type **MODIFY** and press **Return**. (You could also type **MODI** to save time, since the first four characters of VP-Info commands are all that are needed.)
4. Notice the following display:

```
Thursday, June 25, 1987
                                  UP-Info Modify                        MEMBERS.DBF

Name        Type    Width   Dec         Name        Type    Width   Dec

NAME         C       25      0
ST_ADR       C       25      0
C_S_Z        C       25      0
AFFIL        C       25      0
JOINED       C        8      0
AGE          N        2      0
PAID_UP      L        1      0
INFO         C       50      0
```

5. Move the cursor to the "S" in the ST_ADR field name and delete "ST_" by pressing **Del** three times.
6. Move the cursor to the C_S_Z field name and delete each underline character with the **Del** key.
7. Move the cursor to the PAID_UP field name and delete "_UP" by positioning the cursor at the underline and pressing **Ctrl-Y**. Your structure should now resemble the following:

```
Thursday, June 25, 1987
                                  UP-Info Modify                        MEMBERS.DBF

Name        Type    Width   Dec         Name        Type    Width   Dec

NAME         C       25      0
ADR          C       25      0
CSZ          C       25      0
AFFIL        C       25      0
JOINED       C        8      0
AGE          N        2      0
PAID         L        1      0
INFO         C       50      0
```

8. Press **End** and press **Return** to save the modified structure.
9. Type **LIST STRU** and press **Return** to examine the changed database structure. Notice the following:

```
1>LIST STRU
Data file:              MEMBERS.DBF
Number of records:         3
File number:               #1
Field    Name         Type   Width  Dec
  1      NAME          C       25
  2      ADR           C       25
  3      CSZ           C       25
  4      AFFIL         C       25
  5      JOINED        C        8
  6      AGE           N        2
  7      PAID          L        1
  8      INFO          C       50
** Record Length **           162
1>
```

10. Type **EDIT 1** and press **Return.** Notice that the three fields you changed are all empty for record 1.
11. Press **Ctrl-Q** to exit the Editing screen.
12. Type **DELETE ALL** and press **Return** to delete the ruined records.
13. Type **PACK** and press **Return** to discard the deleted records. (DELETE and PACK are covered in Module 21.)
14. Type **APPEND FROM B:TEMP1 SDF** and press **Return.**
15. Type **LIST** and press **Return** to confirm that your new records are OK. Compare with the following screen:

```
1>DELETE ALL
    3 DELETE(S)
1>PACK
    0 TOTAL PACKED
1>APPEND FROM B:TEMP1 SDF
    0 APPEND(S)
1>LIST
00001  Williams, David          3456 Fresno Circle        Tampa, FL 32656
 U.S. Air Force (Ret)     19801115 56 Y Active

00002  Phillips, George W.      11205 Dawn Drive          Lago Vista, TX 78641
 Austin Medical Center    19810601 39 Y Enthusiastic

00003  Galvin, Theodore A.      5545 Gulch Road           Culver City, CA 96750
 Miracle Micro Shop       19830215 42 N May cancel membership

1>
```

16. Type **COPY TO TEMP2** and press **Return** to make a standard database backup. (Remember, the SDF backup does not work if you change field lengths or locations.)
17. Type **MODI** and press **Return**.
18. Using the cursor keys, go to the Width specification for the field INFO, type **40** and press **Return** to reduce its size.

NOTE

The largest INFO record only contains 21 characters, so 40 characters is probably a generous space; if your MEMBERS database contains 1000 records, the ten saved characters remove ten thousand bytes from the file space used up by the database.

19. Press **End** and then **Return** to conclude modification of the database.
20. Type **LIST** and press **Return** to confirm that your data was not lost.
21. Type **CLEAR ALL** and press **Return** to close all files.
22. Turn to Module 30 to continue the learning sequence.

Module 43

NOTE, *, ;

DESCRIPTION

The asterisk character (*) is used in command files to insert comment lines. These lines are used to display the name of the command file or to annotate command files with descriptive comments explaining the functions of the command lines. The NOTE command does precisely the same thing as the asterisk (*) character, and it is used interchangeably.

The semicolon (;) is another comment designator. It is used to insert comments on the same line as a command. The VP-Info command interpreter reads the semicolon as a continue-on-the-next-line marker and ignores the following text. When you are typing in the editor and you type a word that passes beyond Column 77, VP-Info wraps the word down to the next line and inserts a semicolon to indicate that the line continues. When the command interpreter reads this semicolon, it goes to the next line to continue the command. A command line can contain up to 256 characters, but the screen displays an 80-character line, so the command line may be broken up with one to three semicolons as continuation signals.

Forms of *, NOTE, and ; are shown in the following lines.

```
NOTE This comment line is for information purposes only.
* This comment line is exactly like the one above.
WAIT                 ; Pauses operation and displays "WAITING"
```

APPLICATIONS

It is a good idea to annotate your command files with comment lines. Following are some suggestions for comment line use.

1. Place the name of the command file at the beginning.

   ```
   * ADD.PRG — Adds a record to the Address Book application.
   ```

2. Enter a version number to the command file for configuration control.

   ```
   * ADD program VERSION 2.1, January 6, 1988
   ```

3. Insert comments liberally to describe the function of different sections of the command file. (Since VP-Info compiles its command files, these have no effect on processing speed.)

   ```
   * Locate NAME field that matches the memory variable MNAME.
   WAIT                 ; Pause operation without a following display.
   ```

4. Write yourself reminders about future changes that are needed in a command file.

   ```
   * Don't forget to modify the DELETE program to display the record
   * before it's deleted.
   ```

TYPICAL OPERATION

In this illustration comment lines are used in a sample command file to demonstrate the use of NOTE (or *) and the semicolon. The sample command file works in conjunction with the PICNIC database created in Module 64. Begin at the VP prompt.

1. Type **WRITE SAMPLE** and press **Return**.
2. Type the following command file. Notice the use of comment lines.

NOTE

The use of comment lines is overdone here. Excessive comment lines increase the compile time for command files, but they do not effect the operating time for the compiled file. The best procedure is to keep a heavily commented copy of a program file as a backup, but do your actual work with compiled files. (See Module 14 on using the COMPILE command.)

```
* SAMPLE.PRG — Makes use of comment lines.
* Version 1.00 December 7, 1988
CLS                          ; Clear the screen.
USE PICNIC                   ; Use PICNIC database.
NOTE          Get a name from the keyboard with ACCEPT.
ACCEPT 'Enter the Name you want to look up ' TO MName
NOTE          Locate name; convert to uppercase to assure match.
LOCATE FOR !(NAME)=!(MName)
DISPLAY NAME,AMOUNT,TRIM(MEASURE),BRING OFF ; Display the record.
WAIT                         ; Pause operation; display prompt.
CLS                          ; Clear the screen.
USE                          ; Close the database.
CANCEL                       ; End operation.
```

3. Press **Alt-F** to format the file and then press **End** and **Return** to write the command file to disk.
4. Type **DO SAMPLE** and press **Return** to run the command file; prompts and responses are shown in the following example.

```
Enter the Name you want to look up  Dickens
Record 4
Dickens, Charles        1 Jar Mustard
WAITING
```

5. When you finish experimenting with the command file, erase the sample file from your disk by typing **DELE FILE SAMPLE.PRG** and pressing **Return**.
6. Turn to Module 47 to continue the learning sequence.

Module 44

ON ERROR, ON ESCAPE, INKEY( )

DESCRIPTION

The ON ERROR and ON ESCAPE commands and the INKEY function are used to intercept the occurrence of a specified condition during VP-Info operation. ON ERROR looks for an error condition and stores its number code to :ERROR and the associated error message to :MESSAGE; ON ESCAPE looks for the Esc key; and INKEY( ) looks for a key press to store as :KEY. Each of these commands and functions is described in the following paragraphs.

The form of the ON ERROR and ON ESCAPE commands is a structure concluded with the command ENDON. When nesting the two commands, be sure to use the Alt-F function to confirm accurate order by indenting structures.

When ON ERROR or ON ESCAPE structure is used, it remains in effect until the program replaces it with another one or an exit occurs.

ON ERROR The ON ERROR command looks for a VP-Info execution or syntax error. By following it with a procedure or a message and some commands, you can trap and respond to potential errors in a predetermined, controlled way. Look at the following sample program.

```
* ERRCHK.PRG — Demonstrates ON ERROR
ACCEPT "Number > " to dummy
ON error
   ? "Oops!",:message
   ? "Press Return"
   WAIT
   @ 10,5 SAY "Leaving"
   RETURN
ENDON
? Dummy/10
RETURN
```

Since Dummy is a string variable, the attempt to divide it by 10 generates an error message and a wait condition.

ON ESCAPE The ON ESCAPE command monitors your keyboard activity for the Esc key. If you press Esc, the structure between the ON ESCAPE command and its ENDON command is executed. The following sample program contains a structure which displays the print message whenever the Esc key is pressed:

```
* ON.PRG — Test ON ESCAPE.
CLS
ON ESCAPE
```

```
        @ 4,10 SAY "You pressed the Escape key."
        CANCEL
    ENDON
    Mvar= ' '
    @ 2,10 SAY "Type a letter, number, or punctuation mark. "
    @ 2,55 GET Mvar PICT 'X'
    READ
    @ 4, 10 SAY 'The ASCII code for '+Mvar+' is '+str(RANK(mvar),3)+'.'
    RETURN
```

When run, this command file first prepares the ON ESCAPE condition and then displays the prompt, "Type a letter, number, or punctuation mark." Typing Z results in a screen that looks like this.

```
          Type a letter, number, or punctuation mark.  Z

          The ASCII code for Z is  90.
 1>
```

Pressing Esc results in a screen that displays the ON ESCAPE message, like the following one.

```
          Type a letter, number, or punctuation mark.

          You pressed the Escape key.
 1>
```

INKEY( ) The number returned by the INKEY( ) function is an integer between 0 and 511. The integer value corresponds to the code value of the key pressed. For the 256 keys assigned ASCII codes, that number is used. For other keys, including Alt combinations and the function keys, the codes are numbers between 256 and 511.

INKEY( ) pauses operation until a key is pressed. Here is a list of some special keys and corresponding INKEY( ) values:

Key	*Value*	*Key*	*Value*
Right Arrow	333	F1	315
Home	327	F10	324
Left Arrow	331	Shift-F1	340
Alt-F1	360	Ctrl-F1	350
Ctrl-Right Arrow	372	Ctrl-F9	358
PgUp	329	Alt-A	286
Ctrl-PgDn	374	Ctrl-A	1
Ins	338	Del	339

The Esc key is used to halt command operations, including a running list on the screen. You can "disarm" this effect by entering SET ESCAPE OFF, but if you do this in a command file, be sure to provide some other exit path, or the program cannot be stopped. For instance, the following example file uses the Esc key to halt operation. Without it, the program would simply run till you turned off the computer. Look at the use of the INKEY( ) in the following command file.

```
* KEYS.PRG — Display value for the key pressed.
CLS
@ 2,5 SAY "Press Return to begin."
DO WHILE .NOT. INKEY()=0
@ 2,5 SAY "Press any key [Press Esc to quit]"
CURSOR 2,60
Pressed=str(inkey(),3)        ; Get key code for last key.
@ 3,5 SAY "The code is "+Pressed+". Press Return."
ENDDO
RETURN
```

APPLICATIONS

The ON ERROR and ON ESCAPE structure provide convenient ways to trap VP-Info syntax errors. The INKEY ( ) function lets you use nonprintable keys within command files to control branching operations.

ON ESCAPE also provides a way to avoid input accidents that can cause ruined record files. For example, you can provide a procedure for deleting a record left incomplete because the user pressed the Esc key in the middle of data entry.

TYPICAL OPERATION

In this illustration ON ERROR is used in a command file to monitor input by types. If data of an unexpected type is encountered, the ON ERROR . . . ENDON structure changes it momentarily. Then a second command file provides error checking and escape routines to a data editing program using the ABC file. Begin at the VP prompt.

1. Type **WRITE TYPER** and press **Return** to use the editor.
2. Type the following command file. (Do not type the explanatory remarks or indentation.)

```
                                                   Remarks
* TYPER.PRG — Check data entry, fix it.
CLS
ACCEPT "Variable > " to Dummy            ; ACCEPT takes only strings.
ON ERROR
   IF :ERROR=1                           ; Error 1 is a type error.
      ? "Converting the variable to numeric for the next step"
      Lngth=LEN(dummy)                   ; Length needed to convert it back.
      Dummy=VAL(dummy)                   ; Convert it to numeric.
   ENDIF
ENDON
Mvar=Dummy/10                            ; Division won't work on strings. ON ERROR
*    is called, performs its task, and sends command back to the line containing the error.
*    After the conversion, the math works.
```

```
? "Variable divided by ten is",Mvar
Dummy=STR(Dummy,Lngth)                ; Convert back to string.
? "It's a string again."
RETURN                                ; Exit from program.
```

3. Press **Alt-F**, proofread, and then press **End** and **Return** to save the file.
4. Type **DO TYPER** and press **Return** to try the program. As written, it can convert numbers entered as strings. However, strings with non-number characters in them give bizarre results.
5. When the prompt "Variable > _" appears, type **88** and press **Return**. Compare the result to this screen:

```
Variable >  88
Converting the variable to numeric for the next step
Variable divided by ten is       8.80
It's a string again.
1>
```

6. When you are finished experimenting with the program, type **DELE FILE TYPER.PRG** and **Return** to erase it. Type **WRITE NEWEDIT** and press **Return** to enter the editor again.
7. Type the following program. (Do not type remarks or indentation.)

```
* NEWEDIT.PRG — Controls editing of data.
USE ABC
GO BOTTOM                           ; Go to last record.
Max=#+1                             ; Set limit of last record.
WINDOW 12,10,20,70
LIST                                ; In window.
WINDOW                              ; Back to main screen.
ON ESCAPE                           ; If Esc pressed during editing.
    Saving=' '                      ; Create variable for Get Table.
    @ 22,10 SAY "SAVE this entry? Y/N " GET Saving PICT 'X'
    READ
    IF !(Saving) = 'Y'
        FLUSH                       ; Update the disk file.
        CANCEL                      ; Exit from program.
    ELSE
        NOUPDATE                    ; Discard current changes.
        CANCEL
    ENDIF Save on ESC
ENDON
DO WHILE T
    RecNo=0                         ; Initialize variable for Get Table.
    @ 2,10 SAY "Select Record to Edit " GET RecNo PICT '99'
    READ
```

```
    IF RecNo<Max                    ; Record exists.
        GO RecNo                    ; Go to it.
        ERASE 22,22                 ; Erase ELSE's error message, if necessary.
    ELSE                            ; Record number too high.
        @ 22,40 SAY "No such record."
        LOOP                        ; Restart DO WHILE.
    ENDIF RecNo checking
    * Create Get Table for data editing, show current record contents.
    @ 4,20 SAY "        Name:  " GET Name
    @ 5,20 SAY "Phone Extn:  " GET Extn
    @ 6,20 SAY " Mail Drop:  " GET Mail
    * Add Data-handling keys to entry possibilities.
    @ 8,10 SAY "Alt-S to Save, Alt-A to Abandon, Alt-X to save and eXit."
    READ
    DO CASE
    CASE :KEY=287                   ; Pressed Alt-S.
        FLUSH                       ; Update disk.
        LOOP                        ; Restart DO WHILE.
    CASE :KEY=286                   ; Pressed Alt-A.
        NOUPDATE                    ; Discard changes to this record.
        LOOP                        ; Restart DO WHILE.
    CASE :KEY>256                   ; Alt-X or other non-alphanumeric pressed.
        BREAK                       ; Exit from DO WHILE.
    ENDCASE
ENDDO
RETURN                              ; Back to prompt.
```

8. Press **Alt-F** to format the file, proofread it, and then press **End** and **Return** to save it.
9. Type **DO NEWEDIT** and press **Return** to run the program. Experiment with the various options by selecting records and editing them, then exiting from the program with either an Esc followed by an N (No save) or an Alt-X (Save). To compare the old list with the new one, type **ERASE 1,2** and press **Return** after exiting, and then use the LIST and DISPLAY commands to examine the changes. The CLS command has been left out to allow these comparisons as long as you don't mind a rather cluttered screen.
10. Use DELE FILE to eliminate the NEWEDIT.PRG file from your disk.
11. Turn to Module 52 to continue the learning sequence.

Module 45

PERFORM, PROCEDURE

DESCRIPTION

A procedure is a series of command lines within a command file that perform some operation. This collection of command lines is given a procedure name, identified by the PROCEDURE . . . ENDPROCEDURE structure, and called by the PERFORM command.

A procedure must be at the end of a command file, after the PERFORM command or commands that call it. The first line within a procedure contains the procedure name in the form:

PROCEDURE *name*

where a procedure name must begin with an alpha character, and can have from 1 to 10 characters consisting of letters, numbers, and underscores. A program may contain up to 32 procedures; each must have a unique name. The body of the procedure contains standard VP-Info commands for performing some operation. The last line in a procedure contains the ENDPROCEDURE command. ENDPROCEDURE completes the procedure and returns control to the line following the PERFORM command line from which the procedure was called.

The following example is a simple procedure file containing three independent procedures.

```
* HRLY.PRG — a procedures file that converts hourly wage rates
INPUT "Enter the hourly rate " to BASE
PERFORM hr_wk
PERFORM hr_mo
PERFORM hr_yr
PROCEDURE hr_wk
   ? 'The weekly income is $',STR(BASE*40,9,2)
ENDPROCEDURE
*
PROCEDURE hr_mo
   ? 'The monthly income is $',STR(BASE*173.333,9,2)
ENDPROC
*
PROC hr_yr
   ? 'The annual income is $',STR(BASE*2080,9,2)
ENDPR
RETURN
```

If you create this file and then run it by typing DO HRLY and type 5.75 as the hourly rate, this screen appears:

```
1>DO HRLY
Enter the hourly rate  5.75
The weekly income is  $     230.00
The monthly income is $     996.66
The annual income is  $   11960.00
1>
```

APPLICATIONS

When a set of programs is compiled, any DO command subroutines are compiled into the main program each time they are called, so that a DO command called five times takes up five times the space it normally would. Procedures are useful for repetitive tasks, because they only need to be compiled once, and then can be performed as often as needed. For example, if you wish to display the same information many times or perform a recurring computation, you can build a PROCEDURE structure like a calculation tool box. This saves disk space and memory space that would otherwise be used by compiling multiple copies of DO files into every command file requiring common subroutines.

TYPICAL OPERATION

In this illustration the procedure file contained in the previous example is used to demonstrate how procedures are called and used. Begin at the VP prompt.

1. Type **WRITE HRLY** and press **Return** to use the VP-Info editor.
2. Type the following command file. (Do not type the explanatory remarks.) Notice that abbreviations are used for both PROCEDURE and ENDPROCEDURE, to avoid typos and save time. Remember that only the first four letters of a command are significant.

```
* HRLY.PRG — a procedures file that converts hourly wage rates
INPUT "Enter the hourly rate " to BASE
PERFORM hr_wk
PERFORM hr_mo
PERFORM hr_yr
PROCEDURE hr_wk
   ? 'The weekly income is $',STR(BASE*40,9,2)
ENDPROCEDURE
*
PROCEDURE hr_mo
   ? 'The monthly income is $',STR(BASE*173.333,9,2)
ENDPROC
*
PROC hr_yr
   ? 'The annual income is $',STR(BASE*2080,9,2)
ENDPR
RETURN   ; Terminate program.
```

3. Press **End** and **Return** to save the procedure command file.
4. Type **DO HRLY** and press **Return**; respond to the rate prompt by typing an hourly rate, **8.25**.
5. Notice that three calculated amounts are displayed:

```
1>DO HRLY
Enter the hourly rate  8.25
The weekly income is  $    330.00
The monthly income is $   1429.99
The annual income is  $  17160.00
1>
```

6. Type **DELE FILE HRLY.PRG** and press **Return** to delete the procedure file from your working disk.
7. Turn to Module 14 to continue the learning sequence.

Module 46

POST

DESCRIPTION

The POST command lets you sum the contents of one database into a master database. The master database must be open and indexed, and the source database should be closed.

The general form of the POST command is:

```
1>POST ON key FROM source file FIELDS field1 WITH expression1
```

If you wish to post several fields, you can use the form:

```
1>POST ON key FROM source file FIELDS field1 WITH expression1,
                              field2 WITH expression, field3
                              WITH expression ...
```

You can also specify a scope at the end of the command in a FOR clause.

The key field must be in both the source and target databases, and it must be in the active index of the master file.

For example, if PICMAST were opened with an index on BRING, you could copy the current totals for each food supply with this command:

```
1>POST ON Bring FROM Picnic Field Amount WITH Amount
```

As a second example, assume that you have the two inventory databases described in Module 67, WHSE and WIP. If you wish to update the WHSE database to those parts presently counted in WIP, you can use the POST command without opening the WIP database.

If the key field name in both databases is PART_NO, the WHSE has an active index including PART_NO, and the field containing the quantity is QTY in both databases, you can proceed as follows:

```
1>USE WHSE INDEX PN
1>POST ON PART_NO FROM WIP FIELD QTY WITH QTY + WIP
```

This series of commands puts WIP and WHSE in work areas 1 and 2, leaving WHSE in the active work area. The UPDATE command adds the contents of the QTY fields and replaces the WHSE quantity values with their present value plus the quantity value in the WIP database. Look at the following list.

WHSE			WIP			WHSE (After Posting)	
PART_NO	QTY	+	PART_NO	QTY	=	PART_NO	QTY
A-1230	5		A-1230	2		A-1230	7
B-1001	12		B-1001	6		B-1001	18
D-3561	7		D-3561	3		B-3561	10
D-3562	8		D-3562	2		D-3562	10
W-1210	4		W-1210	2		W-1210	6

If no record exists in the master that matches the indexed field for a record in the transaction file, the POST can create a new master record for the new data. To activate this ability, include the command SET ADD ON before using the POST command.

The POST, TOTAL, and UPDATE commands perform similar functions. Here is a list of key differences:

	POST	TOTAL	UPDATE
Main file:	master, indexed	source, indexed	target
Second:	source, closed	summary, new	source,open,indexed
	refer to by name	refer to by name	refer to by area #

APPLICATIONS

The POST command is for transferring individual records, typically transactions, to a master record.

TYPICAL OPERATION

In this illustration, a DAILYS database and a MASTER database are created, and then the POST command is used to pass new transaction records into the MASTER database. Begin at the VP prompt.

1. Type **CREATE DAILYS** and press **Return** to set up the first database.
2. Create this structure, then press **End** and **Return** to save it:

```
Name        Type    Width    Dec

INVNO        C        4       0
QTY          N        2       0
PRICE        N        5       2
DATE         C        8       0
TRANSNO      C        4       0
<End>
```

3. Type **CREATE MASTER** and press **Return** to set up the second database.
4. Create this structure, then press **End** and **Return** to save it:

```
Name        Type    Width    Dec

TRANSNO      C        4       0
TSALE        N        6       2
TAX          N        5       2
<End>
```

5. Type **INDEX ON TransNo TO MTRANS** and press **Return** to create an index for MASTER.
6. Type **WRITE DAYDATA.TXT** and press **Return**.
7. Copy the six data lines on the following screen exactly, paying special attention to spacing, to create an SDF data file.

```
DAYDATA.TXT                      VP-Info WRITE                    INSERT

....+....1....+....2....+....3....+....4....+....5....+....6....+....7....+....8
A1110220.50198712021001◄
A1110330.75198712021002◄
A1220115.75198712021002◄
A1320115.75198712051003◄
C1110721.00198712061004◄
A1110220.50198712071005◄
```

8. Press **End** and then press **Return** to save this file.
9. Type **USE DAILYS** and press **Return.**
10. Type **APPEND FROM DAYDATA.TXT SDF** and press **Return.**
11. Type **GO TOP** and press **Return** to go to the first record, then type **BROWSE** and press **Return** to proofread for accurate appending of the text file. Compare your screen to the following, and use the editing keys to fix any errors:

```
#1 DAILYS.DBF                    VP-Info BROWSE
       INVN QT PRICE DATE     TRAN
00001  A111 02 20.50 19871202 1001
00002  A111 03 30.75 19871202 1002
00003  A122 01 15.75 19871202 1002
00004  A132 01 15.75 19871205 1003
00005  C111 07 21.00 19871206 1004
00006  A111 02 20.50 19871207 1005
```

12. When the data is OK, press **End** to return to the VP prompt.
13. Type **USE MASTER INDEX MTRANS** and press **Return.**
14. Type **SET ADD ON** and press **Return** so new records can be created.
15. Type **POST ON TransNo FROM DAILYS FIELDS TSale WITH Price, Tax WITH Price*.06** and press **Return.** Do not be alarmed if POST ERROR messages appear; they are warnings that new records are being added.
16. Type **LIST** and press **Return.** Notice that the two sales in DAILY with TransNo = '1002' have been summed, and all the taxes have been computed. Before going on, use DELETE FILE to erase MASTER.DBF and DAILYS.DBF, MTRANS.NDX, and DAYDATA.TXT.
17. Turn to Module 11 to continue the learning sequence.

Module 47

PRINT STATEMENT (?)

DESCRIPTION

Use of the question mark as an interactive mode operator was described in Module 39. In this module, the question mark is described in its role as a print statement. If you are familiar with the BASIC programming language, then you know that when the command lines

```
10 PRINT "A blank line follows this line."
20 PRINT
30 PRINT "This is another line."
```

are run, the following lines are displayed.

```
A blank line follows this line.

This is another line.
```

Notice that PRINT without following text displays a blank line. You can think of the question mark as being equivalent to the BASIC PRINT statement. The statements required to produce the above display in VP-Info are:

```
? 'A blank line follows this line.'
?
? 'This is another line.'
```

Displayed text is enclosed in either single or double quotes. If the text includes a single quote within it, then surround your text using double quotes. On the other hand, text that includes a double quote should be enclosed in single quotes. The following lines demonstrate these principles.

```
? 'Press "Q" to quit'
?
? "Don't press the Esc key"
```

The REMARK command is a functional synonym for the print (?) command; the two can be used interchangeably. For example, the command REMARK 'HELLO' prints the word HELLO on the next line; REMARK by itself on a line prints a blank line. REMARK can also be combined with memory variables and quoted text to create screen messages.

To see additional examples of the print statement, review the MENU command file example in Module 71.

VP-Info provides many approaches to putting text on the screen. The print statement is used for short pieces of text, often in conjunction with either field contents or memory variables. For example, you can display the value of a field or memory variable following a descriptive caption. Check the following examples. Assume the DESCRIP, AMOUNT, and TAX are field names, and MVar is a memory variable.

```
    ? 'The cost of',TRIM(DESCRIP),'is
$'LTRIM(STR(AMOUNT+TAX,6,2))

    ? 'The value of the memory variable is',MVar

    ? 'A double vertical bar looks like ',CHR(186)
```

NOTE

In the first example the TRIM statement is used to eliminate trailing blanks; the LTRIM(STR( )) statement converts the numeric value of AMOUNT + TAX to a character string. Once converted, the LTRIM string function trims leading blanks to eliminate unwanted spaces.

APPLICATIONS

The print statement is easy to use for displaying menus and prompts. The ability to follow the print statement with the contents of fields and memory variables makes its use in command files convenient. The print statement is also used with the CHR( ) function, described in Module 11, to combine graphic characters and text. The following command lines demonstrate this application by drawing a double-line box. (This command file does by hand what you can do with the BOX command described in Module 6.)

```
                                              Remarks
* BOX.PRG — Displays a box
STORE CHR(201) TO A                    ; Stores upper left-hand corner graphic to A.
STORE CHR(187) TO B                    ; Stores upper right-hand corner graphic to B.
STORE CHR(200) TO C                    ; Stores lower left-hand corner graphic to C.
STORE CHR(188) TO D                    ; Stores lower right-hand corner graphic to D.
STORE CHR(205)+CHR(205) TO H           ; Stores two horizontal lines to H.
STORE CHR(186) TO V                    ; Stores vertical bar to V.
CLS                                    ; Clears the screen.
?
? '          ',A+H+H+H+H+H+H+H+H+H+H+H+H+H+H+H+H+H+H+H+H+H+H+H+B
? '          ',V,'                                              ',V
? '          ',V,'                                              ',V
? '          ',V,'                                              ',V
? '          ',C+H+H+H+H+H+H+H+H+H+H+H+H+H+H+H+H+H+H+H+H+H+H+H+D
?
WAIT
CLS
RETURN                                 ; Terminates program.
```

This command file displays the following information and block characters on most personal computers when you type DO BOX and press Return.

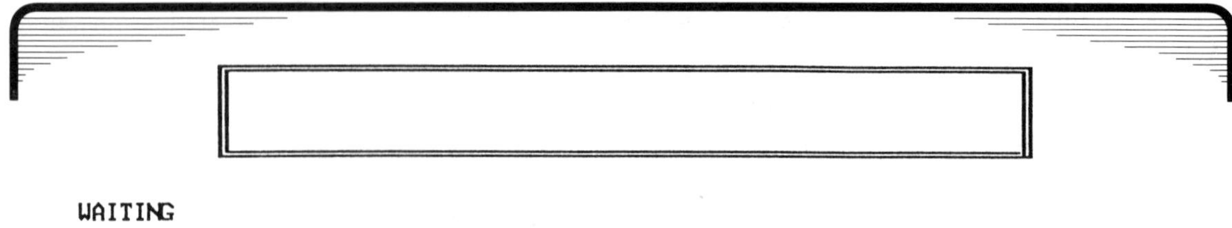

WAITING

The same box can be created with the command, BOX 2,9,6,66 DOUBLE.

TYPICAL OPERATION

In this illustration the print statement is used in a command file to display information in the STOCK database created in Module 15. Print statements are used in the command file to display a menu, prompts, memory variables, and field values. If necessary, turn to Module 15, create the STOCK database structure, and add the records shown. Then perform the following steps, beginning at the VP prompt.

1. Type **WRITE PRINT1** and press **Return** to use the editor.
2. Type the following command file. (Do not type the explanatory remarks or indentation.)

```
                                 Remarks
* STOCKER.PRG—Demonstrates use of the Print Statement.
DO WHILE T                       ; Begins DO WHILE loop; operates until CHOICE = 4.
* Display a menu:
CLS                              ; Clears screen.
? '                                   STOCK MAINTENANCE'
?
? '                                                                    Press'
?
? '                              Add new stock                          [1]'
? '                              Change inventory information           [2]'
? '                              Delete a stock record                  [3]'
? '                              Exit stock maintenance                 [4]'
?
* Pause, display prompt, and store keyed response as Choice.
ACCEPT 'MAKE YOUR SELECTION ' TO Choice
USE STOCK                        ; Put STOCK database in use.
CLS                              ; Clear screen.
DO CASE                          ; Start CASES statement.
* Add a record:
CASE CHOICE='1'                  ; If CHOICE = '1,' use following command line.
APPEND                           ; Add (append) record to bottom of database.
* Change a record:
```

```
CASE CHOICE='2'          ; If CHOICE = '2,' use following command lines.
LIST OFF PART_NO,DESCRIP
? "   To make a change, type the stock number"
? '   and press RETURN.'
ACCEPT '   ==================>' TO MPN     ; Accept keyboard input to
*                                            memory variable MPN.
CLS                      ; Clear screen.
* Locate field PART_NO = memory variable MPN.
LOCATE FOR !(PART_NO)=!(MPN)
* If the item isn't found:
IF EOF                   ; If end-of-file, do IF statement.
CLS                      ; Clear screen.
? "                    Can't find ",MPN
WAIT                     ; Pause and display "WAITING" prompt.
* Return control to line below first DO WHILE statement.
LOOP
ENDIF                    ; End the IF statement (if end-of-file).
* If the name is found, display the record:
DO WHILE T               ; Begin interior DO WHILE loop.
? PART_NO,DESCRIP        ; Display PART_NO and DESCRIP fields.
?
? '          Press          To'
? '            C            Change'
? '            R            Return to the Menu'
ACCEPT TO Option         ; Pause and store response to Option.
CLS
* Return to the menu:
IF !(Option)='R'         ; If Option = 'R' or 'r,' do IF statement.
BREAK                    ; Exit interior DO WHILE loop.
ENDIF                    ; End IF statement (OPTION = R).
* Edit the record:
IF !(Option)='C'         ; If uppercase Option = C, do IF statement.
EDIT #                   ; Edit current record.
BREAK                    ; Exit interior DO WHILE loop.
ENDIF                    ; End IF statement (OPTION = C).
ENDDO                    ; End current DO WHILE statement.
* Delete a record:
CASE CHOICE='3'          ; If CHOICE = '3,' use following commands.
? "   To Delete a record, type the part number"
? '   and press RETURN.'
* Next, accept keyboard input to variable MPN.
ACCEPT '   ==================>' TO MPN
CLS
LOCATE FOR !(PART_NO)=!(MPN)    ; Search for PART_NO = MPN.
* If the item isn't found:
IF EOF                   ; If end-of-file encountered, do following.
CLS
? "              Can't find ",MPN
WAIT                     ; Pause and display "WAITING" prompt.
* Return control to line after first DO WHILE statement.
LOOP
```

```
ENDIF                        ; End current IF statement (If end-of-file).
• If the item is found:
DO WHILE T                   ; Begin interior DO WHILE loop.
? PART_NO,DESCRIP            ; Display PART_NO, DESCRIP fields.
?
? '          Press              To'
? '            D              Delete'
? '            R              Return to the Menu'
ACCEPT TO Option             ; Pause and store response to Option.
CLS
• Return to the menu:
IF !(Option)='R'             ; If uppercase Option = R, do IF statement.
BREAK                        ; Exit interior DO WHILE loop.
ENDIF                        ; End current IF statement (OPTION = R).
• Delete the record:
IF !(Option)='D'             ; If uppercase Option = D, do IF statement.
DELETE                       ; Mark current record for deletion.
PACK                         ; Delete marked record.
BREAK                        ; Exit interior DO WHILE loop.
ENDIF                        ; End current IF statement (OPTION = D).
ENDDO                        ; Completes interior DO WHILE loop.
• Return to VP-Info:
CASE CHOICE='4'              ; If CHOICE = '4,' use following commands.
CANCEL                       ; Cancel command file and return to prompt.
ENDCASE                      ; Ends CASE statement.
ENDDO                        ; Ends exterior (initial) DO WHILE loop.
RETURN                       ; Terminate program.
```

3. Before saving the program, press **Alt-F** to format the file, and proofread it for all necessary END statements by checking the indentation. Each IF should have its own ENDIF indented to the same degree, each DO WHILE has its ENDDO and the DO CASE its own ENDCASE.
4. Press **End** and then press **Return** to write the command file to disk.
5. Run the STOCKER command file by typing **DO STOCKER** and pressing **Return**. The following menu and prompts are displayed. Try your own variations to test the program. (You may want to use this file as a model for your own command file.)

NOTE

To save space, the sample screens are displayed as if they were not being erased with the CLS command.

```
                    STOCK MAINTENANCE
                                                   Press

               Add new stock                        [1]
               Change inventory information         [2]
               Delete a stock record                [3]
               Exit stock maintenance               [4]

MAKE YOUR SELECTION
```

(Type **1** and press **Return**)

```
#1 STOCK.DBF                UP-Info APPEND
Record       5
PART_NO........   RV-123-44
DESCRIP........   WIPER BLADES
COST...........        .99
PRICE..........       4.99
QTY_IN.........         20
QTY_OUT........          1
```

Page 1
(Add a record with the following data)

(Finish the record by pressing **End**)

```
                    STOCK MAINTENANCE
                                                  Press

                 Add new stock                     [1]
                 Change inventory information      [2]
                 Delete a stock record             [3]
                 Exit stock maintenance            [4]

MAKE YOUR SELECTION  2
```

(Type **2** and press **Return**)

```
TX-345-02        BOOT, TIRE
GG-4544-15       TUBE, INNER
BR-78R-14        TIRE, RADIAL
FS-3455-120W     BATTERY, MAINT.FREE
RV-123-44        WIPER BLADES
  To make a change, type the stock number
  and press RETURN.
  =================> RV-123-44
```

(Type **RV-123-44** and press **Return**)

```
Record 5
RV-123-44        WIPER BLADES

       Press              To
         C               Change
         R               Return to the Menu
```

Type **R** to return to the Main Menu)

```
                    STOCK MAINTENANCE
                                                  Press

                 Add new stock                     [1]
                 Change inventory information      [2]
                 Delete a stock record             [3]
                 Exit stock maintenance            [4]

MAKE YOUR SELECTION  4
```

(Type **4** and press **Return**)

6. Turn to Module 6 to continue the learning sequence.

Module 48
QUIT

DESCRIPTION

The QUIT command is one that you should become familiar with right away. It is used to "quit" VP-Info and return to the operating system prompt. QUIT closes all files in use, clears all memory variables, and ends the VP-Info session.

You should never end a session without either typing QUIT at the prompt or including QUIT in a command file as the last statement. (Command files are lists of VP-Info commands that execute in the order entered. These are described in more detail as you progress through this book.) If you turn off your computer without using QUIT, you may damage open files.

Before starting VP-Info, be sure that you have the proper configuration file (named CONFIG.SYS) and the DOS files on your system disk. This file takes effect when you turn on your computer's power. The CONFIG.SYS file is described in Module 2 and Appendix B, and contains the following lines:

```
FILES=20
BUFFERS=20
```

There should also be a VPI.CNF file (not to be confused with the CONFIG.SYS file) on the VPI program disk, used to set VP-Info default conditions when it is started.

Remember to always respond to the date and time prompts if you do not have an automatic system clock in your computer, to ensure that your files are marked with the current date and time.

To begin, type VPI and press Return.

A preliminary information screen is displayed followed by the VP prompt. At this point VP-Info is waiting for your instructions. You can create files, edit them, print reports, and so on.

Once you are finished with your VP-Info work, you must exit from VP-Info. This is done by typing QUIT and pressing Return.

The QUIT command returns you to the operating system prompt.

APPLICATIONS

The QUIT command is used every time you end a VP-Info session. It closes all files and returns you to the operating system prompt. The QUIT command is either typed at the VP prompt or included in a command file. (More about command files later.) In either case, the QUIT command is always used to exit from VP-Info.

TYPICAL OPERATION

In this illustration VP-Info is started and then the QUIT command is used to return to the operating system prompt.

1. With the VP-Info program located in the default drive (the A drive if you have two floppy disks, or the C drive on a hard disk system), type **VPI** and press **Return**.
2. At the VP prompt type **QUIT** and press **Return**.
3. Notice the following display, assuming that the default disk drive is A. The information below "Remarks" is not displayed. It is a comment set off with a semicolon, like comments in command files.

```
VP-Info  Version 1.1    10/29/86
Copyright (c) 1984, 1985, 1986 Sub Rosa Inc.


1>QUIT                                        Remarks
A:\                                           ; System prompt is displayed
```

4. Turn to Module 23 to continue the learning sequence.

Module 49

RENAME

DESCRIPTION

The RENAME command, like the DOS version, changes the name of a file. The general form of the RENAME command is:

```
1>RENAME oldname to newname
```

VP-Info's RENAME does not accept * or ? wildcard names. Although it uses the location defaults established by your VPI.CNF file, you must specify the drive on both filenames if you specify it on the first, or a "file not found" error is reported.

Some examples of the RENAME command are shown in the following list. Notice that you can rename files on any disk drive by placing the disk drive designator in front of the filename. Open files should not be renamed. If you wish to rename a file, you can close it with the CLOSE ALL command and then use the RENAME command.

1. RENAME *oldname* TO *newname* Changes the original filename to the filename following the TO statement on the default disk drive. If no extension name is given for either filename, then VP-Info assumes the file is a database and automatically assigns a DBF extension to the new filename. The TO is optional.

   Examples:

   ```
   1>RENAME MEMB TO MBRS              ; Only works if MEMB is a DBF file.
   1>RENAME PHONELST.PRG to LISTER.PRG
   ```

2. RENAME B:*oldname* TO B:*newname* Changes the original filename to the filename following the TO statement on disk drive B. With no extension, *oldname* must be a DBF file.

   Example:

   ```
   1>RENAME A:MEMBERS TO A:MBRS
   ```

3. RENAME *oldname.ext* TO *newname.ext* Changes the original filename and extension to the filename and extension following the TO statement. Notice that you must specify drive B: with the FIL extension, because FIL is not listed in your VPI.CNF file, so VP-Info assumes that files with such an extension are on the startup drive.

   Examples:

   ```
   1>RENAME B:LIST.FIL TO B:LETTER.FIL
   1>RENAME LISTER.PRG PHONELST.PRG          ; The TO is optional.
   ```

APPLICATIONS

The RENAME command is used to maintain your files just as with the DOS REN command. If you decide to change your file naming scheme, you can use RENAME to assign a new name to the file of your choice. If you wish to change names on a batch of files, use the DOS RENAME command.

TYPICAL OPERATION

In this illustration the RENAME command is used to change the name of a small practice file. Next, the DELETE FILE command is used to remove the temporary practice file from your disk. Begin at the VP prompt.

1. Type **WRITE TEMP** and press **Return** to use the VP-Info editor. Notice that the editor automatically assigns the extension PRG to the file.

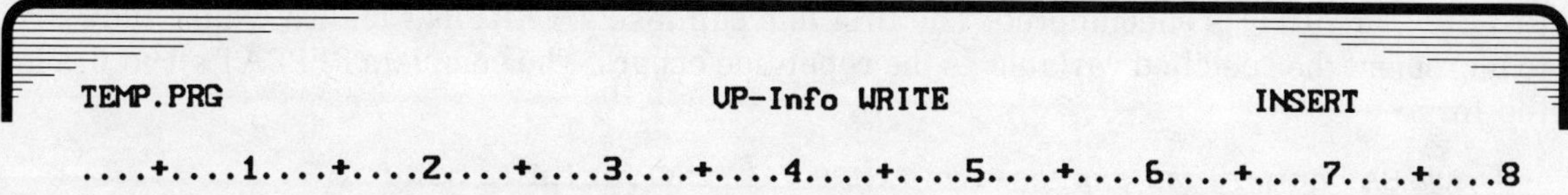

2. Type **This is a practice file.**
3. Press **End** and compare your screen to this:

```
TEMP.PRG                           VP-Info WRITE                      INSERT
Save this file as TEMP.PRG
....+....1....+....2....+....3....+....4....+....5....+....6....+....7....+....8
This is a practice file.
◄
```

4. Press **Return** to write the file to disk.
5. Type **DIR B:*.PRG** and press **Return**. Notice that a TEMP.PRG program is in the directory listing.
6. Type **RENAME TEMP.PRG TO TEMP1.TXT** and press **Return**.
7. Type **DIR B:*.TXT** and press **Return**. Notice that the renamed file is listed as TEMP1.TXT.
8. Type **DELETE FILE B:TEMP1.TXT** and press **Return**.
9. Type **DIR B:*.TXT** and press **Return**. Notice that TEMP1.TXT is gone.
10. Turn to Module 36 to continue the learning sequence.

Module 50

REPEAT

DESCRIPTION

The REPEAT command is an *iterative* command that performs its operation a specified number of times. The first line of the REPEAT structure has the form:

```
REPEAT number TIMES
```

The operation repeats the number of times specified, unless an exit command (BREAK, CANCEL, RETURN, or QUIT) is encountered. The first line can take a VARYING clause which allows you to increment the specified variable as the repetition occurs. The complete REPEAT structure has the form:

```
REPEAT numerical expression TIMES VARYING variable name
   :
   (command lines)
   :
   (increase variable by 1)
ENDREPEAT
```

You can "nest" REPEAT . . . ENDREPEAT structures with the other structures and within each other. The following example, which writes a calendar, contains an IF . . . ENDIF structure. It also combines two REPEAT structures. Notice also that indentation is used to signal the structural relationships of the END terms.

```
* Calendar Program for a month beginning on Sunday.
CLS
? 'SUN    MON    TUE    WED    THU    FRI    SAT'
?
REPEAT 5 TIMES VARYING Week
    REPEAT 7 TIMES VARYING Day
        Today= Day+((Week-1)*7)
        ?? PIC(Today,'999'),'  '
        IF (Today)>30
            CANCEL
        ENDIF
    ENDREPEAT
    ?
ENDREPEAT
```

Be sure to conclude your WRITE tasks by pressing Alt-F, to indent all structures for proofreading.

APPLICATIONS

The REPEAT structure is ideal for writing delay loops or filling matrix variables. Use it any time a repetitious operation is required.

TYPICAL OPERATION

In this illustration REPEAT is used to create a delay loop. Compare this program to the similar program in Module 27. Begin at the VP prompt.

1. Type **WRITE RDELAY** and press **Return** to use the editor.
2. Type the following command file. (Do not type the explanatory remarks or the indentations.)

```
                                Remarks
* RDELAY.PRG — Displays a message for specified number of seconds.
CLS                          ; Clears the screen.
INPUT "How many seconds of delay? : " TO Sec
? '      THIS MESSAGE WILL DISAPPEAR IN ',PIC(Sec,'999'),'SECONDS.'
X = Sec * 99                 ; The operation of the REPEAT loop takes
*                              approximately 1/99 of a second.
InTime=TIME(3)               ; Store system time as seconds since midnight.
REPEAT X TIMES               ; Do operation X times.
Ok=22/7
ENDREPEAT                    ; When the REPEAT expression has been
*                              executed enough, control passes to
*                              the next line.
OutTime=TIME(3)              ; Get system time again.
Ok=TIME(1)                   ; Reset :TIME format.
Lapsed=VAL(OutTime)-VAL(InTime)
? PIC(Lapsed,'999'),' seconds have passed.'
RETURN                       ; Returns control to VP prompt.
```

3. Press **Alt-F** to reformat the file, then proofread, checking for uniform indentation of structures.
4. Press **End** and then press **Return** to write the command file to disk.
5. Run the command file by typing **DO RDELAY** and pressing **Return**.
6. At the "How many seconds" prompt, type **10** and press **Return**. The REPEAT operation is accurate enough for any delay under five minutes.
7. Turn to Module 59 to continue the learning sequence.

Module 51

REPLACE

DESCRIPTION

The REPLACE command is used to REPLACE the contents of one or more specified fields within either the current record or all records, depending on the form of the command. You can also restrict replacements to certain records by using the FOR *expression* clause. Forms of the REPLACE command are shown in the following list.

1. REPLACE *field name* WITH *string* Replaces the contents of the named field in the current record with the string, which can be character, numeric, or logical.

   Example:

   ```
   1>REPLACE PART_NO WITH '250987-01'
         1 REPLACE(S)
   ```

2. REPLACE *field1* WITH *string*, *field2* WITH *string*, . . . Replaces the contents of the named fields in the record with the corresponding strings. Use commas as separators.

   Example:

   ```
   1>REPLACE QTY WITH 125, PART_NO WITH '250987-01'
         8 REPLACE(S)
   ```

3. REPLACE *scope field name* WITH *string* Replaces the contents of the named field(s) with the corresponding string(s) for a range of records, such as ALL or NEXT 5.

   Examples:

   ```
   1>REPLACE ALL PRICE WITH PRICE*1.05
       128 REPLACE(S)
   ```

   ```
   1>REPLACE NEXT 3 PRICE WITH PRICE*1.05
         3 REPLACE(S)
   ```

4. REPLACE *field name* WITH *string* FOR *expression* Replaces the contents of the named field(s) with the corresponding string(s) for all records that match the FOR expression.

   Example:

   ```
   1>REPLACE COST WITH COST*1.1 FOR DESCRIP='Tire'
         7 REPLACE(S)
   ```

5. REPLACE *fieldname* WITH *memory variable* Replaces the contents of the named field with the named memory variable.

   ```
   1>REPLACE DATE WITH MDATE
         1 REPLACE(S)
   ```

You may wish to display the active database file with the LIST command so you can see which records require changing. You can move the record pointer to the first record requiring replacement by typing the record number and pressing Return. Then type the REPLACE command to make the needed changes. If every record requiring a replacement has a common expression, you can use the expression in your command to fix all records with one entry.

APPLICATIONS

The REPLACE command is commonly used to change the contents of the fields within a database in the interactive mode. In addition, the REPLACE command is often used in command files to replace the value of a field with a memory variable. The following three command lines create a memory variable with the name MZip, open a database named PLACES, and then replace the contents of the ZIP field with '75074' in all records having a ZIP value of '75089.'

```
1>MZip = '75074'
1>USE PLACES
1>REPLACE ZIP WITH MZip FOR ZIP = '75089'
```

Inclusion of the ALL, NEXT, and FOR *expression* statements lets you make replacements on a *global* basis, that is, for all records in a database file that meet a specified condition or contain a common expression.

TYPICAL OPERATION

In this illustration the REPLACE command is used with the ABC database created in Module 5 to replace the MAIL fields containing "84" with "2084." Begin at the VP prompt.

1. Type **USE ABC** and press **Return**.
2. Type **LIST** and press **Return**. Compare your screen to the following:

```
1>USE ABC
1>LIST
00001  Sergio, Vincent      3596 84
00002  Bishop, Sam          2234 430
00003  Collins, Arthur      4554 323
00004  Harris, Robert       3353 2230
00005  Alexander, T.G.      1104 84
00006  McAllister, Mick     8957 5267
1>
```

NOTE

Your sixth record is the one you added.

3. Type **REPLACE ALL MAIL WITH '2084' FOR MAIL = '84'** and press **Return**. Notice the message, "2 REPLACE(S)."

4. Type **LIST** and press **Return**. Notice that "84" has been replaced with "2084" in Sergio's and Alexander's records.

```
1>USE ABC
1>LIST
00001  Sergio, Vincent      3596 2084
00002  Bishop, Sam          2234 430
00003  Collins, Arthur      4554 323
00004  Harris, Robert       3353 2230
00005  Alexander, T.G.      1104 2084
00006  McAllister, Mick     8957 5267
1>
```

5. Type **CLEAR ALL** and press **Return** to close all files.
6. Turn to Module 15 to continue the learning sequence.

Module 52
REPORT, REPORT FORMS, SPOOL

DESCRIPTION

The REPORT command prints a report using a form file created in the full-screen editor with the WRITE command. Before the REPORT command is used, a database file must be in use or specified in a FILE clause in the report form, and the specified report form must exist. The report can be sent to the screen (the default), the printer, a communications port, or a text file.

Here are two sample REPORT commands, using a hypothetical report form file called MONTHLY.FRM:

`1>REPORT Monthly WHILE TransDate<'87000'` ; With the current record set to the first 1986 record in a database indexed or sorted on TransDate, this command uses MONTHLY.FRM to create a report for 1986.

`1>REPORT Monthly FOR TransDate<'870201'.and. TransDate>'870100'` ; Creates a similar report, but containing all transactions with a January 1986 date on them.

REPORT FORMS Report forms are written in the editor. Begin a report form by typing REPORT *filename*.FRM. You can assign a different extension, but if the form file's extension is not FRM, then you must include the extension when you call the report.

There are eighteen keywords you can include while creating a report form. The following list includes all of them. All keywords except FIELDS are optional; however those that appear must be carefully ordered. The first nine keywords must be in the same order as their order on the following list whenever they are used, and the other nine may follow them in any order. Keywords which take expressions require that the expression be separated from the keyword by a blank space, a hyphen, and another blank, as indicated in the list.

1. FILE - *data file* — Opens the named file for use with the report. If the file is already open, it is closed and reopened. You may open up to six files by writing a FILE clause for each; the first FILE is assigned number 1, the second number 2, etc. Only record data from file number 1 can be reported, however.
2. INDEX - *key* TO *filename* — Indexes the last file opened on the key to an index file. Must follow a FILE clause. If the index already exists, you can combine the FILE keyword with an INDEX reference just as you would with a USE command:

   `FILE - filename INDEX index filename`
3. RELATION - *key* TO *file number* — Relations are defined from file 1 and otherwise operate just as they do in the SET RELATION command (Module 58). There must be a file opened into the work area referenced by the file number, either prior to calling the report form or through FILE keywords.

4. SELECT - *conditional expression* — Specifies conditions records must meet in order to be reported. If the form is called with a FOR clause in the REPORT command, the FOR clause conditions take precedence over the conditions in the SELECT clause.

5. SUBTOTAL - *expression* — Generates a subtotal whenever the *expression*, usually the index key, changes. You can have up to two levels of subtotals in a report.

6. MESSAGE - *string* — Writes a message to go on the line with the specified subtotal each time the subtotal is calculated. You can have one message for each subtotal.

7. FIELDS - *field 1, field2 . . .* — All report forms must include the FIELDS keyword. Fieldnames are separated with commas. Use *fieldname#* designations to include fieldnames from other open files.

8. HEADING - *text1,text2 . . .* — Creates column headings for the fields. This list should have as many commas as the number in the FIELDS list; if you want to print a field without a column heading, type two consecutive commas.

9. PICTURE - *format1, format2 . . .* — Uses PICTURE strings (described in Module 54) to create formats for totalling numeric fields. If a field is not to be totalled, use consecutive commas to skip it, as with the HEADING keyword.

The remaining keywords are optional as well, and they may be in any order as long as they do not occur before any of the keywords already discussed.

10. COMPRESS - — Sends the "015" control code to the printer, which sets compressed print (15 or 17 pitch) on an EPSON and certain IBM-compatibles. If your printer uses different codes than the EPSON, then use SETUP to send the actual code numbers. Note that the blank space, the first hyphen, and the additional blank after COMPRESS are a necessary part of the keyword.

11. SETUP - *value* — Sends the specified code message to the printer. The code can be decimal values (27,28, 72), hexadecimal values (1BH,1CH,48H), or quoted literal characters when accessible (27 and 28 have no accessible character values, decimal 72 is "H"). For example, shifting the Okidata 92 to compressed mode requires a decimal code of "29," which can be sent with the command

```
SETUP - 29
```

or

```
SETUP - 1DH
```

For information about codes, see your printer manual.

12. DOUBLE - — Double-spaces the report.

13. EJECT - — Starts a new page. Affected by the LENGTH keyword and by SET EJECT ON and SET LENGTH TO commands. With nested subtotaling (multiple levels), only the first level causes a page to eject.

14. LENGTH - *number of lines* — Sets number of lines per pages. Must be less than the setting in the SET LENGTH TO command (or less than the default of 66 if it has not been changed).

15. PRINT - — Synonym for SET PRINT ON. Sends the report to the printer.
16. SPOOL - *filename* — Sends the report to a text file. Only works if a print command has already been issued, either the PRINT - keyword or SET PRINT ON, before calling the file.
17. NODETAIL — Suppresses FIELDS and only reports totals and subtotals.
18. TITLE - *string* — A string or string expression to be used as a title, which is printed in the center of the third line of the report. If no TITLE is specified, the system variable :TITLE is used.

The Typical Operation demonstrates the use of many of these keywords.

SPOOLING VP-Info also provides a SPOOL command with two forms that can be used to send print information to a disk file or set up background printing. The forms of the command are

1. SPOOL *filename* This is the redirection command, used after a SET PRINT ON command. This is effectively a synonym for the SET ALTERNATE TO and SET ALTERNATE ON commands, sending all output that would go to the printer to a disk file or a device, such as "com1," instead. To stop spooling, type SPOOL without a filename (remember to also stop printing by typing SET PRINT OFF).
2. SPOOL *filename* TO *device* PAGE *number* This is the background printing command, which takes an optional PAGE clause, prints an existing file without interrupting other work. The filename is an existing text file and the device is specified by its device name (such as "lpt1" for a typical parallel printer). If a PAGE clause is included, then printing begins on the specified page.

To halt the spool printing, type SPOOL/T and press Return.

APPLICATIONS

The REPORT command, combined with form files, provides a fast way to create simple, standard reports. For more elaborate formatted reporting, use the print commands with SAY formatting options.

The ability to print summaries and subtotal values quickly and easily is also a valuable by-product of the VP-Info report generator. The optional keywords for forms let you add information to your heading, print selective records, or output the report to either the printer or a file on demand.

The SPOOL keyword and command allow you to use your printer without tying up other operations on the computer.

TYPICAL OPERATION

In the following illustration, a report form file is created for the PICNIC database and then used to print a report on a disk file. Begin at the VP prompt.

1. Type **WRITE PICNIC.FRM** and press **Return**.

2. Type the following file, carefully duplicating the placement of commas, spaces, and hyphens.

```
PICNIC.FRM                          VP-Info WRITE                        INSERT

....+....1....+....2....+....3....+....4....+....5....+....6....+....7....+....8
FILE - PICNIC INDEX THINGS◄
SUBTOTAL - bring◄
MESSAGE - "  Bringing "+Bring◄
FIELDS - name,guests,amount,measure,bring◄
HEADINGS - Employee,No. of Guests,,Bringing◄
PICTURE -,,99◄
TITLE - Interim Report on Picnic◄
```

3. Press **End** and then press **Return** to save the form.
4. Type **REPORT PICNIC** and press **Return** to view the report. Compare your screen to the following:

```
Thursday, July 16, 1987                                              Page 1

                         Interim Report on Picnic

Employee              No. of Guests      Bringing
  Bringing Beans
Cantwell, Julie         3             2  Pot
                                     --
                                      2

  Bringing Buns
Crandal, Phil           4             5  Packs
Tolliver, Greg          4             6  Packs
                                     --
                                     11

  Bringing Chips
Johns, Bill             3             5  Bags
Johnson, J.D.           4             3  Bags
Stevens, Jan            3             5  Bags
                                     --
                                     13

Press any key to continue ...
```

5. Press **Return** twice to move to page 3. Notice that the report totals all the Amount fields together, for a total of 44 items. Since we want to remove that meaningless number from the final version of the report, the report must be sent to a disk file for editing before going to the printer.

6. Type **WRITE PICNIC.FRM** and press **Return.**
7. Type the following two lines as the last lines in the file:

   PRINT -
   SPOOL - PICRPT.TXT

8. Press **End** and then press **Return** to save the new file.
9. Type **REPORT PICNIC** again and press **Return**. Notice the drive activity.
10. When the VP prompt returns, type **WRITE PICRPT.TXT** and press **Return.**
11. When Page 1 of the report appears, press **PgDn** twice to reach the end of the report, and then press **Ctrl-T** to delete the double line, the number 44, and any extraneous terminal characters, so that the last line in the file simply contains the number 2.
12. Press **End** and then press **Return** and save the file.
13. If you have a printer and it is ready to receive text, then you can print the file now with the SPOOL command. (Do not attempt this without a fully operational printer, or your computer may lock up.)
14. Type **SPOOL PICRPT.TXT TO lpt1** and press **Return.**
15. While the printer is operating, type **LIST** and press **Return**. Notice that the printer and the computer are operating simultaneously. This is only possible in VP-Info with the SPOOL command.
16. To clear disk space, use DELETE FILE to remove PICNIC.FRM and PICRPT.TXT from the disk.
17. Turn to Module 20 to continue the learning sequence.

Module 53

RUN

DESCRIPTION

The RUN command is used to load and run programs outside of the VP-Info program environment. For example, if you wish to check the integrity of a disk in the B drive, and you have the DOS program CHKDSK on your A drive disk, use the command:

```
1>RUN CHKDSK b:/f
```

To use the RUN command, you must add a SET MEMORY TO command to your VPI.CNF file to limit the amount of memory VP-Info uses. If your computer has sufficient memory (more than 256K), the program executes. If there is not enough memory available, an error message is displayed.

You can also run common DOS commands such as DIR and DEL with RUN. The form for this command is

1>RUN COMMAND /C *DOS internal command or batch filename*

When the program or DOS command finishes operation, control is returned to VP-Info, on the line below the RUN command.

NOTE

This can create a distracting display if your RUN command generated lines of text. Use CLS to clear the screen of any overwritten lines.

APPLICATIONS

There are a number of DOS utilities that are useful from within VP-Info. For example, the ability to delete multiple files having the extension BAK is accomplished with RUN COMMAND /C DEL *.BAK, which takes advantage of the DOS wildcard (*) feature. Also, the VP-Info COPY command only works with open data files. Access to the DOS COPY command allows copying of other files as well. In an emergency, you can use RUN COMMAND /C to format a disk in your B drive, being careful to protect your program disk from the hazards of careless executions of the FORMAT command.

It is also possible to execute external programs, which provides a degree of interactive capability between VP-Info and other programs. For example, you can use a small external editor or any COM or EXE file utilities without exiting from VP-Info.

TYPICAL OPERATION

This operation does not work unless you have included the SET MEMORY TO 64 clause in your VPI.CNF file as described in Module 2. First you use RUN COMMAND /C to copy your .CNF file to the B drive; then you use RUN to execute a CHKDSK command. Here, the CHKDSK checks the B drive disk. If you install CHKDSK on your VP-Info program disk, or copy it to a RAMDisk, or are using a hard disk, you can use the command on other drives. Begin at the VP prompt.

CAUTION

Never remove your VP-Info program disk while VP-Info is running, or you can suffer one of a variety of serious crashes.

Never use CHKDSK/F on your VP-Info program disk while VP-Info is running, or the disk may be seriously damaged.

1. Type **RUN COMMAND /C COPY VPI.CNF B:** and press **Return**.
2. Type **DIR B:*.CNF** and press **Return** to confirm the copy. Notice that VPI.CNF is now listed on your B drive directory.
3. Place your DOS utility disk containing CHKDSK.COM in the B drive.
4. Type **RUN COMMAND /C B:CHKDSK** and press **Return**. Compare your display with the following. Differences of detail are caused by differences in file sizes and system configurations. If any other messages appear, such as references to errors, file allocation, or lost clusters, then consult your DOS manual, because you have uncovered a faulty file or disk.

```
1>RUN COMMAND /C B:CHKDSK
1> 362496 bytes total disk space
     45056 bytes in 2 hidden files
   310272 bytes in 9 user files
      7168 bytes available on disk

   655360 bytes total memory
     67264 bytes free
```

5. Turn to Module 25 to continue the learning sequence.

Module 54

SAY, SAY GET, SAY USING, CLEAR GETS, READ

DESCRIPTION

This module deals with a set of VP-Info statements used to display text and accept keyboard entries into database fields and memory variables. The information in this module describes forms of the SAY statement. Because the SAY statement is often used in conjunction with the GET and @ *row,col* statements, information about these statements is also included. For more information about @ *row,col* and GET, see Modules 6 and 34.

@ *row,col* SAY "..." Some forms of the @ *row,col* SAY statement are described in the following list.

1. @ *row,col* SAY '*text*' The text enclosed in single or double quotes is displayed beginning at the specified *row,col* coordinates.

   Example:

   ```
   @ 5,20 SAY 'Read the information and press any key...'
   ```

2. @ *row,col* SAY *field name* The contents of the named field are displayed beginning at the specified *row,col* coordinates. The named field in the current record is used.

   Example:

   ```
   @7,15 SAY CITY
   ```

3. @ *row,col* SAY *memory variable* The contents of the named memory variable are displayed beginning at the specified *row,col* coordinates.

   Example:

   ```
   STORE 25 TO Amount
   @ 12,35 SAY Amount
   ```

4. @ *row,col* SAY '*text*' + *memory variable* Displays text and contents of specified memory variable as a single expression.

   Example:

   ```
   @ 3,1 SAY 'The value of the memory variable is ' + MVar
   ```

5. @ *row,col* Erases specified row from the specified col position to the left edge of screen.

   Example:

   ```
   @ 3,40
   ```

When SET FORMAT TO PRINT is active, the displayed output is directed to your printer instead of to your screen. To bring it back to your screen, you can enter SET FORMAT TO SCREEN. This is VP-Info's default (normal) mode. When the printer is active, be sure to use @ *row,col* positions sequentially, from top to bottom, left to right. This is critical when information is printed, because your printer can't move backwards; it prints a row and a column at a time.

THE ROW( ) AND COL( ) FUNCTIONS The ROW( ) and COL( ) functions contain the current row and column position of the cursor. This is where text is displayed. If the cursor is presently at row 3, column 12, the expression

```
@ ROW()+1,COL() SAY TRIM(CITY) + STATE + ZIP
```

positions the contents of the CITY, STATE, and ZIP fields to row 4, column 12. These functions let you output information in a location relative to the current cursor or printer position, rather than having to compute absolute row and column position values.

You may wish to try the ROW( ) and COL( ) functions from the VP prompt. Type the following three lines to see the positions.

```
1>CLS
1>? ROW()
1>? COL()
```

Compare your screen with the following result:

```
1>? ROW()
      1.00
1>? COL()
      9.00
1>
```

Notice that the locations are reported as real numbers, and that the position reported is your location at the time you issued the command. (The cursor was in the ninth column, at the right of the "COL( )" statement when you pressed Return.)

@ row,col* SAY *"text"* GET *field name The SAY statement can incorporate the GET statement to display text and designated field contents. Because GET is used to display or display and modify field contents, it is not used for printing, nor is it usable in immediate mode. If one or more SAY . . . GET statements are followed by a command line containing the CLEAR GETS statement, the field contents are only displayed. However, if they are followed by the READ statement, the cursor is positioned in the first displayed field. The READ statement lets you enter information directly into the displayed field from your keyboard, and the entered information is inserted into the record. Some examples of this form of the SAY statement follow.

```
USE MEMBERS
@ 5,15 SAY "                    Member's Name "  GET NAME
@ 6,15 SAY '                  Street Address '   GET ADR
@ 7,15 SAY '       City, State, and Zip Code '   GET CSZ
CLEAR GETS
@ 8,15 SAY "Are this member's dues paid (T/F)?" GET PAID
READ
```

The NAME, ADR, and CSZ fields are only displayed in rows 5, 6, and 7; the CLEAR GETS statement prevents the field contents from being modified. However, the cursor is positioned at the PAID field to allow modification. This is caused by the READ statement on a line following the last @ *row,col* SAY . . . GET statement.

@ row,col* SAY *field name* USING *expression The USING clause lets you control the format of displayed or printed information. For example, if you wish to display all text in uppercase form, you can use:

```
@ 10,12 SAY NAME USING '!!!!!!!!!!!!!!!!!!!!!!!!!'
```

Notice that the ! sign is the uppercase control character. The Name field is 25 characters long, so the USING specification must be the same size. If the template is too short to display the contents of the field, a string field is left blank, a number field is indicated with a row of asterisks as long as the template.

@ row,col* GET *field name* PICTURE *expression This command form also lets you control the format of information from displayed fields. The GET . . . PICTURE structure is the GET equivalent of the SAY . . . USING structure and handled in the same way. However it also lets you control the way that information is entered into a database. This is particularly helpful when consistency of data entry is important. For example, you might want all social security numbers in the SSN field of your database to be stored as nine digits but represented on screen with the appropriate hyphens. The statement to force this entry (assuming you have a database containing the character field SSN) is:

```
@ 10,12 GET SSN PICTURE '999-99-9999'
```

NOTE

Because the hyphen is an alphanumeric character, you must create SSN as a character field.

If you were to list the files from such a database, and Record #1 contained the social security number 000-00-0000, it would appear in the record list as "000000000," saving two bytes per record. A similar trick could force formatting of phone numbers as "[999] 999-9999" while saving the phone numbers as alphanumeric fields of only ten characters rather than fourteen.

These examples illustrate one type of formatting clause. Many more can be used with PICTURE and USING clauses or the PIC( ) function to create entry templates and display formats. In the following table, Type N applies to numeric fields, C to character fields, and B to both.

Table 54-1 Format and Template Expressions

Character	*Type*	*Description*
A	C	Allows only alphabetical characters. `@ 12,20 GET TITLE PICTURE 'AAAAAAAAAAAAAAAAAAAA'`
X	C	Allows alphanumeric characters, including symbols. `@ 5,5 SAY "Part Number? " GET PN PICTURE 'XXXXXX-XX'`

!	C	Converts lowercase to uppercase. `@ 5,5 SAY 'NAME  ' GET NAME PICTURE '!!!!!!!!!!'`
9	B	Allows only digits, periods, and commas for data, with signs and leading blanks permitted. `@ 5,5 SAY 'Salary? :' GET Salary PICT '99,999.99'`

$	N	Displays a $ sign next to the left-most digit (if the format specified uses $ signs to represent all whole number positions, as in '$$$,$$$.99') or in the farthest left position in the format (PICTURE '$999,999.99').
		`@ 8,26 GET Cost * 1.1 PICTURE '$,$$$.99'`
		`If COST is $1000.00, the displayed number is "$1,100.00."`
		`@ 8,26 GET COST * 1.1 PICTURE '$99999.99'`
		`The displayed number is "$ 1100.00."`

APPLICATIONS

The various SAY statements have many applications. With the @ *row,col* position statement, SAY is used to display and print text and the contents of fields and memory variables at specific row and column positions. The ability to use SAY with GET lets you display or print field contents at any *row,col* position. The contents are only displayed when GET statements are followed by CLEAR GETS; they may be changed when GET statements are followed by READ.

Finally, the PICTURE . . . USING clause is used to control the way field contents are displayed, and in some cases, the format in which they are entered. For example, you can display dollars and cents with dollar signs and decimals; large numbers with commas and decimal points. One popular application of the PICTURE '$9999.99' clause is to print dollar signs on checks.

TYPICAL OPERATION

In this illustration several variations of @ *row,col* . . . SAY are used in a command file named SAY.PRG. The command file uses the ABC database last modified in Module 38. Begin at the VP prompt.

1. Type **WRITE SAY** and press **Return** to use the VP-Info editor.
2. Type the following command file. (Do not type the explanatory remarks or indentation.)

Remarks

```
* SAY.PRG — Uses variations of the SAY statement.
CLS
SET INTENSITY OFF          ; Turns off reverse video display.
* @ ... SAY positions text.
@ 2,15 SAY 'THIS PROGRAM ALLOWS UPDATING OF EMPLOYEE INFORMATION'
ACCEPT 'Press "Q" to Quit, any other key to proceed  ' TO Check
IF !(Check)='Q'            ; If uppercase Check = 'Q'
    CLS
    CANCEL                 ; Cancels command file operation.
ENDIF                      ; Completes IF statement; passes control on.
USE ABC                    ; Puts ABC database file in use.
DO WHILE .NOT. EOF         ; Continues operation while not end-of-file.
```

```
    CLS
  • The following @ row,col lines display text and field values.
    @ 5,10 SAY 'Name            ' GET NAME PICTURE '!!!!!!!!!!!!!!!!!!!!'
    @ 6,10 SAY 'Age             ' GET AGE PICT '99'
    @ ROW(),COL()+13 GET DATE PICT '9999/99/99'
    CLEAR GETS                 ; Prevents modification of preceding fields.
    @ 7,10 SAY 'Telephone X  ' GET EXTN
    @ 8,10 SAY 'Mail Drop #  ' GET MAIL
  • READ allows modification of field values on rows 7 and 8.
    READ
    ACCEPT 'Press "Q" to Quit, any other key to proceed ' TO Check
    IF !(Check)='Q'
       BREAK                   ; Exits DO WHILE loop if Check is 'Q' or 'q.'
    ELSE                       ; If Check is not "Q," uses following commands.
       SKIP                    ; Positions record pointer to next record.
    ENDIF                      ; Completes IF statement; passes control on.
  ENDDO                        ; Completes DO WHILE statement.
  USE                          ; Closes the database file.
  SET INTENSITY ON             ; Turns reverse video back on.
  CLS
  RETURN                       ; Exits from command file.
```

3. Press **Alt-F** to add formatting and proofread the file.
4. Press **End** and **Return** to write the command file to disk.
5. Run the command file by typing **DO SAY** and pressing **Return**. Compare your screen with the following, and respond to the prompts as indicated. Also notice how CLEAR GETS prevents data entry while READ lets you make changes.

```
                THIS PROGRAM ALLOWS UPDATING OF EMPLOYEE INFORMATION
Press "Q" to Quit, any other key to proceed          (Press a key and Return)
          Name           SERGIO, VINCENT
          Age            29              1982/10/21
          Telephone X 3596                           (Press Return twice)
          Mail Drop # 2084
Press "Q" to Quit, any other key to proceed          (Type Q and press Return)
```

6. Continue experimenting with your command file. Any changes you make in the last four fields are modified in the database. You can edit these fields just as you would with the EDIT or BROWSE commands, and the Arrow keys allow you to move all around in the active fields until you press Return while in the PAID field. Try using alternate PICTURE clauses and rearranging the position of the displayed text.
7. When finished, type **DELE FILE SAY.PRG** and press **Return** to delete the command file from your disk.
8. Turn to Module 65 to continue the learning sequence.

Module 55
SCOPE

DESCRIPTION

The SCOPE command restricts the record range of other VP-Info commands to a specified portion of an indexed database. It affects the GO TOP and GO BOTTOM commands and the End-of-File (EOF) value.

The SCOPE command can be specified in two ways, both requiring use of the active index. To turn off a SCOPE, type the command by itself.

If you type SCOPE *indexed field name*, where the active index is for that field, all other commands except FIND and GO operate on those records whose indexed field data is the same as that in the current record.

If you type SCOPE *string*, then the scope range is from the first record whose indexed field fits the string to the end of the file.

CAUTION

If you attempt to declare a SCOPE that is not appropriate to the currently active index, a STACK OVERFLOW error may occur, causing VP-Info to crash and return to the DOS prompt.

The declared SCOPE should be the master index field or a lefthand portion of that field (See LEFT( ) in Appendix D). SCOPE should be used carefully, because it can create some unwanted results. When using it, the SCOPE should be in effect for the minimum necessary time. Specifically, do not use FIND or REPLACE ALL while a SCOPE is in effect. Cancel any SCOPE declaration before closing data or index files.

VP-Info 1.4 includes the new SET command, SET FILTER TO *expression* (See Module 60), that is less tricky than SCOPE to use.

APPLICATIONS

A SCOPE command can be used to restrict command operations to the specific portion of the indexed database which fits the field specifications.

TYPICAL OPERATION

The value of the search functions in VP-Info can only be hinted at with examples drawn from tiny databases. This operation begins by creating an artificial database larger than any you have used so far, and then demonstrates the use of SCOPE to limit functions within that file. Begin at the VP prompt.

1. Type **USE ABC** and press **Return.**
2. Type **COPY TO BIGLIST** and press **Return.**
3. Type **USE BIGLIST** and press **Return**, and then type **APPEND** and press **Return.**
4. Add the following two records:

```
Name                 Extn Mail Date     Age

Burrows, Andrew      1234 4321 19861010 27
Billings, Paul       3456 2344 19860912 38
<End>
```

5. Type **COPY TO TEMP** and press **Return.**
6. Type **WRITE DATAMAKE** and press **Return** to enter the full-screen VP-Info editor.
7. Type the following program. (Do not type explanatory remarks.)

```
                                    Remarks
* DATAMAKE.PRG – Creates a large test file.
USE BIGLIST
REPEAT 10 TIMES                     ; Command structure for repetition.
APPEND FROM TEMP                    ; Add copies of records in TEMP.
ENDREPEAT                           ; After appending 7 records 10 times.
INDEX ON !(NAME) TO
BIGNAME                             ; Index the BIGLIST file.
CANCEL                              ; Back to the VP prompt with index active.
```

8. Press **Alt-F** then press **End** and **Return** to save the file.
9. Type **DO DATAMAKE** and press **Return.** Notice the conversation report for each of the ten appends and the indexing function.
10. Type **GO BOTTOM** and press **Return.**
11. Type **DISP** and press **Return.** Notice that record 91 is displayed.
12. Type **SCOPE 'B'**, being sure to use an uppercase "B", and press **Return.**
13. Press **Up Arrow** three times to retrieve the command GO BOTTOM. When it is on the line with the cursor, press **Return** to re-execute it.
14. Type **DISP** and press **Return.** Notice that with SCOPE set, the last "Burrows" file is considered the bottom.
15. Type **? EOF** and press **Return.** Notice that the computer responds "F" for false.

16. Type **SCOPE !(Name)** and press **Return**. Now the computer only works with those files which share the same Name field as the current record.
17. Type **LIST** and press **Return**. Notice that only the eleven Burrows files appear.
18. Type **LOCATE FOR Extn = '4554'** and press **Return**.
19. Type **DISP** and press **Return**. Notice that the current record is not the one searched for (Extn 4554 belongs to Collins). SCOPE excludes Collins from consideration.
20. Type **? EOF** and press **Return**. Notice that now the computer reports "T" for True, even though Burrows is not the actual last record.
21. Type **SCOPE** and press **Return** to disable the SCOPE setting.
22. Press **Up Arrow** four times to retrieve the LOCATE command, and then press **Return** when it appears under the cursor. Compare your screen to the following:

```
1>LOCATE FOR Extn= '4554'
1>disp
00098  Burrows, Andrew        1234 4321 19861010 27
1>? eof
T
1>SCOPE
1>
1>SCOPE
1>? eof
1>disp
1>LOCATE FOR Extn= '4554'
Record 3
1>
```

23. When you are finished experimenting with the SCOPE command, type **QUIT** and press **Return** to go back to the DOS prompt.
24. At the DOS prompt, type **DEL B:BIG*.*** and press **Return** to erase the DBF and NDX files, then type **DEL B:TEMP.DBF** and press **Return** to erase the TEMP file. Finally, type **DEL DATAMAKE.PRG** and press **Return**.
25. Turn to Module 63 to continue the learning sequence.

Module 56

SCREEN

DESCRIPTION

The SCREEN command is used to store up to three alternate screens which you may write to or swap displays among. This command requires at least 320K of RAM.

When you use the WINDOW command, the material written over is not recoverable upon closing the window. If you wish to superimpose a message and then return to the former screen data, the SCREEN command allows you to do this, creating "pop-up" effects. You can also use it to store display material to an background screen and pop it up later.

Here are examples of the SCREEN command:

	Remarks
1>SCREEN 1,2	; Copies the current screen image, including cursor position and color attribute, to background Screen 2 (Screen 1 is always the display screen).
1>SCREEN 2,3	; Copies the contents of background Screen 2 to background Screen 3.
1>SCREEN 3,1	; Copies (displays) Screen 3 to Screen 1.
1>SCREEN 3	; Directs output to Screen 3. In conversational mode rather than command files, this creates a confusing screen appearance, because everything except the actual keyboard input is going to the background screen. As a result, the VP prompt and the new line for the next command are suppressed until output is redirected to Screen 1, the display screen.

To explain this last example, consider the following:

A list is sent to Screen 2 from the VP prompt. First, these are the commands to perform that transfer, each entered with a Return:

```
1>CLS
1>USE ABC
1>SCREEN 2
1>CLS
1>LIST
1>SCREEN 1
```

At this point, however, your display looks like this:

```
1>USE ABC
1>SCREEN 2CLSLISTSCREEN 1
```

Next, after you type the command SCREEN 2,1, the display looks like this:

```
1>
1>_01  Sergio, Vincent       3596 2084 19821021 29
00002  Bishop, Sam           2234 430  19811110 34
00003  Collins, Arthur       4554 323  19830612 43
00004  Harris, Robert        3353 2230 19850131 38
00005  Alexander, T.G.       1104 2084 19820202 26
00006  McAllister, Mick      9857 5267 19830625 41
00007  Johns, Bill T.        2332 4544 19850915 24
1>
```

Notice that the prompt is located in the display of the first record, another hazard of using SCREEN in the conversational mode.

APPLICATIONS

The SCREEN command is very useful in command files for pop-up applications like help screens because it allows you to store the current screen and recover it.

TYPICAL OPERATION

This operation adds to the ABC database an INFO field and a library file containing memos keyed to that field. This requires modifying the database before using the new command file to create memos. To avoid listing the records repeatedly, a single list is stored on Screen 2. Begin at the VP prompt.

1. Type **USE ABC** and press **Return** to open the database.
2. As a safety precaution, type **COPY TO TEMP** and press **Return**, making a backup copy of the database.
3. Type **MODIFY** and press **Return** to change the database.
4. Press **PgDn** five times to create a new field line, and add the following field:

   ```
   INFO     N    5
   ```

5. Press **End** and then **Return** to save the new database.
6. Type **WRITE MEMO** and press **Return** to write the following command file. (Do not type the remarks or indentations.)

```
* MEMO.PRG – Creates LIB memos keyed to the INFO field of ABC.
USE ABC
CLS
STORE 1 to RecNo                ; Initialize RecNo.
SET LIBRARY TO ABCMEMO          ; Open Library.
LIST                            ; Display records.
SCREEN 1,2                      ; Copy that display to a background screen.
```

```
DO WHILE T                               ; Do command loop.
   ?
   ? "Select a record [by number] to add a memo to. "
   INPUT "Choose Zero to Quit.   Choice: " to RecNo
   IF RecNo = 0                          ; Zero selected.
      BREAK                              ; Quit command structure.
   ENDIF                                 ; Exit loop.
   GO RecNo                              ; Move record pointer to selected record.
   STORE :AVAIL TO Next                  ; Store next volume number to Next.
   REPLACE INFO WITH Next                ; Put Next in INFO field.
   @ 23,5 SAY Name+"      [WRITE and SAVE your memo as a text volume.]"
   WINDOW 0,20                           ; Open editor, leaving message on line 23.
   WRITE .Next                           ; Create the memo.
   WINDOW                                ; Return to full-screen window.
   SCREEN 2,1                            ; Replace the screen with the list on 2.
ENDDO                                    ; End DO WHILE structure.
RETURN                                   ; Terminate program.
```

7. Press **Alt-F** to format the program, proofread it, and then press **End** and then **Return** to save it.
8. From the VP prompt, type **SET LIBRARY TO ABCMEMO** and press **Return**.
9. Type **WRITE .1** and press **Return** and use the editor to create a first volume containing the message "No memo for this record."
10. Type **DO MEMO** and press **Return**.
11. Type **1** and press **Return** to select writing a memo on Sergio.
12. Notice that the editor opens a library file keyed to the variable NEXT, and that the WINDOW function has allowed you to display a message at the bottom of the editor screen.
13. Type the following memo: **Vincent is available for overtime on Thursdays.**
14. Press **End** and then press **Return** to save the library volume. Notice that the SCREEN commands retrieve the original list, allowing you to select another record or quit.
15. Type **0** and press **Return** to exit from the memo writer.
16. Type **LIST**and press **Return**. Notice that Sergio now has a "2" in the last field, indicating the presence of a memo keyed to volume 1 of the ABCMEMO library.
17. Type **? :AVAIL** and press **Return**. Notice that the next volume available is 3.

CAUTION

Never attempt to access or print a non-existent library volume (in this case, volume 3, which is not yet written). The result will be a computer lockup with possible damage to the data on the disk containing the LIB file.

18. Type **TEXT .2** and press **Return**. Compare your screen to the following display, which shows all the screen activity from step 14 on:

```
00001  Sergio, Vincent      3596 2084 19821021 29
00002  Bishop, Sam          2234 430  19811110 34
00003  Collins, Arthur      4554 323  19830612 43
00004  Harris, Robert       3353 2230 19850131 38
00005  Alexander, T.G.      1104 2084 19820202 26
00006  McAllister, Mick     9857 5267 19830625 41
00007  Johns, Bill T.       2332 4544 19850915 24

Select a record (by number) to add a memo to.
Choose Zero to Quit.  Choice:  0
1>list
00001  Sergio, Vincent      3596 2084 19821021 29      2
00002  Bishop, Sam          2234 430  19811110 34
00003  Collins, Arthur      4554 323  19830612 43
00004  Harris, Robert       3353 2230 19850131 38
00005  Alexander, T.G.      1104 2084 19820202 26
00006  McAllister, Mick     9857 5267 19830625 41
00007  Johns, Bill T.       2332 4544 19850915 24
1>? :avail
      3.00
1>text .2.
Vincent is available for overtime on Thursdays.
1>
```

19. Type **DELE FILE MEMO.PRG** and press **Return** to remove the memo program from your work disk.
20. Type **SET LIBRARY TO** and press **Return** to close the library, then type **CLEAR ALL** and press **Return** to clear the working environment.
21. Turn to Module 18 to continue the learning sequence.

Module 57

SCROLL

DESCRIPTION

The SCROLL command scrolls the active window up or down one line. If the display screen is the "active window," the entire display is scrolled. The command works in both conversational mode and command files, but has more useful applications in command files. These are the forms of the SCROLL command:

	Remarks
1. SCROLL UP	; Scrolls the screen or active window up one row. Alternatively, SCROLL DOWN.
2. SCROLL 8,10	; Scrolls only the contents of rows 8, 9, and 10 up one row. (This cannot be combined with UP/DOWN.)

APPLICATIONS

If you are using an area framed by messages for your display, the SCROLL command can be used to keep the frame on screen while the center scrolls. A similar effect can be achieved by placing the scrolling information inside a window. See the example in the Typical Operation section of this module.

TYPICAL OPERATION

This operation creates a display window with messages at the top and bottom and scrolls record data between them. The database used is ABC. Begin at the VP prompt.

1. Type **WRITE SCANNER** and press **Return.**
2. Create the following command file (do not type remarks or indentation):

```
* SCANNER.PRG        Reads data from ABC to the screen.
CLS
USE ABC
@ 5,10 SAY "Employee database for My Company"
WINDOW 9,10,16,45 BLANK             ; Create borderless window.
SET COLOR TO 3                      ; Cyan characters on black in window.
CLS                                 ; Clear window.
STORE ' ' to Continue               ; Initialize Continue and SLine
SLine = 12
@ 10,11 SAY "Name              Mail Ext"     ; Top window line message.
@ 15,11 SAY "More . . . .   Press Return"    ; Bottom window line message.
DO WHILE .NOT. EOF                           ; DO entire file.
   @ SLine, 12 SAY Name+Extn GET Continue    ; Begin at 12,12.
```

```
    READ                          ; Get Continue.
    SKIP                          ; Next record.
    SLine = SLine+1               ; Add 1 to line number
    IF SLine >14                  ; If line number exceeds 14
      SCROLL 12,14                ; Scroll lines 12, 13, and 14.
      SLINE=14                    ; Reset line number to 14.
    ENDIF                         ; End of IF routine.
  ENDDO                           ; EOF encountered; go on.
  @ 16,0                          ; Erase "More . . . ." prompt.
  SET COLOR TO 7                  ; Reset original colors.
  CURSOR 0,0                      ; Go to screen top.
  WINDOW                          ; Exit from the window.
  CLEAR                           ; Close database.
  RETURN                          ; Exit from the command file.
```

3. Press **Alt-F** to format the file, proofread it, then press **End** and **Return** to save it.
4. Type **DO SCANNER** and press **Return** to see the program in operation; press **Return** to scroll the fields. Notice that the window area is printing in a different color than the main screen. Also, notice that only the field data is scrolling.
5. When you are through experimenting with the program, return to the VP prompt and type **DELE FILE SCANNER.PRG** and press **Return** to clear space on your work disk.
6. Turn to Module 34 to continue the learning sequence.

Module 58

SELECT, SET RELATION TO, SET LINK TO

DESCRIPTION

With the USE# command (described in Module 68), you can open a file directly into an inactive work area. The SELECT command then lets you select any 1 of 6 possible database *work areas.* A work area contains a database, and if you like, up to seven corresponding database index files.

The SET RELATION TO function lets you establish a relationship between two databases sharing a common field. For example, you may have two employee database files, each using a common NAME field. One may contain phone number and mail station information, while the other contains job code and salary information. The relation can be established on the NAME field. More information and an example is provided on the next few pages, following a more detailed description of the SELECT command and work areas.

The SET LINK TO function allows you to connect two databases by record number rather than by shared fields. If the first record of one database contains the address and phone data on an employee and the first record of a second database contains the same employee's social security number, salary, etc., and the entire database is set up "in parallel," so to speak, then you can LINK the two files and maintain them simultaneously.

SELECTING WORK AREAS VP-Info uses work areas in which database and index files are stored and from which they are called. The SELECT command is used to associate a database file with a work area. The general form of the SELECT command is:

```
SELECT 1
USE dbfile1
SELECT 2
USE dbfile2
```

Now that dbfile1 is associated with work area 1, you can make it the active work area with the command:

```
SELECT 1
```

Notice that SELECT always is used with a number. It cannot take a variable or macro specification.

You can select work areas and name databases until you reach 6. However, you must have begun with a CONFIG.SYS file that contains:

```
FILES=20
BUFFERS=20
```

in order to organize your computer's memory to support seven database files and the operation of corresponding index and command files. Even with a capacity of twenty files, keep in mind that VPI.EXE counts as one of them, a database with seven indexes counts as eight, and you need at least one for any PRG files you try to use. In other words, three open databases with six indexes each would exhaust your supply of files. On the other hand, few databases require that many indexes; the chances are that you would exhaust the memory capacity of a 640K system long before you opened twenty files.

The SELECT command allows you to move through work areas. The current work area is indicated by the number of the VP prompt. If you last selected work area 2, even a CLOSE ALL command does not shift you back to area 1. To return to area 1, you must type SELECT 1.

To open a database in a different work area without shifting into that area, you can type USE#*n filename*. For example, the following series of commands keeps you in the first work area while opening PICNIC.DBF into the second, and then shifts to the third and opens MEMBERS there:

```
1>USE ABC
1>USE#2 PICNIC
1>SELECT 3
3>USE MEMBERS
```

At this point, a LIST command would list the MEMBERS data. However, you can also list either of the other databases without SELECTing it, using LIST#1 for ABC or LIST#2 for PICNIC.

COMMAND REDIRECTION You can send a command from one work area to another by including a reference number with the first word of the command. To list the PICNIC data from work area 3, type LIST#2 OFF. To see the structure of ABC, type DISP#1 STRU. The third work area remains active until a new SELECT command is given.

You can also reference fields from more than one database by the same method. For example, typing DISP name#1,name#2,name#3 causes a display of the Name field for the current record in each datafile, with the current record number for the active work area. If you are in work area 3, you do not need to include a reference number for the Name field in MEMBERS.

RECORD POINTER CONTROL The ability to display mixed data from multiple databases is not much use without a way to link the files. The key to changing information within any database file is to position the record pointer at the desired location. The record pointer stays in place within each database until moved by some command addressed to that database. This is true for individual database operation as well as when you are using several databases in different work areas. Look at the following illustration.

Work Area	1	2	3
Database	Equip	Bldg	Land
Record No.	1 2< – pointer 3 4 5	1 2 3 4< – pointer 5	1< – pointer 2 3 4 5
Field Names	Des Price AccDep BookVal	Des Price Deprec BookVal	Des Price AccApp MktVal

The three databases (Equip, Bldg, and Land) are selected into work areas 1, 2, and 3 with the following commands:

```
1>SELECT 1
1>USE EQUIP
1>SELECT 2
2>USE BLDG
2>SELECT 3
3>USE LAND
```

To verify the active databases and their work areas, you can type STATUS and press Return to see the settings:

```
Thursday, July 16, 1987              UP-Info STATUS

Rec #              File name         Indexed by
00001  File 1 ... EQUIP.DBF
00001  File 2 ... BLDG.DBF
00001 *File 3 ... LAND.DBF
00000  File 4 ...
00000  File 5 ...
00000  File 6 ...
```

Since the database files have just been opened, all three files are positioned at Rec # 00001 (the asterisk next to File 3 indicates that the third work area is selected). As the files are used, the pointers get moved, and their new positions are available in the STATUS list. Notice that the record pointer is positioned at a different record in the preceding diagram. Commands that affect field contents and structure only operate on the active database file. You can extract, exchange, or edit information within any of the pointed records, or within records that match some expression in the selected databases.

For example, if you want to add the BookVal and MktVal fields (these names stand for *book value* and *market value*) of the current records and store them to a memory variable named TOTVAL, you can use:

```
3>TOTVAL=BOOKVAL#1 + BOOKVAL#2 + MKTVAL#3 TO TOTVAL
```

This command totals BookVal from EQUIP's second record with BookVal from the fourth record of BLDG and MktVal from the first record in LAND. Notice that the # symbol is used to establish to which database's field we are referring. If you wish to find the value of all buildings, equipment, and land in the databases, position the record pointer to the first record in each database by typing GO#1 TOP, GO#2 TOP, and GO TOP, pressing Return after each entry. Then type: SUM BOOKVAL#1 + BOOKVAL#2 + MKTVAL#3 TO TOTVAL.

The variable TOTVAL is now available no matter which work area is selected, until it is released or discarded in some other way.

Commands that move the record pointer only affect the selected database. For example, you can append a blank record to EQUIP with APPEND#1 BLANK, and then position the record pointer to the blank record with GO#1 BOTTOM. Next, you can find a record in BLDG with the LOCATE#2 command. Once at the desired record, you can use the REPLACE command to move field contents from the second database to first database with: REPLACE *field name*#2 WITH *field name*#1.

The command REPLACE NAME#2 WITH NAME#1 would add the name located in PICNIC to the previously blank record in ABC.

You can also transfer the contents of memory variables to databases using field names. Look at the following example:

```
3>MVar = 12                          ; Stores 12 to memory variable MVar.
3>SELECT 1                           ; Selects database in work area 1.
1>REPLACE AMOUNT#2 WITH MVar         ; Replaces the contents of the AMOUNT field in
                                       database#2 with the contents of MVar (12).
```

SET RELATION The general form of the SET RELATION function is:

```
SET RELATION ON key expression TO work area number
```

A relationship can be established between two databases using a common field. The field must be indexed in the second database (called the lookup database), both databases must be selected into work areas, and the lookup database must have an active index using the chosen key expression. An indexed field is referred to as a *key field*.

Restated, the SET RELATION ON *key expression* TO *work area* establishes a relationship between the two databases that contain a common key field.

The database in the active work area is linked to a second database residing in the named work area. The record pointer is coordinated between the two databases by moving both to records containing the key expression. Remember, the key expression must exist in the active index of the lookup database.

SET LINK The SET LINK command simply connects two databases on the assumption that the first record of one database is related to the first record in the other, the tenth to the tenth, the 211th to the 211th, etc. It can be used with unindexed files, but the records must be in the same order and there should be the same number of records in each file.

An example should help clarify the distinction between RELATION and LINK. Both commands are used in the Typical Operation in this module.

APPLICATIONS

Many applications require large amounts of data, such as accounting applications that combine sales order-entry, accounts receivable, and inventory. A residential real estate database can require close to 150 data elements when considering all information required in a multiple-listing agreement (ownership information, terms, legal descriptions, structural descriptions, land descriptions, room sizes, appliances, utilities, tax districts, and so on).

On a networked system, you may be keeping simultaneous databases on employees, students, or customers, with one record containing public information like phone numbers, addresses, etc.

and another containing confidential information like grades, social security numbers, memos, or salaries. These two files can be linked with limited access to the data in the confidential one.

Setting a relationship, on the other hand, allows cross-linking of indexed files to keep a transaction database linked to files of customers, commissioned salespeople, and inventory, with only one data field duplicated. Rather than having one gigantic transaction database in which each transaction record includes the full address of the customer, one data field from the customer file and one data field from the inventory file can cross link three unique databases.

The ability to simultaneously use up to six database files lets you work with about 750 fields instead of 128. By combining this amount of power with available memory variables, you can design extremely versatile applications.

TYPICAL OPERATION

In this illustration the linking commands are used to create and modify a new database related to ABC. Begin at the VP prompt.

1. Use the ABC database created in Module 5 and last modified in Module 56. If necessary, recreate it and enter the data as shown.

```
1>USE ABC
1>DISP STRU
Data file:                 ABC.DBF
Number of records:             8
File number:                  #1
Field      Name       Type     Width    Dec
  1        NAME        C        20
  2        EXTN        C         4
  3        MAIL        C         4
  4        DATE        C         8
  5        AGE         N         2
  6        INFO        N         5
** Record Length **             44
1>LIST
00001  Sergio, Vincent          3596 2084 19821021 29    2
00002  Bishop, Sam              2234 430  19811110 34    1
00003  Collins, Arthur          4554 323  19830612 43    1
00004  Barris, Robert           3353 2230 19850131 38    1
00005  Alexander, T. G.         1104 2084 19820202 26    1
00006  McAllister, Mick         8957 5267 19830625 41    1
00007  Johns, Bill T.           2332 4544 19850915 24    1
00008  Sergio, Alice            1234 5432 19861227 39    3
```

2. Once the database is ready, type **COPY FIELD NAME TO ABC1** and press **Return**.
3. Type **INDEX ON NAME TO PBX** and press **Return**.
4. Type **USE ABC1** and press **Return**. Then type **MODIFY** and add fields 2 through 4 as shown.

```
Data file:                  ABC1.DBF
Number of records:              8
File number:                   #1
Field      Name         Type     Width    Dec
   1       NAME           C        20
   2       JOB_CODE       C         4
   3       EMP_DATE       C         8
   4       RATE           N         7       2
   5       <End>                          Press End to complete modify.
** Record Length **                40
```

5. Because the records are in the same order, you can use SET LINK ON to transfer the DATE field from ABC to the EMP_DATE field in ABC1. First, type **USE#2 ABC** and press **Return** to open the file.
6. Type **LIST name, name#2** to confirm the records' order. Notice that the name "Sergio, Vincent" is listed repeatedly in the last column. ABC is not advancing through the records.
7. Type **GO TOP** to return ABC1 to the first record.
8. Type **SET LINK TO 2** and press **Return**, type **GO 4**, and then type **LIST name, name#2** again. (Or press the Up Arrow three times to repeat the second-to-last command.) Notice that the records are now synchronized.
9. Type the following series of commands.

NOTE

As a short cut, you might try typing REPLACE Emp_Date WITH Date#2 and pressing Return, then typing SKIP and pressing Return, and then pressing the Up Arrow twice to retrieve the REPLACE command from the command buffer. When the REPLACE command appears on the command line, press Return. Then type SKIP and press Return. Continue this process until you have executed the REPLACE command eight times. Alternatively, a small command file containing a REPEAT structure could do this task economically if there were more than a dozen records to change.

```
1>GO TOP
1>REPLACE Emp_Date WITH Date#2
1>SKIP
1>REPLACE Emp_Date WITH Date#2
1>SKIP
1>REPLACE Emp_Date WITH Date#2
1>SKIP
1>REPLACE Emp_Date WITH Date#2
```

```
1>SKIP
1>REPLACE Emp_Date WITH Date#2
1>SKIP
1>REPLACE Emp_Date WITH Date#2
1>SKIP
1>REPLACE Emp_Date WITH Date#2
1>SKIP
1>REPLACE Emp_Date WITH Date#2
1>LIST NAME, EMP'DATE,NAME#2,DATE#2
```

10. Compare your listing with the following:

```
1>LIST NAME, EMP_DATE,NAME#2,DATE#2
00001  Sergio, Vincent      19821021 Sergio, Vincent      19821021
00002  Bishop, Sam          19811110 Bishop, Sam          19811110
00003  Collins, Arthur      19830612 Collins, Arthur      19830612
00004  Harris, Robert       19850131 Harris, Robert       19850131
00005  Alexander, T.G.      19820202 Alexander, T.G.      19820202
00006  McAllister, Mick     19830625 McAllister, Mick     19830625
00007  Johns, Bill T.       19850915 Johns, Bill T.       19850915
00008  Sergio, Alice        19861227 Sergio, Alice        19861227
1>
```

11. Now type **SET LINK OFF** and press **Return**, then type **GO TOP**.
12. Type **BROWSE** to add the necessary information for the Job_Code and Rate fields as follows:

```
#1 ABC1.DBF                                     VP-Info BROWSE
        NAME                             JOB_  EMP_DATE    RATE
00001   Sergio, Vincent                  232   19821021 2150.00
00002   Bishop, Sam                      320   19811110 4300.00
00003   Collins, Arthur                  214   19830612 2350.00
00004   Barris, Robert                   114   19850131 2425.00
00005   Alexander, T. G.                 898   19820202 1900.00
00006   McAllister, Mick                 721   19830625 2200.00
00007   Johns, Bill T.                   123   19850915 3110.00
00008   Sergio, Alice                    155   19861208 3250.00
```

13. Type **INDEX ON NAME TO EMPL** and press **Return**.
14. Type the following instructions from the VP prompt, ending each with **Return**.

```
1>SELECT 2
2>SET RELATION ON Name TO 1
2>STAT
```

```
Thursday, July 16, 1987          VP-Info STATUS

Rec #              File name     Indexed by
00001   File 1 ... ABC1.DBF      NAME
00001  *File 2 ... ABC.DBF
00000   File 3 ...
00000   File 4 ...
00000   File 5 ...
00000   File 6 ...
```

15. Press **Esc** to return to the VP prompt, and then type the following command line, press **Return**, and notice the resulting display.

    2>LIST NAME, EXTN,MAIL,JOB_CODE#1,RATE#1

```
2>LIST NAME, EXTN,MAIL,JOB_CODE#1,RATE#1
00001  Sergio, Vincent        3596 2084 232  2150.00
00002  Bishop, Sam            2234 430  320  4300.00
00003  Collins, Arthur        4554 323  214  2350.00
00004  Harris, Robert         3353 2230 114  2425.00
00005  Alexander, T.G.        1104 2084 898  1900.00
00006  McAllister, Mick       8957 5267 721  2200.00
00007  Johns, Bill T.         2332 4544 123  3110.00
00008  Sergio, Alice          1234 5432 155  3250.00
```

16. Notice how information from both databases is displayed simultaneously.
17. Type **CLOSE ALL** and press **Return**.
18. Turn to Module 66 to continue the learning sequence.

Module 59

SEQUENTIAL AND NON-SEQUENTIAL FILES

DESCRIPTION

The APPEND and COPY modules discuss the use of SDF and SDF DELIMITED clauses to transfer data in and out of DBF files and TXT files. In addition to these functions, familiar to users of the dBASE family, VP-Info also provides a complete set of file-handling functions for direct access to sequential (TXT) and non-sequential (DBF) files.

A sequential file stores data in a linear sequence, like a ribbon or a cassette tape. Consider, for example, the PICNIC.TXT file and the PICNIC.DBF file, both containing the thirteen records entered in Module 64. Stored as text, the first record of PICNIC.TXT stops as soon as the last meaningful character is recorded, the last letter in the field MEASURE. Then the record is terminated and the next byte of space is used to write the first character of the next record. In PICNIC.DBF, however, each record takes up 48 bytes. Once you deduct the 521 bytes used in the file to keep *data file header* information, like the names and sizes of fields, you can depend on every 48th character being the first character of a record's NAME field. The result? In this case, PICNIC.DBF is 580 bytes larger than PICNIC.TXT. Subtracting the file header, we are still left with an average of 4.7 more bytes per record in the DBF file than in the TXT file; for every ten records in the DBF file, you can have eleven records in the TXT file.

You may be wondering why bother with DBF files, then. As you are about to see, sequential files are efficient places to store data, but very inefficient places to retrieve it from. A sequential file is like a novel with no chapter breaks, page numbers, or even space between the words! To find your place, you have to guess and sample. A DBF file, to pursue the analogy, has page numbers, chapter breaks, a table of contents, and indexes. Another name for a non-sequential file is *random-access*, so called because you can select any part of the file and go directly to it.

VP-Info provides a dozen functions you can use to manipulate files directly. Some are character oriented, and therefore more useful for non-sequential files; others are line oriented, reading the carriage returns used as record terminator in TXT files, and thus more useful with sequential files.

FILE FUNCTIONS These twelve functions are not commands, but many of them are variations of command words, like GET, WRITE, READ. All of them, because they work directly on files, must be used with great care, or they can go so far as to lock up the computer or even scramble the contents of a disk.

The form for most of these functions is:

```
FUNCTION(expression,n)
```

where n is an optional code number assigned to a file. You may have up to four files open at once, assigned numbers 1 through 4. Any time you fail to include a file code, the program assumes you mean file number 1. Most of the functions take variables as their expressions. All the functions are capable of working with both file types, but some of them work better with one type than with the other.

Because these are functions rather than commands, you must avoid using them in command syntax. For example, if you type

```
1>WRITE(NewRec,1)
```

the program takes WRITE to be a call for the editor, and you suddenly find yourself set up to edit a file with the bizarre name "(NEWREC.PRG." This accident is merely a nuisance, but a similar error with READ( ) or GET( ) could lock up the computer.

To avoid this problem, always use one of two approaches to these functions:

1. Use a dummy variable: Ok = READ(Curr,1). Then you can type ? OK and confirm, with a response of logical True, that the function worked.
2. Use a print (?) command: ? READ(Curr,1). This is faster than the first method, but the first leaves you with a variable to manipulate.

NOTE

The following examples use a hypothetical file, PICNIC.TXT. You may create this file to try the examples, if you kept PICNIC.DBF, by following these steps:

```
1>USE PICNIC
1>COPY TO PICNIC.TXT SDF
1>WRITE PICNIC.TXT
```

Edit the final blanks in each record, so that the triangular Return marker is touching the last character in each record. (Do not remove the triangles, however, because they are used as record terminators.) Save this modified file and the result is a truly sequential file that conforms to the examples below.

If you do attempt the examples, be sure to back up your work disk first, because direct access to files has great potential for locking computers and scrambling disks — both minor annoyances if you take proper precautions.

FUNCTIONS FOR USE WITH EITHER FILE TYPE A file can be opened to read from it or write to it. You can always read from a file, but some of the write functions do not work once you have performed a read function. Here are the three basic functions and some notes on how each works:

1. ROPEN(*variable representing DOS filename,n*) Open file to read, position pointer at beginning of file. You can use DOS filenames, set off with quotation marks, in an Open

function, but if you do, you have no record of the open file's name. If you first set DATAFILE1 = "PICNIC.TXT" then you can always type ? DATAFILE1 to refresh your memory about file assignments. A file opened with ROPEN( ) can be read a number of ways, but only one write function, PUT( ), works with it.

2. WOPEN(*variable representing DOS filename*,n) Open file to write, position pointer at end of file. This is not the EOF you can use with DBF files, and once you have done any search or read function, you must WOPEN( ) the file again in order to write to it with any function except PUT( ). The other write functions all append things to the end of the file. All search and read functions work on a WOPENed file.

3. CLOSE(n) Closes the file assigned that code number, or closes file number 1 if no number is specified. Always close all files when you are through with them. A QUIT command closes them, but in the meantime a neglected open file, like an open bottle, is an accident waiting to happen.

FUNCTIONS FOR SEQUENTIAL FILES Four functions manipulate the file based on line markers, and therefore they work most effectively with sequential files. The sequential file functions are:

4. READ(*variable*,n) Reads the current line into the variable specified, and advances the pointer to the beginning of the next line. In PICNIC.TXT, this function would read the first record into the variable.

5. WRITE(*variable*,n) Appends the contents of the variable to the end of the file. Only works if no search or read operations have been performed on a WOPENed file. If PICNIC.TXT were WOPENed, you could assign a string representing a new record to this variable, then WRITE( ) the variable to append a new record to the file.

6. SSEEK(*line number*,n) Since a record is a line, the number is a synonym for the record number. Hence in PICNIC.TXT, line 8 is the record,

   "Cantwell, Julie   3 Beans   1 Pot."

   SSEEK( ) moves the pointer to the specified line. The line number can be a number, a variable, or even a mathematical expression.

7. OUT(*variable*,n) The OUT( ) function can be used to write one and only one character at the end of a file. If the variable contains more than one character, only the first character is written. This character replaces the standard EOF marker (^ Z, or ASCII 26), and a file closed with some other EOF marker should never be recalled into VP-Info except under very controlled circumstances using the character reading functions described below. The OUT( ) function is used primarily to format files for software that uses special EOF markers. Since VP-Info provides character reader functions as well (primarily for use with non-sequential files), you could also use the OUT( ) function to create your own proprietary EOF marker. The only danger is that a text file lacking the ASCII 26 EOF marker can lock up the computer if accessed by the normal TEXT, WRITE, and APPEND routes.

   Here is an example of a complete set of functions in use from the VP prompt, with explanatory remarks:

```
1>DATAFILE1="PICNIC.TXT"          ; Assign variable name to DOS file.
1>? ROPEN(DATAFILE1,1)            ; Open PICNIC.TXT to read.
T                                 ; True means the task was done.
1>? SSEEK(8,1)                    ; Go to line (record) 8.
T                                 ; Done.
1>? READ(Current,1)               ; Read line 8.
T
1>? Current                       ; Print its contents, now the variable Current.
Cantwell, Julie       3 Beans          1 Pot
1>? READ(NextR,1)                 ; Read next line.
Hicks, Ginger        3Hot Dogs        3Packs
```

FUNCTIONS PRIMARILY FOR USE WITH NON-SEQUENTIAL FILES Five functions are available for use with non-sequential (DBF) files. Since they all depend on searching, reading, and writing a file one character at a time, they are most easily used in the structured environment of a non-sequential file. However, as the Typical Operation demonstrates, they can be combined with the line/record functions to provide some powerful tools for manipulating sequential files. Here is a list of the last five functions:

8. LOC(*n*) A numerical rather than a logical function, LOC( ) returns the current pointer position as a number. If you ROPEN a file, the initial value of LOC( ) is 0.00. If you WOPEN the file, LOC( ) is the position of the end-of-file marker.

9. SEEK(*number,n*) Like the SSEEK( ) function, SEEK( ) moves the pointer, but the pointer is moved to the character position corresponding to the number. Since the positions begin with 0, to position the pointer on the 44th character, you should specify SEEK(43,1). If you know that the non-sequential file contains records of 48 bytes, that the first one begins at byte 522, and that the first field is twenty bytes long, then you can apply a formula to access the second field of any record in the database (in this case, PICNIC.DBF):

```
POS=(521+((RecNo-1)*48)+20)
SEEK(Pos,1)
```

10. IN(*variable,n*) The counterpart of OUT( ), IN( ) reads the character at the counter position LOC( ), then moves the counter one character left.

11. GET(*variable,width,n*) The GET( ) function reads a string of the specified width into the variable, beginning at the current character position, and moves the counter to the next character after the string. For example, after using SSEEK(10,1) to move to the beginning of the tenth line (synonymous with the tenth record), the value of LOC( ) is 390.00. Type ? GET(name,20,1) to store the name field to the variable, then the value of LOC( ) is 420.00. Type ? Name, and the name in record 10, "Tolliver, Greg," appears.

12. PUT(*variable,n*) Of all the writing functions, only PUT( ) can work on an ROPENed file or a WOPENed file after it has been subjected to a search or a read. Unlike WRITE( ) and OUT( ), PUT( ) overwrites the file at the current position rather than appending its variable at the end of the file. So, for example, if you wanted to change the name in the first record of PICNIC.TXT from "Johns" to "Jones," this series of commands would do it:

```
1>ok=seek(0,1)
1>ok=put(>>Jones<<,1)
```

```
1>ok=seek(0,1)
1>ok=read(curr,1)
1>? curr
Jones, Bill            3Chips            5Bags
```

APPLICATIONS

Direct access to files is a powerful tool, and it must be used with the caution and respect we accord other powerful tools, like chain saws. With these functions, you can find out which of the three possible data file types you are working with, by reading information stored in the otherwise inaccessible first byte of the data file header. You can access the rest of the header's data and even (cautiously) change the data. You can repair damaged files and translate files into or out of otherwise inaccessible data formats. You can use the empty portions of the data header to hide passwords, copyrights, and other protective devices.

TYPICAL OPERATION

In this illustration data file header information is retrieved from a DBF file in immediate mode, and then file functions are used to create a TXT file field reader. Begin at the VP prompt.

1. To print the type code for PICNIC.DBF on the screen, type the following series of commands. (Do not type the explanatory remarks.)

```
1>DATAFILE1="PICNIC.DBF"          ; Assign the DOS filename to a memvar.
1>OK=ROPEN(DATAFILE1,1)           ; Open PICNIC.DBF for reading.
1>OK=IN(TypeCode,1)               ; Assign the first byte to TypeCode.
1>? RANK(TypeCode)                ; Change the ASCII code to its number value.
      2.00                        ; PICNIC.DBF is a Type 2 file.
1>CLOSE(1)                        ; Always close opened files.
```

2. Type **WRITE READER** and press **Return** to use the editor.
3. Type the following command file. (Do not type the explanatory remarks or the indentations.)

```
                                         Remarks
* READER.PRG — Displays requested field data.
CLS
RecNo=0                                  ; Variables used in structures must be initialized.
Ttl=0
Go=' '
DATAFILE1="PICNIC.TXT"                   ; Assign DOS filename to a memvar.
OK=Ropen(DATAFILE1)                      ; Open Picnic.TXT to read.
DO WHILE READ(OK,1)                      ; This structure reads to the last record, to count
    READ(OK)                             ; the records. After the last record, READ( ) = F.
    Ttl=Ttl+1                            ; Tally the passes to count the records.
ENDDO                                    ; Finished; Ttl = number of records; go on.
DO WHILE T                               ; Main program structure.
    CLS                                  ; Begin each loop with a clear screen.
    @ 2, 9 SAY "Which Record?              [  0] to Quit."
    @ 2,24 GET RecNo PICT >999<          ; Insert the GET in the gap in Row 2.
    READ                                 ; Read Get Table
    IF RecNo=0                           ; User wants to exit.
        BREAK                            ; Exit past ENDDO to closing procedure.
```

```
ENDIF RecNo                           ; Add ID remarks to IF structures.
IF RecNo>Ttl                          ; Record number too high.
    @  2, 9 SAY "  No such record is in the file. "
    ACCEPT TO Go                      ; Wait for user to read message.
    LOOP                              ; Restart DO WHILE structure.
ENDIF
RecStr="RECORD "+PIC(RecNo,>999<)  ; A string for all record messages.
•     Use MENU( ) to create 2-column lightbar, select from 3 choices.
TEXT Reader                           ; Use READER.TXT for menu. See Below.
CURSOR 4, 9                           ; Place the cursor at Row 4, Column 9.
Mselect=MENU(3,2)
DO CASE                               ; Start CASE structure.
CASE Mselect=1                        ; Selected NAME.
    OK=GET(Mname,20,1)                ; Read 20 characters from file 1 to Mname.
    @ 15,10 SAY RecStr+" is for "+TRIM(Mname)+"." ; Create message.
    ACCEPT TO Go                      ; Notice that TRIM( ) discards trailing blanks.
    LOOP                              ; After a key is pressed, restart DO WHILE.
CASE Mselect=2                        ; Selected GUESTS.
    Pos=LOC()+20                      ; SSEEK( ) made LOC( ) the beginning of this record,
    OK=SEEK(Pos,1)                    ; so LOC( ) + 20 skips NAME.
    OK=GET(Mguests,2,1)               ; Read the 2 characters of GUEST to MGuests.
    @ 15,10 SAY RecStr+" includes "+Mguests+" guests."
    ACCEPT TO Go                      ; Wait for key press, then
    LOOP                              ; Restart DO WHILE structure.
CASE Mselect=3                        ; Selected BRINGING.
    Pos=LOC()+22                      ; SSEEK( ) made LOC( ) the beginning of the record,
    OK=SEEK(Pos,1)                    ; so LOC( ) + 22 skips the first two fields.
    OK=GET(MBring,12,1)               ; Get BRING and advance LOC( ).
    OK=GET(MAmount,3,1)               ; Get AMOUNT and advance LOC( ).
    TopStr=RECSTR+" is bringing "+MAmount ; Create substring for message.
•    Because of the variable length of the record in a TXT file, we cannot just retrieve the
•    final field, or we also retrieve carriage returns and even the end-of-file marker.
•    This routine uses the Return symbol to terminate the retrieval process.
    MMeasure=''                          ; Initialize memvars for the structure.
    Mchar=' '
    DO WHILE .NOT. Mchar=CHR(13)         ; Keep going until Return symbol is read.
        OK=IN(Mchar,1)                   ; Retrieve character at LOC( ), advance.
        IF .NOT. Mchar=CHR(13)           ; If it isn't a Return symbol, then add
            MMeasure=MMeasure+Mchar      ; it to the string.
        ENDIF                            ; Don't save Return.
    ENDDO                                ; We read the Return.
•   The next line assembles a message from the memvars and fields.
    @ 15,10 SAY TopStr+" "+MMeasure+" of "+TRIM(MBring)+"." ; Make message.
    ACCEPT TO Go                      ; Wait for user to press a key.
    LOOP                              ; Restart main DO WHILE structure.
OTHERWISE                             ; If 0 or any wrong input pressed at Menu,
    BREAK                             ; then exit from main structure.
    ENDDO
    OK=CLOSE(1)                       ; Close PICNIC.TXT.
    RETURN                            ; Return to VP prompt.
```

4. Press **Alt-F** to reformat the file, then proofread, checking for uniform indentation of structures.
5. Press **End** to write the command file to disk.

6. Before running the program, you must create the READER.TXT and PICNIC.TXT files. Type **WRITE READER.TXT** and press **Return.**
7. Type your text so that your screen looks exactly like this one (begin each line at column 11).

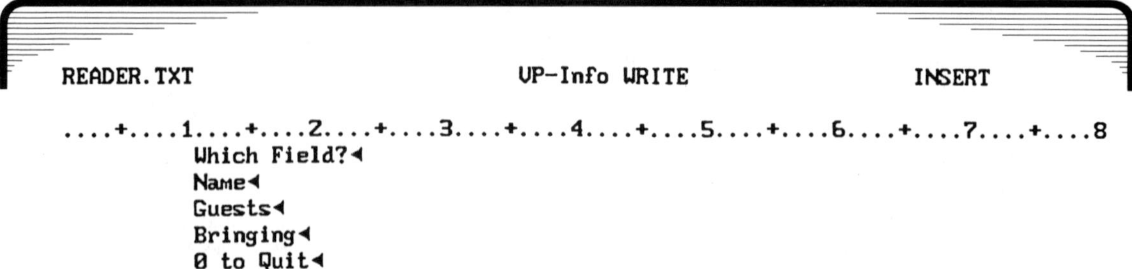

8. Press **End** to save the file.
9. To create PICNIC.TXT, type **USE PICNIC** and press **Return**, then type **COPY TO PICNIC.TXT SDF** and press **Return.**
10. The new file will need some editing. Type **WRITE PICNIC.TXT** and press **Return.**
11. Delete blanks at the ends of lines, so that your file looks like this (the triangular Return markers up against the last character in each line):

```
PICNIC.TXT                          UP-Info WRITE                        INSERT

....+....1....+....2....+....3....+....4....+....5....+....6....+....7....+....8
Johns, Bill         3Chips         5Bags◄
Collins, Ric        4Dip           3Cartons◄
Miller, Gary        3Hot Dogs      6Packs◄
Dickens, Charles    2Mustard       1Jar◄
Crandal, Phil       4Buns          5Packs◄
Johnson, J.D.       4Chips         3Bags◄
Struthers, Susan    4Pickles       1Jar◄
Cantwell, Julie     3Beans         1Pot◄
Hicks, Ginger       3Hot Dogs      3Packs◄
Tolliver, Greg      4Buns          6Packs◄
Stevens, Jan        3Chips         5Bags◄
Farris, Jody        3Relish        1Jar◄
Jasper, Dave        2Dip           2Cartons◄
```

12. Press **End** and **Return** to save the file.
13. Run the command file by typing **DO READER** and pressing **Return**. When the first prompt appears, type a record number (other than 0). When the menu appears, press **Return** to select "Name." The program responds by writing the appropriate message and positioning the cursor below it, waiting for you to press any key.
14. Press **Return** again. When the menu reappears, either move the lightbar with the cursor controls or type **1**, **2**, **3**, or **0**.
15. When you finish experimenting with this file, you may wish to delete it to save disk space; if so, type **DELE FILE READER.PRG** and press **Return**.
16. Turn to Module 58 to continue the learning sequence.

Module 60

SET FUNCTIONS

DESCRIPTION

VP-Info has a large repertoire of SET functions used to control the VP-Info operating environment. For example, SET PRINT ON directs displayed information to your printer. SET PRINT OFF turns simultaneous printing back off. These and many other SET functions are summarized in this module.

The SET commands are written in one of two forms:

```
SET switch ON
SET default TO
```

When you start VP-Info, a number of pre-established SET values exist. These existing values are called *defaults*. You can change default values of both types of SET defaults by entering the appropriate SET function in a command file or from the prompt.

For example, if you want to change the default drive to B, you can type SET DEFAULT TO B. If you want to turn on the explanations of editing keys, you can type SET MENU ON.

By typing STAT, you can call a screen listing the current status of 27 SET *switch* ON/OFF commands. The following information is displayed below the familiar files list:

```
Echo      N  Step      N  Talk      Y  Print     N  Console   Y
Alternate N  Debug     N  Zero      Y  Colon     N  Bell      N
Escape    Y  Exact     N  Intensity Y  Terminal  N  Trim      Y
Confirm   N  Ansi      N  Raw       N  Delete    N  Prompt    N
Lines     Y  Menu      N  Function  Y  Mono      Y            N
Add       Y  Eject     Y
```

Each of the SET functions is described in the following list. The boldfaced parameter is the default value.

SET ADD ON/**OFF** — Used with the POST command (Module 46). If there is no record in the master file for the indexed key in the transaction file, then VP-Info APPENDs a blank record to the master file, transfers all non-numeric data to it, and then posts the specified numeric data to it.

SET ALTERNATE TO *filename* — Directs displayed information to a file. The filename has the extension TXT unless another is specified.

SET ALTERNATE ON/**OFF** — Turns output to alternate file ON or OFF. You cannot close a file by typing SET ALTERNATE TO without a filename.

SET BELL **ON**/OFF — Speaker "beeps" during data entry when cursor reaches the end of a field or if the data being typed is illegal (the letter "A" typed into a numeric field, for example).

SET COLON ON/**OFF** — When ON, it places a colon on either side of an editing field set for input.

SET COLOR ON/OFF, SET COLOR TO *number* — The SET COLOR command is used to set colors on a color monitor. If you have a monochrome monitor, the SET COLOR command is used to set text attributes, like bold, flashing, or underlined text. The SET COLOR command is controlled by the type of monitor controller you have, monochrome or color.

The general form of the SET COLOR command is:

```
SET COLOR TO attribute
```

where *attribute* is a value between 1 (blue on black) and 255 (blinking bright white on white). If you have a color monitor, add together the values from this chart to create the screen appearance you want:

Foreground (Characters)	Background (Screen)	Flash	Intensity
0 Black	0 Black	0 No	0 Low
1 Blue	16 Blue	128 Yes	8 High
2 Green	32 Green		
3 Cyan	48 Cyan		
4 Red	64 Red		
5 Magenta	80 Magenta		
6 Brown	96 Brown		
7 White	112 White		

Keep in mind that many combinations are unreadable. Particularly, combining the same foreground and background color effectively makes invisible text.

Monochrome systems use 7 for normal text, 1 for underline, 112 for reverse video. To make text brighter, add 8 to the selected attribute; to make text flash, add 128. Attribute values are additive, so 7 + 112 + 128, an attribute value of 247, would create a reversed flashing grey text.

A SET COLOR command only affects those parts of the screen used after the setting. If you were to type SET COLOR TO 4 from the VP prompt, the next prompt would be red, but the rest of the text on the screen would stay gray. If you then typed ERASE, the prompt and the letter "E" would be red, but the rest of the word would still be gray. After the ERASE was executed (by pressing Return), all screen writing would then be red until a new SET COLOR command.

SET CONFIRM ON/**OFF** — When ON, a Return is required to complete data entry within a field, even if the field is full.

SET CONSOLE **ON**/OFF — When OFF, screen output is not visible. Use this feature sparingly, because once the screen is off, you literally cannot see what is going on.

SET DATE TO *format* — Sets the default format for reading date strings. Any string called by the DATE( ) function is read according to the currently set format. In other words, if "040612" is the string in the variable Birthday, how it is read is determined by the current setting. If you have SET DATE TO 'mmddyy' and specify ? DATE(2,Birthday), the response is "04/06/12." However, if you SET DATE TO 'yyddmm' then the same value, "040612," is read as "12/06/04."

Do not use SET DATE to change the display of the :DATE variable. To change the display of the system variable to conform to the current SET DATE setting, type OK = DATE(7) and press Return. For more information, see Module 19, DATE( ) and TIME( ).

SET DEBUG ON/**OFF** — When ON, expressions in DEBUG commands (Module 20) are printed and programs are recompiled even if a CPL file already exists.

SET DEFAULT TO *drive* — Resets location of all DBF and NDX files. Should not be combined with FILES . . . ENDFILES (Module 31).

SET DELETED ON/**OFF** — Commands like LIST and COPY ignore records marked for deletion when ON. The GO command never ignores deleted records.

SET DO **ON**/OFF — When ON, all DO subroutines contained in a PRG file are compiled with the PRG file. When OFF, subroutines are compiled as used. Used primarily to facilitate debugging files (see Module 20).

SET ECHO ON/**OFF** — Echoes command lines to the screen during command file compilation when ON. Used as a debugging tool.

SET EJECT **ON**/OFF — ON causes EJECT to send the printer a form feed command; OFF causes EJECT to send enough line feed commands (based on the value in SET LENGTH TO) to advance to the next page.

SET END **ON**/OFF — When ON, function keys are terminated with a Ctrl-W (End). When OFF, function keys are terminated with a carriage return/line feed combination.

SET ERROR **ON**/OFF — When ON, the defined ON ERROR structure (Module 44) is active. When OFF, the active ON ERROR structure is temporarily suppressed.

SET ESCAPE **ON**/OFF — Pressing Esc halts program operation, unless you use the SET ESCAPE OFF command. SET ESCAPE is normally ON. When OFF, pressing Esc does not interrupt program operation. Like SET CONSOLE OFF, SET ESCAPE OFF should be used cautiously.

SET EXACT ON/**OFF** — When OFF, you can use the first few characters of an index key in a FIND command. When ON, the search expression must be an EXACT match, including even trailing blanks.

SET EXECUTE ON/**OFF** — When OFF, the commands in an ON FIELDS structure (Module 34) are not re-executed upon exit from the structure.

SET FIELDS TO **0**/*value between 128 and 512* — The SET FIELDS command reconfigures the data field table. If the setting is 0, then 32 fields are allocated for each data file opened. If the setting is a number between 128 and 512, then that number of fields is made available to the open data files, as needed. Use the SET FIELDS command with data file Types 1 and 3. Do not use SET FIELDS in programs. It may be used at the prompt or in CNF files only.

For example, an ADDRESS database might need only 10 fields while a concurrently opened INVNTORY file needs 40 fields. INVNTORY could not be a Type 2 file, since the field limit is 32. A SET FIELDS TO 128 would allocate room for the 10 ADDRESS fields and the 40 needed by INVNTORY, leaving more than enough room for the 40 fields that would be needed temporarily for re-indexing and transferring data.

SET FILTER TO *expression* — Restricts the record range of a data file to those records that fit the conditions of the filter. Typing SET FILTER TO with no conditions cancels a filter. Do not mix a SET FILTER command with a SCOPE (Module 55).

SET FORMAT TO **SCREEN**/PRINT — Determines whether "AT" @ commands are sent to the screen or the printer. With SET FORMAT TO PRINTER, conversation commands do not format in their familiar pattern on the screen; a Return does not return the cursor to column 2, next to the prompt.

SET FUNCTION **ON**/OFF — When ON, pressing a function key produces the value assigned to the system variable for that key. When OFF, the key sends its Key value to the system variable :KEY. Reading the variable allows the function keys to be used as selection keys for a menu.

SET INDEX TO *filename,filename . . .* — Opens the named index file(s), with the first file active.

SET INTENSITY **ON**/OFF — Turns reverse video on and off for editing fields.

SET KEEP ON/**OFF** — If OFF, any TEXT command (Module 65) must read the specified file or volume each time it is called. With KEEP ON, the text is held in a buffer for use again.

SET LENGTH TO *length* — Sets the page length in lines, with a default of 66. The value is based on a unit of six lines per inch.

SET LIBRARY TO *filename* — Selects or creates a LIB file and sets the value of :AVAIL to the next available volume number. Never swap disks while a LIB file is open; always close LIB files when done with them by typing SET LIBRARY TO.

SET LINE **ON**/OFF — When ON, line numbers are stored while files are compiled, allowing VP-Info to report the line number of any errors. Helpful for debugging.

SET LINK TO *filenumber*, SET LINK OFF — Links to open data files by record number. No index is needed. Numerous links can be in effect, but only one from a given file. If work area 1 was linked to work area 5 and work area 2 was linked to work area 4, and then a second link command was issued linking work area 1 to work area 2, the link from 1 to 5 would be broken, but the link between 2 and 4 would remain. To break a link, type SET LINK OFF.

SET LOCK ON/**OFF** — If OFF, the current record is not locked in a network. With SET LOCK ON, the record is locked. Networking is discussed in Appendix E.

SET MARGIN TO *n* — Sets the left margin a specified number (*n*) of spaces from the left edge of the printed page.

SET MEMORY TO *n* — Sets the number of kilobytes (10K is 10,240 bytes) of high memory that VP-Info may use for operations. The number available is listed on the STATUS screen in the message "Space in high memory. #####" (total available memory in bytes). To use the RUN command (Module 53), you must include a SET MEMORY restriction in your VPI.CNF file. Usually SET MEMORY TO 64 leaves VP-Info adequate working space in a 300K + RAM system.

SET MENU **ON**/OFF — Turns full-screen command menus on and off. When ON, help information about action keys is displayed when commands like EDIT and MODIFY are used.

SET MONO **ON**/OFF — If you have both monochrome and color monitors attached to your system, this command switches your configuration to suit the one in use.

SET NETWORK TO **0**/1 — Set at 0, VP-Info ignores networking commands (covered in Appendix E). If you SET NETWORK TO 1, networking commands are active.

SET PRINT ON/**OFF** — Directs floating point text to your printer when ON. This includes text displayed with the print statement (?) and the LIST and TEXT commands.

SET PROMPT ON/**OFF** — When ON, the VP prompt is replaced with the dBASE-style dot prompt.

SET RAW ON/**OFF** — When OFF, the single space normally used to separate fields in DISPLAY and print commands is suppressed.

SET RELATION ON *key expression* TO *file number* — Establishes a relationship between two databases that contain a common key expression. The database in the active work area (see Module 58) is linked to a second database in a selected work area. The second database is indexed on a key including the key expression, which is a field present in both databases. The record pointer is coordinated between the two databases by moving to the record containing the key expression or a specified numeric value.

```
Example:                                 Remarks
 1>USE INVNTORY                          ; INVNTORY includes field PN.
 1>USE#2 INVPRICE INDEX PR               ; PR is an index on field PN.
 1>SET RELATION ON PN TO 2
 1>DISPLAY  DES, PN, PRICE#2             ; DES in 1, PRICE in 2, PN in both.
 Battery    ER-1500    .47
```

SET SAVE **ON**/OFF — When OFF, editing changes are not saved to disk. Only changes made with the REPLACE command are saved.

SET SCREEN **ON**/OFF — If ON, the SCREEN command works as described in Module 56. If OFF, the cursor position and color attribute are not saved. In versions prior to 1.4, these parameters were not saved by SCREEN. Use SET SCREEN OFF if you need backward compatibility with early versions of VP-Info.

SET SNOW ON/**OFF** — IBM graphics adapters generate "sparks" of color while writing the screen at full speed. If you wish to have fastest operation, leave SNOW ON, but if you find the effect distracting, you can disable it, at some cost in screen refresh speed, by typing SET SNOW OFF.

SET STEP ON/**OFF** — When ON, halts command file operation after each command line. Lets you run a program one step at a time while debugging it. If you have not SET LINE OFF, then line numbers are displayed in the upper left corner of the screen.

SET TALK **ON**/OFF — Turns VP-Info's user conversation on and off. Having the conversation on during command file operation displays extraneous text. Talk is always ON while in conversational mode.

SET TEXT ON/**OFF** — When ON, SAY variables are saved in Get Tables and updated if changed by Get entries.

SET TRIM ON/**OFF** — When ON, trailing blanks are trimmed from TEXT & macros.

SET UPPER ON/**OFF** — When ON, all character entries are displayed and stored in uppercase.

SET WIDTH TO *page width* — Sets the line width for display of TEXT.

SET ZERO **ON**/OFF — When OFF, a zero value is displayed as a blank.

As you can see, there are many helpful SET functions for controlling the way information is displayed, printed, and interpreted by VP-Info. There are several SET functions that you will rarely use, but there are others that you will use in often, like SET PRINT ON.

APPLICATIONS

SET functions are used in both the interactive mode and within command files. Some of the most frequently used SET functions are used to send displayed information to your printer (SET PRINT ON), to turn off half-intensity (or reverse video) display (SET INTENSITY OFF), and to turn off the VP-Info message conversation.

TYPICAL OPERATION

In this illustration the SET ALTERNATE TO function is used with the PICNIC database, created in Module 64, to save displayed information to a text file. Then you view the text file using the VP-Info editor. Begin at the VP prompt.

1. When ALTERNATE is on, the cursor does not move in response to the Return key, even though commands are being executed. Type the following four commands. Watch the behavior of the cursor as you conclude each by pressing **Return**.

```
SET ALTERNATE TO B:TEST
SET ALTERNATE ON
USE PICNIC
LIST
```

2. Notice that the Return key does not return the cursor to column 2 of the next line. This is because output is being directed to a file buffer to be saved as TEST.TXT.

```
1>SET ALTERNATE TO TEST
1>SET ALTERNATE ONUSE PICNICLIST
00001  Johns, Bill          3 Chips       5 Bags
00002  Collins, Ric         4 Dip         3 Cartons
00003  Miller, Gary         3 Hot Dogs    6 Packs
00004  Dickens, Charles     2 Mustard     1 Jar
00005  Crandal, Phil        4 Buns        5 Packs
00006  Johnson, J.D.        4 Chips       3 Bags
00007  Struthers, Susan     4 Pickles     2 Jar
00008  Cantwell, Julie      3 Beans       2 Pot
00009  Hicks, Ginger        3 Hot Dogs    3 Packs
00010  Tolliver, Greg       4 Buns        6 Packs
00011  Stevens, Jan         3 Chips       5 Bags
00012  Farris, Jody         3 Relish      2 Jar
00013  Jasper, Dave         2 Dip         2 Cartons
```

3. Type **SET ALTERNATE OFF** and press **Return** to close the **TEST.TXT** file. Notice the drive activity.
4. Type **WRITE TEST.TXT** and press **Return**. Notice that only the LIST command sent output to the file. The ALTERNATE is effectively a PRINT file, so it receives any output that would normally go to the printer after a SET PRINT ON command.
5. Press **End** to re-save the file (this ensures that any odd characters in the file, such as can occur at the end of a file, are disposed of). You're now back at the VP prompt.
6. If you want to conserve disk space, delete the TEST.TXT file by typing **DELE FILE TEST.TXT** and pressing **Return**.
7. Turn to Module 44 to continue the learning sequence.

Module 61
SORT

DESCRIPTION

The SORT command gives you the ability to copy the records and structure of a database to another database file arranged in either alphabetical, numerical, or alphanumeric order. The SORT is done on one or more named fields within the active database, in ascending (A to Z or 0 to 9) order.

The following examples show forms of the SORT command accompanied by explanations of each. The specified database must be in use to be sorted.

1. SORT ON *field name* TO *filename* Copies database structure and contents, sorted on the named field in alphanumeric order, to the named file.

```
1>SORT ON CITY TO NEWADR
```

2. SORT ON *field1* + *field2*, . . . TO *filename* Copies the database to the specified filename organized on the specified string variables or fieldnames, in the order they are specified. The total number of characters in the key fields cannot exceed 60. This is called a *multiple-variable sort*. When entries in *field1* are identical, *field2* determines the order, etc.

```
1>SORT ON ADR+NAME+JOINED TO NEWFILE
```

The SORT command resembles the COPY command (Module 15) except that you can organize your records in alphanumeric order while copying, and you must copy the entire database when using SORT. Unlike COPY, SORT cannot use the FOR, WHILE, SDF, or SDF DELIMITED clauses. It also resembles the INDEX command (Module 38) except that a new data file is created with SORT.

APPLICATIONS

The SORT command lets you put data in order after entering it into a database in random order. Once the data is entered, you can sort it in alphanumeric order. For example, you may wish to print a list of names contained in a database and use the list as a telephone directory. You will probably want to sort them alphabetically before you print them. The SORT command is an excellent tool to use in the preparation of an address or telephone list. If you want to arrange an inventory database in part number order, you can use the SORT command for this too.

If you want to convert a database to standard data file format in sorted order, you can use a simple 2-step process. First sort the database; then use the target file and the appropriate COPY . . . SDF or COPY . . . SDF DELIMITED commands (Module 15) to convert the file to a .TXT file.

TYPICAL OPERATION

In this illustration the SORT command is used to rearrange the ABC database to a temporary database named ABCSORT. Begin at the VP prompt.

1. Type **USE ABC** and press **Return**.
2. Type **LIST** and press **Return**. Compare your screen to the following:

```
1>USE ABC
1>LIST
00001  Sergio, Vincent      3596 2084
00002  Bishop, Sam          2234 430
00003  Collins, Arthur      4554 323
00004  Harris, Robert       3353 2230
00005  Alexander, T.G.      1104 2084
00006  McAllister, Mick     8957 5267
1>
```

3. Type **SORT ON NAME TO ABCSORT** and press **Return**.
4. Type **USE ABCSORT** and press **Return**. Then type **LIST** and press **Return**. Check for the following display.

```
1>SORT ON NAME TO ABCSORT
    6 RECORDS READ
    6 COPY(S)
1>USE ABC
1>LIST
00001  Alexander, T.G.      1104 2084
00002  Harris, Robert       3353 2230
00003  Bishop, Sam          2234 430
00004  Collins, Arthur      4554 323
00005  McAllister, Mick     8957 5267
00006  Sergio, Vincent      3596 2084
1>
```

5. Type **USE** and press **Return** to close the database.
6. Type **DELE FILE ABCSORT** and press **Return** to delete the practice file.
7. Turn to Module 38 to continue the learning sequence.

Module 62

STATUS

DESCRIPTION

The STATUS command displays screens of information about the current status of your system, telling you which files are open, which file is currently selected (indicated with an asterisk next to the word "File"), which SET switches are on, and what memory variables are in use.

For example, a typical STATUS display might look like this:

```
Thursday, June 25, 1987            VP-Info STATUS

Rec #               File name       Indexed by
00003  File 1 ... MEMBERS.DBF       NAME , AGE
00001 *File 2 ... PHONE.DBF         NAME
00000  File 3 ... ABC.DBF
00000  File 4 ...
00000  File 5 ...
00000  File 6 ...
```

Add...... N	Debug.... N	End...... Y	Intensity Y	Print.... N	Step..... N
Alternate N	Delete... N	Error.... Y	Keep..... N	Prompt... N	Talk..... Y
Bell..... N	Display.. Y	Escape... Y	Line..... Y	Raw...... N	Text..... N
Colon.... N	Do....... Y	Exact.... N	Lock..... N	Save..... Y	Trim..... Y
Confirm.. N	Echo..... N	Execute.. N	Menu..... Y	Screen... Y	Upper.... N
Console.. Y	Eject.... Y	Function. Y	Mono..... Y	Snow..... N	Zero..... Y

```
Program name ......... SHOWLAST.PRG    Files used ........... 1
Data space ........... 24582           Space in high memory . 43376
Line width ........... 79              Left margin .......... 0

Press <Enter> to continue
```

When you press Return (also called "Enter"), VP-Info displays all memory variables currently in use, pausing each time the screen fills. When the final screen appears, VP-Info reports total number of variables in use and their total length in bytes.

APPLICATIONS

The STAT command provides a quick way to check the information it displays. You can display only the memory variables by typing DISP MEMO.

TYPICAL OPERATION

This operation executes the SET PROMPT ON command (which switches the standard VP prompt to the familiar "dot prompt" of dBASE), opens the database MEMBERS and creates two variables, then uses STAT to confirm these settings.

1. Type **SET PROMPT ON** and press **Return**. Notice the change in the appearance of the screen prompt.
2. Type **USE MEMBERS** and press **Return**.
3. Type **STORE # TO RecNo** and press **Return**.
4. Type **STORE '1987' TO Year** and press **Return**.
5. Type **STATUS** and press **Return**. Notice that the STATUS screen reports only one unindexed database in use, positioned at Record 1. Notice that the word "Prompt" is now followed by a "Y," indicating that it is on.

```
Thursday, June 25, 1987           VP-Info STATUS

Rec #                File name    Indexed by
00000 *File 1 ... MEMBERS.DBF
00000  File 2 ...
00000  File 3 ...
00000  File 4 ...
00000  File 5 ...
00000  File 6 ...

 Add...... N| Debug.... N| End...... Y| Intensity Y| Print.... N| Step..... N
 Alternate N| Delete... N| Error.... Y| Keep..... N| Prompt... N| Talk..... Y
 Bell..... N| Display.. Y| Escape... Y| Line..... Y| Raw...... N| Text..... N
 Colon.... N| Do....... Y| Exact.... N| Lock..... N| Save..... Y| Trim..... Y
 Confirm.. N| Echo..... N| Execute.. N| Menu..... Y| Screen... Y| Upper.... N
 Console.. Y| Eject.... Y| Function. Y| Mono..... Y| Snow..... N| Zero..... Y

Program name .........                  Files used ........... 1
Data space ........... 34480            Space in high memory . 46774
Line width .......... 79                Left margin .......... 0

Press <Enter> to continue
```

6. Press **Return** and compare your screen to the following:

```
Name            Type    Width    Contents
RECNO            N        8      1
YEAR             C        4      1987
** Total ** 2 variables, 12 bytes
```

7. Press **Return** to go back to the prompt.
8. Type **SET PROMPT OFF** and press **Return** to restore the original VP prompt.
9. Turn to Module 68 to continue the learning sequence.

Module 63

STORE, RELEASE, SAVE, RESTORE, VARIABLE

DESCRIPTION

Memory variables, often referred to as "memvars," are storage locations within your computer's main memory in which you can save character string, numeric, or logical values. You have used memory variables in some of the examples contained in previous modules, and until now, you have used them on faith. This module should take the mystery out of these powerful little "pigeon holes" by describing the STORE, RELEASE, SAVE, and RESTORE commands, where:

STORE	Creates memory variables.
RELEASE	Removes memory variables.
SAVE	Writes memory variables to disk.
RESTORE	Reads memory variables from disk back to memory.

Memory variables are created with the STORE, ACCEPT, INPUT, AVERAGE, and SUM commands. They are also created with an expression like:

```
1>X = 'Hello'
```

where the character string "Hello" is stored to the memory variable X.

Forms of the ACCEPT and INPUT commands are described in Module 4; the SUM and AVERAGE commands are described in Modules 64 and 7.

CHARACTERISTICS You can have as many as 128 active memory variables at a time. (And a matrix variable, described in Module 22, can contain many values but only counts as one variable.)

A character memory variable can contain up to 256 characters. Numeric memory variables are only accurate to 17 significant digits. Numbers are formatted on the screen by a special system variable, :PICTURE, with a default of 7 digits and 2 decimals. To display larger numbers, use the command:

```
1>:PICTURE = '999999999999999.99'
```

using as many 9's as you want number places for. Keep in mind that a :PICTURE of more than 17 places cannot report the number accurately.

Memory variable names are assigned when they are created. The name can have up to ten characters. It must begin with a letter, but may contain numbers and the underscore character. It is a good idea to make the name meaningful. If the memory variable contains the contents of a field, you might use the fieldname preceded with an M, like Mname for the contents of a database Name field.

STORE Several forms of the STORE command exist. These are shown with examples in the following list.

1. STORE *expression* TO *memory variable* Stores the expression to the memory variable, which can be up to ten characters long.

```
1>STORE 'Gov. Johnson' TO MGov
```

or

```
1>MGov = 'Gov. Johnson'              ; This command line stores a string expression to memory
                                       variable MGov.
1>STORE T TO Run                     ; Stores the logical true value to memory variable Run.
1>STORE 144 TO MGross                ; Stores numeric value 144 to memory variable MGross.
1>STORE 2*MGross TO M2Gross          ; Stores the product of two times the value of MGross to the
                                       memory variable M2Gross.
1>STORE MGov+' elected.' TO MResult ; Stores memory variable MGov and the string 'elected'
                                       to the memory variable MResult. "Gov. Johnson
                                       elected." is displayed when you type ? MResult.
```

2. STORE *field name* TO *memory variable* Stores contents of named field to the memory variable. When this form of STORE is used, a database must be in use and the record pointer positioned to the record containing the desired field value.

```
1>STORE NAME TO MName   ; Stores contents of the NAME field to the memory variable MName.
```

3. STORE *field1* + *field2* + . . . TO *memory variable* Stores contents of named fields to memory variable. Trailing blanks are also stored when the plus sign is used.

```
1>STORE NAME + ST_ADR TO Mvar
1>? Mvar
Miller, Gary            3270 Garden Brook
```

This form inserts a single space between field values:

```
1>STORE TRIM(NAME)-' '+ST_ADR TO Mvar
1>? Mvar
Miller, Gary 3270 Garden Brook
```

If you want to see a list of the memory variables in use, you can type DISPLAY MEMORY and press Return at the VP prompt. Information similar to the following is displayed.

```
1>DISPLAY MEMORY

Name         Type   Width   Contents
MGOV          C      12     Gov. Johnson
RUN           L       2     .T.
MGROSS        N       8     144
M2GROSS       N       8     288
MRESULT       C      21     Gov. Johnson elected.
** Total **   5  variables, 51 bytes
1>
```

RELEASE You can remove memory variables individually or in total with the RELEASE command. Forms of the RELEASE command are in the following list:

1. RELEASE *memory variable* Removes the specified memory variable from use.

   `1>RELEASE M2Gross`

2. RELEASE *memory variable1, memory variable2, . . .* Removes specified memory variables from use.

   `1>RELEASE MGov, MResult`

3. RELEASE ALL Releases all current memory variables from use.

   `1>RELEASE ALL`

4. RELEASE EXCEPT *memory variable1, memory variable2, . . .* Releases all memory variables except those listed.

   `1>RELEASE EXCEPT MGross`

Other commands that clear all memory variables from use are CLEAR ALL and QUIT.

RELEASE should be used only when necessary, which should be seldom since up to 128 memory variables can be active at once, including up to 20 matrix variables. Since VP-Info attains its speed by compiling files, and compilers can be easily confused by changes in the operating environment, variables should be maintained throughout a given command file. Never use a RELEASE command inside a branching structure (such as an IF. . .ENDIF or DO CASE. . .ENDCASE).

SAVE and RESTORE There are times when you would like to SAVE your memory variables to disk for later use and then RESTORE them when you need them. That is precisely what the SAVE and RESTORE commands do. SAVE writes the named memory variables to a named disk file. You do not have to type a filename extension, as VP-Info assigns MEM as an extension automatically. The RESTORE command erases current memory variables (unless you use the ADDITIVE clause), and then it restores memory variables from disk back to your computer's memory. Forms of the SAVE and RESTORE commands are contained in the following examples.

1. SAVE TO *filename* Saves all memory variables to the named file, which is automatically given a MEM extension.

   `1>SAVE TO MemFile`

2. RESTORE FROM *filename* Reads all memory variables previously saved to the named file. This command replaces all active memory variables with the restored memory variables.

   `1>RESTORE FROM MEMFILE`

3. RESTORE FROM *filename* ADDITIVE Reads all memory variables previously saved to the named file. The ADDITIVE clause adds the restored memory variables to those already in use instead of writing over them. (However, a misspelled ADDITIVE clause is simply ignored, causing loss of the current memory variables, so type the clause carefully in immediate mode.)

   `1>RESTORE FROM MEMFILE ADDITIVE`

MACROS You can store portions of command lines in memory variables called *macros* which you can then add to command lines. A macro variable is signalled with the addition of the & sign to the variable. The & sign tells VP-Info to operate on the contents of the variable rather than the variable itself. A pair of examples can clarify the distinction:

- Using the ABC database, indexed on NAME, you STORE "SERGIO" TO Mname, then you issue the command, FIND Mname. VP-Info searches unsuccessfully for the word "MNAME" in the index. You issue the command, FIND &Mname, and it looks for the contents of Mname, the string SERGIO.
- Again using ABC, you STORE "NAME, EXTN" TO Mvar, then you type LIST Mvar. The result is not a list of names and extns. You type LIST &Mvar, and VP-Info understands that you want to execute the command made up of LIST and the contents of Mvar.

Macros are demonstrated in many of the Typical Operations sections in this manual, notably in Modules 32, 46, and 67.

VARIABLE The VP-Info documentation recommends defining all memory variables at the beginning of a command file. In practice, this seems to have little effect on the operation of the files.

APPLICATIONS

The ability to STORE selected information to memory variables is important in managing the contents of database files. When writing extensive applications, you will find yourself using the STORE command to duplicate the contents of certain fields into memory variables. Once the contents are in a memory variable, you can move the record pointer around in the database and selectively replace field contents with the contents of memory variables.

Often, memory variables are used as "scratch pads," where mathematical results, like subtotals, are STORED for later use.

If you find yourself approaching the maximum memory variable limit, which is 128 memory variables or 6,000 characters, the RELEASE command is available. Used it judiciously to eliminate memory variables that are no longer needed.

The SAVE command let you save active memory variables to disk, like "putting them on the shelf" for future use. Once this is done, you can begin with a new set of memory variables. When you need the old ones back, you can SAVE the current ones to another disk file and retrieve the original set with the RESTORE command. Remember to use the ADDITIVE clause if you do not want to overwrite active memory variables.

TYPICAL OPERATION

In this illustration the STORE, RELEASE, and SAVE commands are used in a command file that interacts with the ABC database. Begin at the VP prompt.

1. Type **WRITE STORE** and press **Return**. A blank screen is displayed and you are in the VP-Info full-screen editor.

2. Type the following command file. (Do not type the explanatory remarks or indentation.)

```
                                             Remarks
* STORE.PRG—Demonstrates use of STORE, RELEASE, and SAVE.
ERASE                                    ; Clears the screen.
USE ABC                                  ; Puts ABC database in use.
TtlAge=0                                 ; Stores 0 to memory variable TtlAge.
DO WHILE .NOT. EOF                       ; Causes continuous operation until the end of the
*                                          file is reached.
   TtlAge=TtlAge+AGE                     ; Adds current record Age to total.
   SKIP                                  ; Positions record pointer to next record.
   IF EOF                                ; Checks for end of file; commands between IF and
*                                          ENDIF are skipped unless the end of file has
*                                          been reached.
      Recs=#                             ; Stores last record number to memory variable Recs.
      AvgAge=TtlAge/Recs                 ; Divides total age by the number of records;
*                                          stores results to memory variable AvgAge.
      ?                                  ; Displays blank line.
      ? 'THE AVERAGE EMPLOYEE AGE IS', STR(AvgAge,4,1)     ; For the STR function
*                                          and the LTRIM function, see Appendix D.
      ? ' FOR ',LTRIM(STR(Recs,6)),' EMPLOYEES.'
      SAVE TO AGES                       ; Saves active memory variables to AGES.MEM file.
      ?                                  ; Displays blank line.
      WAIT                               ; Pauses operation until a key is pressed.
      USE                                ; Takes database out of use.
      RELEASE ALL                        ; Releases all memory variables.
      CANCEL                             ; Returns control to the VP prompt.
   ENDIF                                 ; Passes control to the next command line.
   LOOP                                  ; Returns execution to the command line after
*                                          the DO WHILE statement.
ENDDO                                    ; Ends DO WHILE; passes control to next statement.
ERASE                                    ; Clears the screen.
CLEAR ALL                                ; Closes all files and releases all variables.
RETURN                                   ; Redisplays VP prompt.
```

3. Press **Alt-F** to format the file, then proofread it.
4. When you are ready, press **END** and then **Return** to write the command file to disk.
5. Type **DO STORE** and press **Return** to run the command file. Compare your screen to the following (the average age varies depending on the contents of your ABC file):

```
THE AVERAGE EMPLOYEE AGE IS 33.5
 FOR 7 EMPLOYEES.

WAITING
```

6. Press any key to redisplay the VP prompt.
7. Verify that no memory variables are active by typing **LIST MEMORY** and pressing **Return.** VP-Info responds with the message "0 variables, 0 bytes."
8. Read the saved memory variables from disk by typing **RESTORE FROM AGES** and pressing **Return.**
9. Verify that the memory variables have been read from disk by typing **LIST MEMORY** and pressing **Return.** Check for the following:

```
1>LIST MEMORY

Name          Type    Width    Contents
TTLAGE         N        8      235
RECS           N        8      7
AVGAGE         N        8      33.5
** Total **    3   variables, 24   bytes
1>
```

Notice that the AVGAGE variable reported in step 5 was not rounded off by the STR( ) function, but simply truncated after the first decimal place. (Rounding would have given an average age of 33.6.)

10. Delete the .MEM file from disk by typing **DELETE FILE AGES.MEM** and pressing **Return.**
11. Delete the STORE.PRG file from your disk by typing **DELETE FILE STORE.PRG** and pressing **Return.**
12. Eliminate the memory variables by typing **RELEASE ALL** and pressing **Return.**
13. Turn to Module 22 to continue the learning sequence.

Module 64

SUM

DESCRIPTION

The SUM command is used to add one or more numeric fields of an active database file. The result can either be stored to a memory variable or displayed. Forms of the SUM command and corresponding examples are shown in the following list.

1. SUM *field name* Sums the contents of the specified field and displays the result.

```
1>SUM QTY
   12 SUM(S)
    168.00
```

2. SUM *field1,field2, . . .* Sums specified fields and displays the results.

```
1>SUM QTY,COST,PRICE*1.05
  105 SUM(S)
   2309     34523.48      74560.86
```

3. SUM *field name* TO *memory variable* Sums specified field to the specified memory variable.

```
1>SUM QTY,COST TO MQTY,MCOST
    4 SUM(S)
     86.00      65.23
```

4. SUM *field name* TO *memory variable* FOR *expression* Sums specified field name to specified memory variable for those records that match the expression.

```
1>SUM QTY TO MQTY FOR COST > .99
```

5. SUM *field name* TO *memory variable* WHILE *expression* Sums field to memory variable while expression is valid. If expression becomes invalid, summing stops.

```
1>SUM QTY TO MQTY WHILE COST <= 100.00
```

APPLICATIONS

The SUM command is used to store the arithmetic total of one or more fields within a database file to a memory variable for later use, or to display an arithmetic total in response to a direct user inquiry. The SUM command is used both in command files and in the interactive mode.

TYPICAL OPERATION

In this illustration a new database is created. Then the SUM command is used to find the sums of various numeric fields. Begin at the VP prompt.

1. Type **CREATE PICNIC** and press **Return.**
2. Prepare the following database structure, then press **End** and **Return** to save it.

Name	Type	Width	Dec
NAME	C	20	0
GUESTS	N	2	0
BRING	C	12	0
AMOUNT	N	3	0
MEASURE	C	10	0
<End>			

3. Type **APPEND** and add the following records, pressing **End** at empty Record No. 14

```
Record No.    1
NAME          Johns, Bill
GUESTS          3
BRING         Chips
AMOUNT          5
MEASURE       Bags

Record No.    2
NAME          Collins, Ric
GUESTS          4
BRING         Dip
AMOUNT          3
MEASURE       Cartons

Record No.    3
NAME          Miller, Gary
GUESTS          3
BRING         Hot Dogs
AMOUNT          6
MEASURE       Packs

Record No.    4
NAME          Dickens, Charles
GUESTS          2
BRING         Mustard
AMOUNT          1
MEASURE       Jar

Record No.    5
NAME          Crandal, Phil
GUESTS          4
BRING         Buns
AMOUNT          5
MEASURE       Packs

Record No.    8
NAME          Cantwell, Julie
GUESTS          3
BRING         Beans
AMOUNT          1
MEASURE       Pot

Record No.    9
NAME          Hicks, Ginger
GUESTS          3
BRING         Hot Dogs
AMOUNT          3
MEASURE       Packs

Record No.   10
NAME          Tolliver, Greg
GUESTS          4
BRING         Buns
AMOUNT          6
MEASURE       Packs

Record No.   11
NAME          Stevens, Jan
GUESTS          3
BRING         Chips
AMOUNT          5
MEASURE       Bags

Record No.   12
NAME          Farris, Jody
GUESTS          3
BRING         Relish
AMOUNT          1
MEASURE       Jar
```

```
Record No.      6                     Record No.      13
NAME          Johnson, J.D.           NAME          Jasper, Dave
GUESTS         4                      GUESTS         2
BRING         Chips                   BRING         Dip
AMOUNT          3                     AMOUNT          2
MEASURE       Bags                    MEASURE       Cartons
```

```
Record No.      7                     Record No.      14
NAME          Struthers, Susan        NAME          <End>
GUESTS         4                      GUESTS
BRING         Pickles                 BRING
AMOUNT          1                     AMOUNT
MEASURE       Jar                     MEASURE
```

Press **End** to stop data entry.

4. List the database by typing **LIST** and pressing **Return**.

```
1>LIST
00001  Johns, Bill          3 Chips      5 Bags
00002  Collins, Ric         4 Dip        3 Cartons
00003  Miller, Gary         3 Hot Dogs   6 Packs
00004  Dickens, Charles     2 Mustard    1 Jar
00005  Crandal, Phil        4 Buns       5 Packs
00006  Johnson, J.D.        4 Chips      3 Bags
00007  Struthers, Susan     4 Pickles    1 Jar
00008  Cantwell, Julie      3 Beans      1 Pot
00009  Hicks, Ginger        3 Hot Dogs   3 Packs
00010  Tolliver, Greg       4 Buns       6 Packs
00011  Stevens, Jan         3 Chips      5 Bags
00012  Farris, Jody         3 Relish     1 Jar
00013  Jasper, Dave         2 Dip        2 Cartons
1>
```

5. Determine how many people will be at the picnic by adding the number of records to the sum of the guests as follows:

```
1>GO BOTTOM
1>STORE # TO RN
1>SUM GUESTS TO TOT_GUEST
   13 SUM(S)
     42.00
1>? RN + TOT_GUEST
     55.00
1>
```

6. Type **SUM AMOUNT FOR BRING = 'Chips'** and press **Return** to determine how many bags of chips will be brought to the picnic.

```
1>SUM AMOUNT FOR BRING = 'Chips'
   3 SUM(S)
     13.00
1>
```

7. Type **CLEAR ALL** to close all files.
8. Keep the PICNIC database. It is used in several other exercises.
9. Turn to Module 7 to continue the learning sequence.

Module 65

TEXT, TEXT . . . ENDTEXT

DESCRIPTION

The TEXT command and the TEXT . . . ENDTEXT structure are used to display or print text, depending upon the status of your printer. A text structure can also be stored in a LIBRARY (see Module 40) for retrieval with the SET LIBRARY TO command.

The TEXT command lets you display multiple lines of text. Any ASCII file, such as a PRG file or a DOS BAT file, can be displayed (but not edited). You may create files containing text and retrieve them using the TEXT command:

```
1>TEXT MENU
```

This causes display of the contents of a file named MENU.TXT. You may also store the contents of MENU.TXT as Volume 1 of a *filename*.LIB file containing numerous text messages, and retrieve it to the screen with the following command sequence:

```
1>SET LIBRARY TO filename
1>TEXT .1
```

The period is a signal that what follows is a volume number.

Both of these methods avoid inclusion of large blocks of text in your compiled PRG files. When you need such blocks, the TEXT . . . ENDTEXT structure can be used to create them. An example of using the TEXT . . . ENDTEXT structure within command files is illustrated below.

```
ERASE
TEXT
This program is used to enter customer information from invoices, change customer
information, or delete obsolete customer information. Before starting, be sure you
have all the latest customer paperwork available.
ENDTEXT
WAIT
ERASE
TEXT
                                 ===============================
                                    Customer Information System
                                 -------------------------------

                                 1  ENTER NEW CUSTOMER INFORMATION

                                 2  CHANGE CUSTOMER INFORMATION

                                 3  DELETE CUSTOMER FROM FILE

                                 4  QUIT THIS PROGRAM

                                 === Select One and Press Return ===
```

```
ENDTEXT
ACCEPT TO Choice
        :
(more command lines)
        :
RETURN
```

You can use the full-screen editor to create your text files. The advantage of the TEXT approach to screen-creation is that you can simply type your text precisely where you want it on the screen, using the Spacebar and Return as well as the cursor keys, and then save the screen as a text file. In addition, all three TEXT formats permit you to include variables for both input and output.

TEXT FORMATTING AND VARIABLES Format variables in a TEXT structure with the *fixed* and *floating* macro symbols. A fixed macro always displays the variable in the same position on the screen; a floating macro merges the variable with surrounding text. Use fixed macros for tables and forms, floating macros for creating message strings.

The input macro symbols operate like the GET command, allowing you to display and then edit a variable. Like GET, input macros are activated with a READ command. The % symbol used in a TEXT structure signals a fixed input macro; the @ symbol signals a floating macro.

The output macro symbols merely display information, either in fixed (with the # symbol) or floating (with the & symbol) display.

NOTE

The TEXT format symbols have different meanings in other contexts.

To format a variable inside a TEXT structure, include formatting instructions at the beginning of the structure of the following form, using a separate line for each formatted variable and preceding each variable name with a double period:

```
..Cost,"$9,999.99"
..Name,!!!!!!!!!!!!!!!!!!!!!!!!!
..Phone,[999] 999-9999
```

APPLICATIONS

The TEXT commands are convenient for displaying long passages of text, menus, and multi-line prompts on the screen. You can route the text to your printer by using SET PRINT ON prior to displaying the information to your screen. By using SET KEEP ON, you can load a text file into memory and then use it repeatedly.

The TEXT . . . ENDTEXT command pair make creating display text as easy as typing. You can display text at any coordinate on the screen by positioning the cursor to the line of your choice and using blank spaces to move from left to right. The print (?) and @ *row,col* commands are also used to display or print text. These commands are described in Modules 6 and 47.

TYPICAL OPERATION

In this illustration the TEXT and ENDTEXT commands are used in a command file to demonstrate their use, then the menu program written in Module 71 is modified to store the menu itself in a TEXT file. Begin at the VP prompt.

1. Type **WRITE ATEXT** and press **Return** to use the VP-Info editor.
2. Type the following command file, including the blank lines. (Do not type the explanatory remarks, however.)

```
                                             Remarks
* ATEXT.PRG – Demonstrates the TEXT and ENDTEXT commands.
CLS                                          ; Clears the screen.
TEXT                                         ; Signals that following lines are text.

                    SOME TEXT DISPLAY COMMANDS ARE:

                    1. DISPLAY
                    2. ? '   '
                    3. @ row,col SAY '    '
                    4. TEXT and ENDTEXT

ENDTEXT                                      ; Ends the text statement.
WAIT                                         ; Pauses operation and displays prompt.
CLS                                          ; Clears the screen.
CANCEL                                       ; Returns control to VP prompt.
```

3. Press **End** and **Return** to write the command file to disk.
4. Type **DO ATEXT** and press **Return** to run the command file. Compare your screen to the following:

```
                    SOME TEXT DISPLAY COMMANDS ARE:

                    1.  DISPLAY
                    2.  ? '   '
                    3.  @ row,col SAY '    '
                    4.  TEXT and ENDTEXT

   WAITING
```

5. When you finish experimenting with this example, type **DELE FILE ATEXT.PRG** and press **Return** to delete the file from your disk.
6. Type **WRITE MENU.TXT** and press **Return** to create the following text file in the editor. Use Alt-G to create the box around the header text:

```
MENU.TXT                        VP-Info WRITE                        INSERT
....+....1....+....2....+....3....+....4....+....5....+....6....+....7....+....8
         ADDRESS BOOK MAIN MENU

                                                      PRESS
                                                      -----
           DISPLAY AN ADDRESS AND PHONE NUMBER          1

           ADD A NEW ADDRESS AND PHONE NUMBER           2

           CHANGE AN ADDRESS OR PHONE NUMBER            3

           DELETE AN ADDRESS AND PHONE NUMBER           4

           PRINT AN ADDRESS AND PHONE NUMBER            5

           PRINT AN ADDRESS AND PHONE LIST              6

           EXIT TO VP PROMPT                            7

      ==============================================================

           Enter your selection:  %Choice
```

7. Press **End** and **Return** to save the text file, and then type **WRITE MENU.PRG** to load the command file.
8. Delete the menu display and the ACCEPT command, and replace them with a TEXT command so that the first ten lines of the file read as follows:

```
* MENU.PRG – A command file for displaying the address book menu.
ERASE
* Use a DO WHILE loop to sustain operation.
DO WHILE T
STORE ' ' TO Choice
TEXT MENU
READ
*
* Use series of CASE statements to run the selected command file,
* Exit to the VP prompt, or exit to the operating system.
```

9. Type **End** to save the revised file.
10. At the prompt, type **DO MENU** to try the new command file. Compare your initial screen to the following:

```
                    ADDRESS BOOK MAIN MENU
                                                      PRESS
                                                      -----
        DISPLAY AN ADDRESS AND PHONE NUMBER             1

        ADD A NEW ADDRESS AND PHONE NUMBER              2

        CHANGE AN ADDRESS OR PHONE NUMBER               3

        DELETE AN ADDRESS AND PHONE NUMBER              4

        PRINT AN ADDRESS AND PHONE NUMBER               5

        PRINT AN ADDRESS AND PHONE LIST                 6

        EXIT TO VP PROMPT                               7
=================================================================

        Enter your selection:  _
```

11. Type **7** to return to the VP prompt.
12. Save these MENU files for use in the following modules.
13. Turn to Module 40 to continue the learning sequence.

Module 66

TOTAL

DESCRIPTION

The TOTAL command is used to transfer the sum of matching fields to a designated database file. Matching fields are consolidated and the designated fields, which must have been previously indexed or sorted, are summed.

Imagine that you have an inventory database with multiple entries for the same part number. The part number field is a *key field* (one that was indexed or sorted). If you wish to determine the total quantity on hand for each part number, you can TOTAL ON the part number field to a database file, specifying the quantity field. This process is demonstrated in the Typical Operation section of this module, using the PICNIC database. Forms of the TOTAL command and corresponding examples are contained in the following list.

1. TOTAL ON *field name* TO *filename* Creates a summary file containing one record for each unique entry in the specified field name, which must be part of the active index key. The structure of the database in use is copied to the specified file, and the contents of the first record with a unique value in the key field are copied into a record, producing a summary file.

```
1>TOTAL ON PART_NO TO LUMBER1
```

2. TOTAL ON *field name* TO *filename* FIELDS *field1,field2* . . . While creating a summary file as described, it also totals the numeric values of the specified fields for those records having the same contents in the designated field name. Without the fields clause, no numeric fields are totaled.

```
1>TOTAL ON PART_NO TO LUMBER1 FIELDS PART_NO, QTY, COST, PRICE
```

3. TOTAL ON *field name* TO *filename* FIELDS *field1, field2*, . . . FOR *expression* This is the same as the previous command except that the FOR clause selects only those records matching the expression.

```
1>TOTAL ON PART_NO TO LUMBER1 FIELDS PART_NO, QTY, COST FOR QTY > 10
```

4. TOTAL ON *field name* TO *filename* WHILE *expression* This command form operates as long as the expression is true. If the expression becomes invalid, the totaling process terminates immediately. In the following example, if a value greater than 10 is encountered in the QTY field, the totaling process stops.

```
1>TOTAL ON PART_NO TO LUMBER1 WHILE QTY <= 10
```

APPLICATIONS

The TOTAL command not only provides arithmetic answers, but it creates a new database that eliminates records having the same value in a key field. This process is accomplished because common records are consolidated as they are copied to the target database file.

TYPICAL OPERATION

In this illustration the TOTAL command is used with the PICNIC database created in Module 64. Begin at the VP prompt.

1. Type **USE PICNIC** and press **Return.**
2. Examine the structure of the database by typing **LIST STRU** and pressing **Return**, and then type **LIST** and press **Return** to see the records. Compare your screen to the following:

```
Data file:              PICNIC.DBF
Number of records:         13
File number:               #1
Field    Name        Type   Width  Dec
  1      NAME         C       20
  2      GUESTS       N        2
  3      BRING        C       12
  4      AMOUNT       N        3
  5      MEASURE      C       10
** Record Length **           48
1>LIST
00001  Johns, Bill           3 Chips         5 Bags
00002  Collins, Ric          4 Dip           3 Cartons
00003  Miller, Gary          3 Hot Dogs      6 Packs
00004  Dickens, Charles      2 Mustard       1 Jar
00005  Crandal, Phil         4 Buns          5 Packs
00006  Johnson, J.D.         4 Chips         3 Bags
00007  Struthers, Susan      4 Pickles       1 Jar
00008  Cantwell, Julie       3 Beans         1 Pot
00009  Hicks, Ginger         3 Hot Dogs      3 Packs
00010  Tolliver, Greg        4 Buns          6 Packs
00011  Stevens, Jan          3 Chips         5 Bags
00012  Farris, Jody          3 Relish        1 Jar
00013  Jasper, Dave          2 Dip           2 Cartons
1>
```

3. Determine the quantities of each picnic supply that have been volunteered by indexing the file and then using the TOTAL command. Type the commands shown at each prompt (but not the remarks).

```
1>INDEX ON BRING TO TEMP              ; Create temporary index.
1>LIST                                ; List the new order.
00008   Cantwell, Julie        3 Beans           1 Pot
00005   Crandal, Phil          4 Buns            5 Packs
00010   Tolliver, Greg         4 Buns            6 Packs
00001   Johns, Bill            3 Chips           5 Bags
00006   Johnson, J.D.          4 Chips           3 Bags
00011   Stevens, Jan           3 Chips           5 Bags
00002   Collins, Ric           4 Dip             3 Cartons
00013   Jasper, Dave           2 Dip             2 Cartons
00003   Miller, Gary           3 Hot Dogs        6 Packs
00009   Hicks, Ginger          3 Hot Dogs        3 Packs
00004   Dickens, Charles       2 Mustard         1 Jar
00007   Struthers, Susan       4 Pickles         1 Jar
00012   Farris, Jody           3 Relish          1 Jar
1>TOTAL ON BRING TO PICNIC2 FIELD AMOUNT ; Total the amounts of each.
1>USE#2 PICNIC2                       ; Open PICNIC2
1>LIST#2 STRU                         ; Notice that the structure is the same, but
                                        database only contains 8 records.
1>LIST#2                              ; List each record entirely.
00001   Cantwell, Julie        3 Beans            1 Pot
00002   Crandal, Phil          4 Buns            11 Packs
00003   Johns, Bill            3 Chips           13 Bags
00004   Collins, Ric           4 Dip              5 Cartons
00005   Miller, Gary           3 Hot Dogs         9 Packs
00006   Dickens, Charles       2 Mustard          1 Jar
00007   Struthers, Susan       4 Pickles          1 Jar
00008   Farris, Jody           3 Relish           1 Jar
1>
```

Notice that the records include irrelevant data — the name and guests field for the first record with each unique BRING field. If this were a permanent file, we might compress it now by typing

```
COPY#2 TO SUPPLIES FIELDS Bring, Amount, Measure
```

to create a database whose records are roughly half as large as they were.

4. Type **CLEAR ALL** and press **Return** to close all files.
5. Turn to Module 67 to continue the learning sequence.

Module 67

UPDATE

DESCRIPTION

UPDATE is another command that lets you combine the contents of two databases. This command allows you to replace the contents of one or more fields in a database with the contents of one or more fields from another database. The updated database must be in the selected work area. The source database must also be in an active, but unselected work area. (For information about selecting work areas, see Module 58.)

The general form of the UPDATE command is:

```
UPDATE FROM filenumber ON key REPLACE field WITH expression
```

If you wish to replace several fields, you can use the form:

```
UPDATE FROM filenumber ON key REPLACE field1 WITH expression1,
        field2 WITH expression, field3 WITH expression ...
```

The key (or indexed) field must have the same field name in both the source and target databases, and it must be in the active index of the source file indicated in the command by its work area number. A key field is one that was used as a basis for sorting or indexing.

Finally, you may include a scope expression and a FOR expression in the command in this form:

```
UPDATE FROM filenumber ON keyREPLACE field1 WITH expression1
          scope FOR expression.
```

For example, if PICNIC were opened with an index on BRING in area 1, and a second copy of the same database were opened at TEMP in area 2, then the command

```
2>UPDATE FROM 1 ON Bring REPLACE Amount WITH Amount+1 FOR Amount<Guests
```

would only adjust the TEMP records of people who were bringing more guests than supplies.

Here is an example of how the UPDATE command is used. Assume that you have two databases that contain inventory quantities. The first database, called WHSE (for warehouse), contains parts in your warehouse. The second database, called WIP (for work-in-process), shows parts presently on the assembly line. Work on the assembly line is commonly called "work-in-process." If you wish to update the WHSE database to those parts presently counted in WIP, you can use the UPDATE command.

If the key field name in both databases is PART_NO, the WIP database has an active index WIPN including PART_NO, and the field containing the quantity is QTY in both databases, you can proceed as follows:

```
1>SELECT 1
1>USE WIP INDEX WIPN
1>SELECT 2
2>USE WHSE INDEX WHSPN
2>UPDATE FROM 1 ON PART_NO REPLACE QTY WITH QTY + QTY#1
```

This series of commands puts WIP and WHSE in work areas 1 and 2, leaving WHSE in the active work area. It activates an index for both databases, though the only one required is WIPN for the source file. The UPDATE command adds the contents of the QTY fields in both databases and replaces each WHSE quantity value with its present value plus the quantity value in the WIP database. Look at the following list.

```
    WHSE                      WIP                     WHSE (After Update)
PART_NO      QTY   +     PART_NO      QTY   =    PART_NO      QTY
-------      ---         -------      ---        -------      ---
A-1230         5         A-1230         2        A-1230         7
B-1001        12         B-1001         6        B-1001        18
D-3561         7         D-3561         3        B-3561        10
D-3562         8         D-3562         2        D-3562        10
W-1210         4         W-1210         2        W-1210         6
```

APPLICATIONS

The UPDATE command is good for establishing a common database that monitors changes in multiple databases. As in the example, counts from several warehouse databases can be consolidated into a master database file. In this way, the total inventory status can be viewed. Inventory information usually includes quantity, cost, price, and sales volume data that changes by the minute. It is often convenient to create and use a transaction database for maintaining those items that change. From the transaction database, you can UPDATE other relevant databases periodically to ensure that you have the latest information.

TYPICAL OPERATION

In this illustration the UPDATE command is used to change information in the PICNIC database file from another file named TEMP. The exercise includes the creation and indexing of this database so you can try the commands on your computer. Start at the VP prompt.

1. Type the following commands to set up the environment, pressing **Return** after each:

```
1>USE PICNIC
1>INDEX ON Bring to THINGS
1>COPY TO TEMP
1>USE#2 TEMP
1>INDEX#2 ON Name to TEMPN
1>SET RELA ON Name to 2
```

2. Type the following command to adjust the Amounts in TEMP:

```
1>REPLACE#2 ALL AMOUNT WITH AMOUNT+1 FOR Guests-1 > Amount
    3 REPLACE(S)
```

3. To assess the effect of making this change, type the following command series, proofreading each line for proper pairing of single and double quotation marks before each press of the Return key.

```
1>Differ-"AMOUNT<>AMOUNT#2"
1>NewAmt="AMOUNT#2,'not',AMOUNT,MEASURE,'of',BRING"
1>LIST NAME,GUESTS,"guests",#NewAmt FOR &Differ OFF
```

NOTE

Notice that the two macros are used to make the entire command fit on a single line. You may type command lines up to 254 characters long; but the screen display after the 79th column is difficult to read or revise.

4. Compare your screen to the following:

```
1>USE PICNIC
1>INDEX ON Bring to THINGS
1>COPY TO TEMP
1>USE#2 TEMP
1>INDEX#2 ON Name to TEMPN
1>SET RELATION ON Name TO 2
1>REPLACE#2 ALL AMOUNT WITH AMOUNT+1 FOR Guests-1 > Amount
1>Differ="AMOUNT<>AMOUNT#2"
1>NewAMT="AMOUNT#2,'not',AMOUNT,MEASURE,'of',BRING"
1>LIST NAME,GUESTS,"guests",&NewAmt FOR &Differ OFF
Cantwell, Julie        3 guests   2 not   1 Pot         of Beans
Struthers, Susan       4 guests   2 not   1 Jar         of Pickles
Farris, Jody           3 guests   2 not   1 Jar         of Relish
1>
```

5. Type **SET RELA OFF** and press **Return** to discontinue the relation.
6. Having screened the effect of the change in TEMP, now save the change into the PICNIC database with the update command keyed to the PICNIC index:

```
1>UPDATE FROM 2 ON NAME REPLACE AMOUNT WITH AMOUNT#2
```

7. Type **LIST** and press **Return** and compare your screen to the following:

```
1>UPDATE FROM 2 ON NAME REPLACE AMOUNT WITH AMOUNT#2
   13 UPDATE(S)
1>LIST
00008  Cantwell, Julie        3 Beans          2 Pot
00005  Crandal, Phil          4 Buns           5 Packs
```

```
00010  Tolliver, Greg       4 Buns        6 Packs
00001  Johns, Bill          3 Chips       5 Bags
00006  Johnson, J.D.        4 Chips       3 Bags
00011  Stevens, Jan         3 Chips       5 Bags
00002  Collins, Ric         4 Dip         3 Cartons
00013  Jasper, Dave         2 Dip         2 Cartons
00003  Miller, Gary         3 Hot Dogs    6 Packs
00009  Hicks, Ginger        3 Hot Dogs    3 Packs
00004  Dickens, Charles     2 Mustard     1 Jar
00007  Struthers, Susan     4 Pickles     2 Jar
00012  Farris, Jody         3 Relish      2 Jar
1>
```

Notice that only the records for Cantwell, Struthers, and Farris have been changed.

8. Type **CLEAR ALL** and press **Return** to close all files.
9. Use the DELETE FILE command to delete TEMPN.NDX and TEMP.DBF from your disk.
10. Turn to Module 46 to continue the learning sequence.

Module 68

USE

DESCRIPTION

To use the information within a database, it must be open, or "in use." The USE command followed by a database filename and Return opens the named database file, or "puts it in use." Associated index files are also opened with the USE command. Index files, which have the extension .NDX, are described in Module 38.

OPENING A DATABASE WITH USE If you try to enter a VP-Info command that interacts with a database file and you do not have a database in use, the VP-Info conversation replies with the error message:

```
38. A database file must be in USE for this command.
```

If this happens, no harm is done. Just type USE *filename*, such as MEMBERS for the MEMBERS database file, and press Return. It isn't necessary to include the database file extension DBF when entering a database filename. The first portion of the filename suffices. This opens the database, or puts it in use.

The conventional way to put a database in use is to type the USE command followed by the database filename, like:

```
1>USE MEMBERS
```

If you want to direct your command to a disk other than the default disk listed in your CNF file, prefix the filename with the drive designator. For example, the command USE C:MEMBERS opens the MEMBERS database on drive C.

If you are using drive B for your database files on a computer with two floppy drives, you should have included the line B:*.DBF in your VPI.CNF files. (See Module 2 or Appendix B.)

If a database has associated index files, you can place the database and index files in use at the same time. To open an index file, use the command:

```
1>USE database filename INDEX index filename
```

For example, assume that the MEMBERS database has two index files named NAMELIST and JOINDATE. You can open the database and the two index files (up to seven index files are possible) with the command:

```
1>USE MEMBERS INDEX NAMELIST, JOINDATE
```

You can have as many as 6 databases in use at the same time. However, the CONFIG.SYS file (see Module 2 or Appendix B) must be in effect to have this many files open. Ensure that it is present on your DOS disk when you start your computer. Then the USE command can be modified to automatically assign a SELECT number to a file and its indexes when it is opened. The command is:

```
>USE#assigned file number database filename INDEX index filename
```

To open PHONE as a second database with its own indexes, type the command:

```
1>USE#2 PHONE INDEX PNAMES
```

The process for having multiple database files open is described in Module 58. For the time being, stick with opening and closing one database at a time.

OTHER OPTIONS WITH USE Because VP-Info compiles its command files, as explained in Module 25, references to databases and indexes that are created in the command file must be handled carefully. Since the files don't exist yet, the compiler can't find them, and the program crashes. To avoid this, you can add a COMPILE clause to the command file. The form of the command is:

```
USE filename COMPILE
```

where *filename* is the name of a datafile which is a model for the file to be created. For example, if you plan to create a temporary copy of MEMBERS, then include the following series of commands:

```
USE MEMBERS COMPILE
USE#2 MEMBERS
FILE = "TEMP"
COPY#2 TO &FILE
```

VP-Info also offers clauses which, when added to USE, allow for networked use of a database. These options are discussed in Appendix E, Networking.

CLOSING A DATABASE FILE WITH USE If USE is typed without a database name, the active database file is closed. Databases are also closed with the QUIT, CLEAR, and CLOSE ALL commands.

APPLICATIONS

The USE command is used in VP-Info's interactive mode (from the prompt) or within command files. In either case it is often one of the first commands issued when starting VP-Info. Prior to issuing the USE command, the information within a database is unavailable, because the database file must be open to be read. Once the database is closed, the database contents can't be displayed, edited, sorted, indexed, or copied.

TYPICAL OPERATION

In this illustration the USE command is used to open the MEMBERS database file modified in Module 42. Begin at the VP prompt.

1. Type **USE MEMBERS** and press **Return**. Notice that the prompt is redisplayed.
2. To verify which database is in use, type **STATUS** and press **Return**.
3. Press **Esc** to interrupt the status display and return to the prompt.
4. Type **USE** and press **Return** to close the database file.
5. Turn to Module 13 to continue the learning sequence.

Module 69

WAIT, WAIT TO

DESCRIPTION

The WAIT command is used to pause command file operation until a key is pressed. While the WAIT command is in effect, the prompt "WAITING" is displayed. Pressing a key continues command file operation. If you press Esc, command file operation is interrupted, and you return to the prompt. The WAIT command can be used to capture a one-character variable in the form WAIT TO *memvar*. To see the WAIT command, you can enter command examples from the prompt:

1. WAIT ; Pauses operation and displays "WAITING."

```
1>WAIT
WAITING
```

2. WAIT TO *MVar* ; Pauses operation, displays the "WAITING" prompt, and stores pressed key to the specified variable.

```
1>WAIT TO Choice
WAITING                ; Type X.
1>? Choice
X
1>
```

If you entered these examples, you can also see the results of the key you typed for WAIT TO CHOICE by typing DISP MEMO and pressing Return. To release the memory variable, type RELEASE ALL and press Return.

Notice that the WAIT TO command stores the value of the pressed key to the designated memory variable. You may recall from Module 4 how the ACCEPT and INPUT commands are used to store either character or numeric strings to a named memory variable. In contrast, WAIT TO stores only a single character or number — the value of the first typed key. WAIT does not require you to press Return to end the input, because it only takes a single character.

APPLICATIONS

There are many applications for the WAIT commands. WAIT is used to pause operation so you can read displayed information or prepare your printer or a disk drive for operation.

WAIT TO is used to store a menu selection or a response to a prompt as a memory variable. Once the variable is stored, you can use an IF or CASE statement to cause a resulting action, as demonstrated in the MENU program contained in Module 71.

The ? command can be used to print a prompt for the WAIT TO command.

One advantage of the WAIT TO command form is that you do not have to follow your keyboard entry with Return. The typed character is stored to the memory variable immediately. This sometimes helps new users, who are not aware of the usual requirement to press Return to complete a command.

TYPICAL OPERATION

In this illustration forms of the WAIT command are used in a command file. Begin at the VP prompt.

1. Type **WRITE WAITCMD** and press **Return** to use the editor.
2. Type the following command file. (Do not type the explanatory remarks.)

```
                                                  Remarks
* WAITCMD.PRG – Demonstrates uses of the WAIT and WAIT TO commands.
ERASE                             ; Clears the screen.
?
? '       THIS COMMAND FILE DEMONSTRATES THE WAIT COMMANDS.'
?
WAIT                              ; Pauses and displays "WAITING" prompt.
DO WHILE T                        ; Continues operation while true.
  ERASE                           ; Clears the screen.
  ?
  ? '                    PICK AN APPLICATION'
  ? '                                      Press'
  ? '               Word Processing          1'
  ? '               Spreadsheets             2'
  ? '               Database Management      3'
  ? '               Exit to VP               4'
  ?
  WAIT TO CHOICE                  ; Pauses and stores keyed character to memory
  *                                 variable CHOICE.
  ERASE                           ; Clears the screen.
  ? '---------------------------------------------------------------'
  DO CASE
    CASE CHOICE='4'               ; If memory variable CHOICE = '4' then the
    *                               commands in this CASE statement operate.
   ERASE
      CANCEL                      ; Returns control to VP prompt.
    CASE CHOICE='1'               ; If CHOICE = '1,' this text is displayed:
      ? 'Word processing is used for text files. Editing functions,'
      ? 'such as insert, delete, and copy, make word processing more'
      ? 'productive than conventional office typewriting.'
    CASE CHOICE='2'
      ? 'A spreadsheet is a planning form made up of rows and columns.'
      ? 'Text, numbers, and equations are entered in cells.'
      ? 'Numerical values may be changed to test financial assumptions,'
      ? 'making the spreadsheet a powerful financial analysis tool.'
    CASE CHOICE='3'
      ? 'Database managers store and maintain frequently-used'
      ? 'information. Database contents can be added to, deleted,'
```

```
        ? 'displayed, recalculated, and printed. VP-Info is a database'
        ? 'management system.'
      OTHERWISE
        LOOP
    ENDCASE                    ; Completes the DO CASE statement.
    ? '-----------------------------------------------------------'
    WAIT                       ; Pauses and displays "WAITING" prompt.
  ENDDO                        ; Completes DO WHILE statement.
  RETURN                       ; Terminates program.
```

3. Press **End** and **Return** to write the command file to disk.
4. Run the command file by typing **DO WAITCMD** and pressing **Return**. Compare the appearance of your screens to the following. (Each response to a WAIT command clears your screen and writes the next screen.) Respond to the prompts as indicated.

```
      THIS COMMAND FILE DEMONSTRATES THE WAIT COMMANDS.

WAITING                                                    Press Return

                    PICK AN APPLICATION
                                   Press
              Word Processing        1
              Spreadsheets           2
              Database Management    3
              Exit to VP             4

WAITING                                                    Type 1

------------------------------------------------------------
Word processing is used for text files. Editing functions,
such as insert, delete, and copy, make word processing more
productive than conventional office typewriting.
------------------------------------------------------------
WAITING                                                    Press Return

                    PICK AN APPLICATION
                                   Press
              Word Processing        1
              Spreadsheets           2
              Database Management    3
              Exit to VP             4

WAITING                                                    Type 4
```

5. When you finish experimenting with the command file, delete it from your disk by typing **DELE FILE WAITCMD.PRG** and pressing **Return**.
6. Turn to Module 45 to continue the learning sequence.

Module 70

WINDOW, COLOR

DESCRIPTION

The WINDOW and COLOR commands can be used separately as well as in tandem to create screen effects.

WINDOW The WINDOW command is used to create partitions on the screen. You can position text or command operations inside a window without affecting the portion of the screen outside the window. Here are some forms of the WINDOW command:

1. WINDOW 5,7 — Creates a window consisting of rows 5, 6, and 7. Any commands issued are executed inside that portion of the screen.
2. WINDOW — Returns to the full screen.
3. WINDOW 5,10,7,60 — Creates a window surrounded by a box whose upper left and lower right corners are Row 4, Col 9 and Row 8, Col 61. Any commands issued are executed inside that box. Notice that WINDOW differs from BOX in that the coordinates represent the usable portion of the screen rather than the locations of the frame's corners.
4. WINDOW 5,10,7,60 BLANK — The single-line box is suppressed.
5. WINDOW 5,10,7,60 DOUBLE — A double-line box is drawn.
6. WINDOW 5,10 COLOR 4 — Creates a window with a color attribute (Red), using the COLOR command.
7. WINDOW 5,10,7,60 COLOR 4,5 — When all four window coordinates are given, you can specify a second color for the frame. If none is specified, the text color is used for the frame.

Although all commands are executed inside the box, row and column specifications are relative to the entire screen. In other words, when you draw a window as described in the examples above and then issue the command

```
1>@20,10 SAY 'Outside'
```

the word "Outside" appears on row 20 of the whole screen.

A CLS or ERASE command from the full screen erases any other windows. Issued inside a window, it only affects the current window.

You cannot use the EDIT command (Module 28) from inside a window.

COLOR The COLOR command takes five numerical specifications. The first is a color attribute number, and the remaining four are row and column specifications like those used with the WINDOW command. All together, they change the screen area specified to a new color combination. The color attribute is determined by adding together the appropriate values from the following table:

Background		Character		Blink		Bright	
0	Black	0	Black	0	Off	0	Off
16	Blue	1	Blue	128	On	8	On
32	Green	2	Green				
48	Cyan	3	Cyan				
64	Red	4	Red				
80	Magenta	5	Magenta				
96	Brown	6	Brown				
112	White	7	White				

For example, consider the following commands:

```
1>COLOR 36,10,10,20,20     ; The display from Row 10, Col 10 to Row 20, Col 20 becomes green
                             with red characters, responding to the value 32 + 4.
1>COLOR 164,10,10,20,20    ; The same area now contains blinking characters (36 + 128).
1>COLOR 0,0,0,23,79        ; The screen is erased to Row 23 (0 is the "color" black on black).
```

A CLS or ERASE command cancels a COLOR command as it clears the screen. The COLOR command only washes a color temporarily across the specified area, rather than permanently changing the screen colors. To make a complete color change, use the SET COLOR TO command with numbers from the color table.

APPLICATIONS

The WINDOW command can be used to control the amount of space a message takes up on the screen and to preserve screen contents while presenting such things as instructions or help screens. A very handy use is to display a database structure or the results of a display command on the upper half of the screen while using the editor in the lower half. For example, the following command series allows you to see the structure of ABC at the top of the screen while writing a command file in the editor displayed between rows 13 and 24:

```
1>USE ABC
1>LIST STRU
1>WINDOW 13,24
1>WRITE filename
```

The COLOR command can be used to call attention to a message.

TYPICAL OPERATION

This illustration adds a WINDOW command to the MENU.PRG last modified in Module 40. Begin at the VP prompt.

1. Type **WRITE MENU** and press **Return** to use the editor.

2. Modify the second CASE statement so that the CASE portion of the file looks like this:

```
DO CASE
CASE Choice='2'
   DO ADD
CASE @(Choice,'123456')>0
   WINDOW 3,10,5,60 DOUBLE
   ? "Not an operative command. Press Return."
   COLOR 207,3,10,5,60
   ACCEPT TO Going
   WINDOW
   ERASE
   LOOP
CASE Choice ='7'
   ERASE
   CLEAR ALL
   RETURN
ENDCASE
```

3. Press **End** to save the modified menu file.
4. Run the command file by typing **DO MENU** and pressing **Return**. Try an inoperative menu selection to observe the action of the window. Notice that the cursor appears in the window while the program waits for a Return command. We changed the WAIT command to an ACCEPT command because any action on the screen returns to the default screen attribute of grey on black. If we had retained the WAIT command, the "WAITING" prompt would have appeared as grey on black. To retain the WAIT command, you could replace the CASE section for inoperative choices with the following:

NOTE

If you make this change, be sure to save the file before you modify it, so that you can use it in the next module.

```
CASE @(Choice,'123456')>0
   WINDOW 3,10,5,60 DOUBLE
   SET COLOR to 207
   CLS
   ? "Not an operative command. Press Return."
   WAIT
   SET COLOR TO 7
   WINDOW
   ERASE
   LOOP
```

5. The order of the commands is critical to the effect; you may wish to experiment with the order to explore the possibilities for various combinations. If so, be sure to restore MENU.PRG to the form specified in step 2 of this operation. That form of MENU.PRG is used in the next module.
6. Turn to Module 56 to continue the learning sequence.

Module 71

WRITE
(Developing Command Files)

DESCRIPTION

If you are working your way through this book using the learning sequence, you have used WRITE in previous modules to create command files.

The general form of this command is:

```
1>WRITE filename
```

If the file exists, it is opened, and if it does not exist, it is created. You can reopen the last file you edited by simply typing WRITE without specifying a filename. The WRITE command starts the built-in VP-Info full-screen editor. This editor creates ASCII text files. Although you can create any kind of document, its intended use is for creating VP-Info command (or program) files.

When using the editor on a text file, you may want to suppress the message line at the top of the screen and the various prompts. To do this, add the term OFF to the end of the WRITE command:

```
WRITE filename OFF
```

This is not recommended for general use, because the Save message is suppressed when you exit from the editor.

FILENAME EXTENSIONS If no extension is included with the filename, it is assigned the extension PRG. If you need a different extension, such as FRM for a report form file or TXT for a text file, you must specify it with the filename. If the file already exists, the named file is displayed, ready to edit or view.

EDITING COMMANDS Once the full-screen editor is in operation, you can use the control sequences listed when you press Alt-H. These sequences are used to move the cursor, insert, delete, and so on.

When the file is typed, you can save it by pressing End or Ctrl-W for "Write." If you display a file, make changes, and then decide not to save the changes, you can abort without saving by pressing Ctrl-Q for Quit. If you accidentally begin a Save and Exit routine by pressing End unintentionally, you can return to editing by pressing Esc.

This is about all there is to using the full-screen editor. You might type WRITE SAMPLE to create a new file. Enter several lines of text and experiment with the control keys. When you are satisfied that you know how they all work, you can either save the document with End or quit without saving with Ctrl-Q.

DEVELOPING COMMAND FILES Creating a command file is easier if you plan ahead. When you're ready to design an application (a database with related indexes and command files), there are several design steps to consider. Once you have blocked out the general structure of your database and the necessary command files, you can write and test command files one at a time. To simplify the file creation process, follow the tips on the next few pages.

1. **Database file structure**—The structure of your database is the first consideration in application design. Jot down a list on paper that includes the following information.

   a. What kind of information must you store and maintain (field names)?
   b. How many characters are needed for each piece (field) of information?
   c. What type is each information element (character, numeric, or logical)? If numeric, how many decimal places are needed?

When you have determined all the fields you will need, their names, and their types and sizes, go ahead and create your database structure. Do not enter all of the data. Limit entry to one or two records for testing.

2. **Data manipulation**—Next, decide what you will do with the information once you have captured it in a database file. Will you:

   a. Add records?
   b. Change records?
   c. Delete records?

3. **Reports**—Once you decide how you will maintain the information, decide upon the kinds of printed or displayed output you will need. Will you want to:

   a. List information to the screen (all or selective)?
   b. List information to your printer (all or selective)?
   c. List information with the date?

Your reports, labels, data entry, and display screens can be designed using the appropriate VP-Info development utilities described in Modules 34, 52, 54, etc. They can also be developed from scratch by using the commands that display and print information.

4. **Application structure**—Once you have an idea of what you want to do with the information, you can block out the structure of the command files that make up your application. It is a good idea to use a modular structure, where separate command files perform different tasks. For example, you may want to write a command file for adding records, one for changing records, and still another for deleting records. You can also write separate command files for each report type you want. This approach lets you develop several small, relatively simple command files instead of putting everything into one large command file that may take forever to debug. The diagram in Figure 71-1 illustrates a series of command files.

5. **Individual command file design**—With the main structure blocked out, you can begin the design of individual command files. If you wish, you can do this directly on your computer using WRITE, with a word processor, or with a compatible pop-up notepad utility.

Begin with a MAIN MENU command file. Call it MENU. From the VP prompt, type WRITE MENU and press Return to access the full-screen editor. Begin typing a command-file skeleton made up of comment lines that begin with an asterisk. These lines are there for reference only and have no effect on command file operation.

```
* MENU.PRG – A command file for displaying the address book menu.
* Use a DO WHILE loop to sustain operation.
* Display selection list.
* Use ACCEPT to display prompt and store selection.
* Use series of CASE statements to run the selected command file, exit
*     to the VP prompt, or exit to the operating system.
```

Save the MENU command file by pressing Ctrl-W.

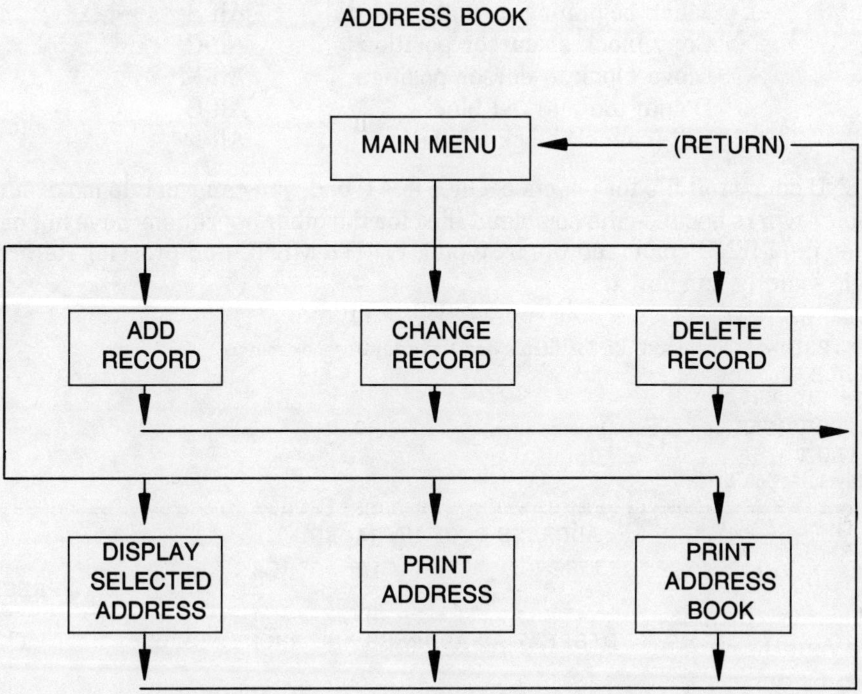

Figure 71-1 Diagramming Command Files

6. **Typing the command file**—Now that your MENU command file is outlined, you can type the command lines under each block. It is a good idea to leave your comment lines in place to show you what each section of the command file, or program, does. You should know that spaces within command files are ignored during operation, but they are counted as part of the 254 allowable characters on a command line.

If a command line exceeds the width of your screen, you can use a semicolon at the end of the line and press Return. The semicolon combines multiple lines into a single statement. If you import a file written in another editor, the VP-Info editor automatically wraps any oversized lines, adding a semicolon to the truncated line. Be sure to check imported files for such lines and fix them in the editor, because they can confuse the command processor.

Remember, when the command file is run, the lines are executed in a top to bottom order. Therefore, be careful to organize your commands in the proper sequence.

TIP: When command files use a series of the same or similar commands, you can copy an existing command file, rename it, edit the contents, and try it out. This technique is faster than retyping everything from scratch. The VP-Info editor lets you mark and manipulate blocks with the following command keys.

Mark beginning or end of block	Alt-B
Copy block at cursor position	Alt-C
Move block to cursor position	Alt-M
Delete the marked block	Alt-D
Kill (cancel) block markers	Alt-K

Type the MENU command file for practice. Once it is typed, you can run it to make sure it works. Only selection 7 works because the command files for the other operations have not been created yet. Redisplay the MENU command file by typing WRITE MENU and pressing Return. Type the command file exactly as shown.

```
* MENU.PRG - A command file for displaying the address book menu.
VARIABLE Choice
ERASE
* Use a DO WHILE loop to sustain operation.
DO WHILE T
* Display selection list.
? '=================================================================='
? '|                      ADDRESS BOOK MAIN MENU                     |'
? '------------------------------------------------------------------'
? '                                                           PRESS'
? '                                                           -----'
? '                   DISPLAY AN ADDRESS AND PHONE NUMBER       1'
?
? '                   ADD A NEW ADDRESS AND PHONE NUMBER        2'
?
? '                   CHANGE AN ADDRESS OR PHONE NUMBER         3'
?
? '                   DELETE AN ADDRESS AND PHONE NUMBER        4'
?
? '                   PRINT AN ADDRESS AND PHONE NUMBER         5'
?
? '                   PRINT AN ADDRESS AND PHONE LIST           6'
?
? '                   EXIT TO VP PROMPT                         7'
```

```
?
? '==============================================================='
*
* Use ACCEPT to display prompt and store selection.
*
ACCEPT 'Enter your selection: ' TO Choice
*
* Use series of CASE statements to run the selected command file,
* exit to the VP prompt, or exit to the operating system.
*
DO CASE
CASE @(Choice,'123456')>0
? "Not an operative command. Press Return."
WAIT
ERASE
LOOP
CASE Choice ='7'
ERASE
CLEAR ALL
CANCEL
ENDCASE
ENDDO
```

Before saving the command file, press Alt-F to take advantage of one of the VP-Info editor's handiest utilities, the automatic formatter. The file is automatically indented to provide a display of the nesting of commands, such as CASE, IF, or REPEAT constructions. If you fail to close such command structures with the necessary END commands, the auto-indent feature shows such oversights to you now.

When the file is ready, save it by pressing Ctrl-W and then pressing Return.

7. **Testing the command file**—Now that your command file is finished, you can test it.

If the first command file runs without any hitches, you are ready to build the second one. But if you encounter problems, you may wish to take advantage of the debugging features (Module 20) provided by VP-Info.

The SET STEP ON command lets you step the program through its paces a line at a time. The command file pauses at every step and waits for you to press Return to go on to the next step. It also gives you the option of typing Esc to exit from the command file. As you step through the program, the line number of the line about to be executed is displayed in the top left corner of the screen.

After any bugs in the first command file are gone, you can move on to the next one, writing and testing each command file as it is developed. It is like "eating an elephant;" you have got to do it one bite at a time.

When the MENU command file, prepared above, is run by typing DO MENU, the following display screen is displayed (if everything was typed in correctly).

```
===================================================================
|                     ADDRESS BOOK MAIN MENU                      |
|-----------------------------------------------------------------|
                                                 PRESS
                                                 -----
          DISPLAY AN ADDRESS AND PHONE NUMBER      1

          ADD A NEW ADDRESS AND PHONE NUMBER       2

          CHANGE AN ADDRESS OR PHONE NUMBER        3

          DELETE AN ADDRESS AND PHONE NUMBER       4

          PRINT AN ADDRESS AND PHONE NUMBER        5

          PRINT AN ADDRESS AND PHONE LIST          6

          EXIT TO VP PROMPT                        7

===================================================================
Enter your selection:
```

TIP: You can create elaborate interactive menu screens with the MENU, WINDOW, BOX, and SCREEN commands, and with the @ *row,col* and @ *row,col* SAY commands described in Modules 6 and 54.

APPLICATIONS

The WRITE *filename* command is generally used to create or edit command files, but is also used to create or edit almost any kind of document. In this respect, VP-Info's full-screen editor can be used as a word processor, capable of creating or changing almost any kind of file containing standard ASCII text characters.

TYPICAL OPERATION

In this illustration an Address Book database structure is designed. Then WRITE is used to write the ADD command file that works in conjunction with the Address Book Main Menu file created in the Description section of this module. Begin at the VP prompt.

1. Type **CREATE ADRBOOK** and press **Return**. Create the database structure shown in the following example.

	Name	Type	Width	Dec	*Remarks*
1	NAME	Character	25		
2	ST_ADR	Character	25		
3	CSZ	Character	25		
4	HPHONE	Character	14		
5	WPHONE	Character	14		
6	NOTES	Character	40		
7	**<End>**				Press **End** and **Return**.

2. Type **WRITE ADD** and press **Return** to use the VP-Info editor.
3. Type the following command file skeleton.

```
* ADD.PRG – Adds records to the Address Book application.
* Erase screen and display data entry instructions.
* Append new records for data entry.
* Clear screen and display instructions to return to Main Menu.
* Erase screen and return to Main Menu.
```

4. Fill in the command file skeleton by typing the ADD command file. (Do not type the explanatory remarks.)

```
* ADD.PRG – Adds records to the Address Book application.
* Erase screen and display introductory information.
ERASE
* Display data entry instructions.
?' TO STOP DATA ENTRY, PRESS END AT THE BEGINNING OF A NEW RECORD.'
?
WAIT  '            PRESS ANY KEY TO START DATA ENTRY...' TO Going
* Append new records for data entry.
USE ADRBOOK
APPEND
* Clear screen and display instructions to return to Main Menu.
ERASE
ACCEPT '           PRESS ANY KEY TO RETURN TO MAIN MENU...' TO Going
* Erase screen and return to Main Menu.
ERASE
RELEASE Going
RETURN
```

5. Press **End** and press **Return** to write the command file to disk.
6. Type **WRITE MENU** and press **Return** to modify the program.
7. Press **Ins** to toggle into Overwrite Mode. (Notice that the word "INSERT" disappears from the top line of the screen.)
8. Go to the series of equals signs used to draw the double bar in Line 8, position the cursor on the *second* equals sign, and press **Alt-G** to activate the graphic line-drawing facility in the editor.
9. Press the **Right Arrow** to replace the equals sign with a solid line.
10. Continue pressing the Right Arrow until you reach the last equals sign, and then press the **Down Arrow** twice.
11. Use the Left Arrow to draw back to the beginning of the bar in Line 10, replacing all but the very first hyphen in the line.
12. Use the Up Arrow to close the box. If you make any errors, press **Alt-G** to exit from Graphics and use your editing keys to fix them. If you get into serious problems, simply press **Ctrl-Q** to abandon your changes.
13. Before going on, confirm that the three modified lines look like the display below. Be sure that the quotation marks have not been overwritten.

14. Go to the line immediately below the DO CASE command, and press **Ctrl-N** to insert a new line. Add these two lines as the first Case:

```
CASE Choice='2'
DO ADD
```

15. Press **Alt-F** to format the new case, and then press **End** and **Return** to save the modified MENU.PRG.
16. Type **DO MENU** from the VP prompt.
17. Type **2** to run the ADD command file. Respond to the next prompt by pressing **Return**.

```
TO STOP DATA ENTRY, PRESS END AT THE BEGINNING OF A NEW RECORD.

     PRESS ANY KEY TO START DATA ENTRY...
```

18. When the APPEND screen appears, add a record of name, address, and phone information. When you are through practicing, press **End** at the beginning of a record to stop data entry.
19. Press **Return** when the following message appears:

```
PRESS ANY KEY TO RETURN TO MAIN MENU...
```

20. When the Main Menu appears, type **7** to return to the VP prompt.
21. Turn to Module 31 to continue the learning sequence.

Module 72

ZAP

DESCRIPTION

The ZAP command is used to remove all records from a database file. The entire file is emptied of all records immediately, with no RECALL allowed.

When the records are "zapped" from the database, all that remains is the database structure.

To empty a database, type ZAP and press Return. The message:

```
1>ZAP
Type YES to have all records deleted from this file
```

is displayed to give you a chance to change your mind. Typing yes (upper- or lowercase) empties the file. Any other input, including an incomplete form of "yes," such as "Y," prompts the message "No records deleted !!!!!" and stops the ZAP.

APPLICATIONS

The ZAP command is handy for quickly deleting all records from within a database file without destroying the database structure. For example, if you are using someone else's database in which you intend to place your own information, the ZAP command becomes a useful tool. However, you should be sure to use ZAP cautiously. If you ZAP a database containing important information, it is lost forever.

TYPICAL OPERATION

In this illustration, the remaining records in MEMBERS are discarded with the ZAP command. After emptying the database, DELETE the file from your disk using the DELETE FILE command. Start at the VP prompt.

1. Type **USE MEMBERS** and press **Return**.
2. Type **LIST** and press **Return** to see the current records.
3. To delete the contents of the database, type **ZAP** and press **Return**. Then type **YES** and press **Return** in response to the prompt.
4. Type **LIST** and press **Return** again. Notice that nothing is displayed, because the contents have been zapped from the database.

5. Type **DISPLAY STRUCTURE** and press **Return** to confirm that the empty database is still there.
6. Close the database by typing **USE** and pressing **Return**.
7. Delete the database from your disk by typing **DELETE FILE MEMBERS.DBF** and pressing **Return**.
8. Verify that the MEMBERS database is gone by typing **DIR B:*.DBF** and pressing **Return**. Notice that MEMBERS.DBF is not displayed in the list of database files.
9. Turn to Module 51 to continue the learning sequence.

Appendix A
TERMS AND DEFINITIONS

INTRODUCTION

Several common terms and definitions encountered in this book are defined in this appendix. In addition to terminology specific to VP-Info, many of the terms are common to computing.

Table A-1 Terms and Definitions

Term	Definition
Alphanumeric	A combination of alphabetical and numeric characters used to form an expression, such as a part number. An example of an alphanumeric expression follows. `PN A-10036-001` Notice that alphabetical, numeric, spaces, and punctuation characters may exist in an alphanumeric expression.
ASCII	American Standard Code for Information Interchange—a standard data code used to represent alphabetical, numerical, and punctuation characters used in Electronic Data Processing systems.
Array	Data stored in a pattern, like a table, and referred to by its location in the pattern.
Attribute	A special characteristic of a value or command.
Batch File	A series of instructions, or commands, that can be called with a command and used to perform a repetitive task. A .PRG file is a batch file, which VP-Info calls with the commands DO and CHAIN.
BIT	A single BInary digiT that has a value of either one or zero (on or off). Produced and used by digital computers to represent data characters and to control computer peripheral devices.
Byte	A single character, symbol, or control code used by a computer; made up of a unique pattern of eight bits, where the pattern specifies the character, symbol, or control code value.
Character	A letter, number, punctuation mark, or symbol.

Clause	A command qualifier; a clause may control the format of displayed or printed information or the structure of a database. Examples of clauses are:
	`BLANK` `PICTURE`
	`DELIMITED` `SDF`
	`FOR` `STRUCTURE`
	`NEXT` `USING`

Command File	See Batch File.

Term	Definition
Command Redirection	A technique for sending a command to a datafile that is open, but not in the selected work area. By adding *#filenumber* to the first word in the command, you direct that command to the other work area. For example, assume you have opened ABC in 1, DEF in 2 and GHI in 3, and look at the following commands: `1>LIST#2 OFF` ; Lists data from DEF. `1>APPEND#3 BLANK` ; Adds a blank record to GHI.
Conversation	The term for the interactive or immediate mode's responses to your commands.
Delimiter	A separator, such as a comma, that designates the end of one field and the beginning of the next.
Environment	The current memory allocations for such things as database fields, matrices, memory variables, and the SET commands. Changed by execution of DO files.
Error Message	A software-embedded message that is displayed when an illegal command or command form is attempted by the system user.

Expression	A combination of constants, variables, and operators. A constant is a fixed value like 'yes' or 7. A variable is a label for a changeable value; MVar might represent 'yes' or 7. Operators are those symbols covered in Appendix C. Example expressions:
	`((7*8)/3+2)*2`
	`7`
	`"John"+LName`
	`.NOT. Paid`

Extension	An optional one- to three-digit suffix which is part of a filename. Examples are: `PHONEBK.DBF` DBF designates a database file. `MENU.PRG` PRG designates a VP-Info command file. `NAMELIST.FRM` FRM designates a report form file.
Field	An entry within a record, such as a name or address field within a customer record.
Field Redirection	Like *Command Redirection*, permits reference to fields in a non-selected but open database. `1>LIST NAME, SALARY#2` ; Lists names from the selected database and salaries from a linked database.
File	A document, database, program, or similar entity that has a filename, a beginning, and an end. Generally made up of discrete records having a length of from one to 8,000 characters (or bytes).
Filename	The name of a file, program, or document stored on magnetic media, such as tape or disk. Filenames are made up of from one to eight characters with an optional one- to three-character extension.
Fixed Position	Always displayed at a specific location on the screen or printed page. Applies to SAY and GET variables, windows and boxes. Fixed position variables are signalled by commands like @ *row,col* SAY.
Floating Position	Displayed at relative rather than absolute locations. Commands like ACCEPT, LIST, and the print (?) command display values relative to the immediate cursor position.

Term	Definition
GET Table	A memory map holding information on up to 64 variables which are to be used by GET commands.
Immediate [Interactive] Mode	Used to enter commands directly from the keyboard. This is the VP-Info default mode which displays a '1>' as a prompt symbol. Besides using commands listed in this table, direct mathematical operations may be used. A few are listed as examples. (Module 39)

```
1>? 25+12               ; The question mark and expression provides an
    37.00               ; immediate on-screen response.
1>GOTO BOTTOM           ; Positions record pointer to last record.
1>? #                   ; What is the current record number?
    29.00               ; The record number is 29.
1>? ((36+25)/10)*3      ; Solve a mathematical expression.
    18.3                ; VP-Info responds with the answer.
1>? MNum*25             ; Multiply MNum by 25.
   125.00               ; VP-Info responds with the answer.
1>?? 10+MNum135.00      ; The double question mark causes the answer to
1>                      ; print on the current screen line.
```

Term	Definition
Memory Variable	A string, numeric, or logical value that is stored in and recalled from memory. (Module 63)

```
1>STORE 25 TO MNum      ; The value 25 is saved to MNum.
1>MNum = 25             ; Identical function.
```

Term	Definition
Record	A collection of information, in one or more fields, about a specific item or person. VP-Info records may contain up to 256 fields and 8000 characters. An entire VP-Info database file may contain millions of records.
Record Pointer	Indicates the record number within a database that is currently being added, edited, displayed, or deleted. Record numbers indicate the sequential position of a record within a database.
String	A series of characters and spaces. String types are either numeric (numbers), character (letters or a mixture of letters, numbers, punctuation marks, and spaces) or logical (true or false; yes or no). Some examples of strings are:

```
"Bill Edwards" "February" "A-100.X"     Character strings.
"25" "456.05" "12345.67"                Numeric strings.
"T" "F" "Y" "N"                         Logical strings.
```

Term	Definition
String Function	String functions are tools that let you control the way strings are stored or displayed, or that let you determine certain characteristics about them. There are string functions that let you convert numbers to characters, characters to numbers, decimal numbers to whole numbers (called *integers*), determine the number of characters in a string, and so on. Appendix D describes string functions and provides examples.
Subroutine	A command file called by another command file; a nested DO file program.
Syntax	The form, spelling, vocabulary, and organization of a command. If the syntax is incorrect, an error message is displayed and procedure execution is halted.
Variable	A value, usually either the contents of a field within a database record or a memory variable. A variable may be a character string (made up of alphanumeric characters, spaces, and punctuation marks), a numeric value, a mathematical expression (equation), or a logical true or false; yes or no. (A blank in a logical field is the same as false or no.)

Term	Definition

Vector	A one-dimensional matrix variable. An open data file is a vector, and its fields may be referred to in most commands with position numbers:
	`1>USE ABC`
	`1>DISP ABC[1]` ; Display first field in current record.
	`Sergio, Vincent`

Volume	The reference block number for the beginning of a text record stored in a Library (.LIB) file. A text record takes up as many whole volumes as its size divided by 256, rounded up.

Appendix B

FILE TYPES

INTRODUCTION

Several different types of files are created and used by VP-Info. These include:

Backup files	.BAK
VP-Info configuration file	VPI.CNF
System configuration file	CONFIG.SYS
Compiled command files	.CPL
Database files	.DBF
Environment files	.ENV
Report form files	.FRM
Library text files	.LIB
Memory variable files	.MEM
Database index files	.NDX
Command files	.PRG
Standard data (or text) files	.TXT

When the files are created by VP-Info, they are assigned appropriate three-character extensions, like CUSTOMER.DBF or MENU.PRG, and these appropriate extensions are assumed when you attempt to use a file. If you attempt to use a file with an extension other than the default, you must specify its extension, as in WRITE INVNTRY.FRM or WRITE MENU.TXT. Table B-1 contains a description and accompanying example for each file type listed.

Table B-1 VP-Info File Types

File Type	*Extension*	*Description*

Backup .BAK Backup files are automatically created as a safety measure when an edited version of a text file is saved. For example, if you use the WRITE *FILENAME* statement to change a file, the previous version of the modified file is kept with a .BAK extension. This happens when you press Ctrl-W to save (write) your modified version.

VP-Info Config. VPI.CNF This file is used by VP-Info when it is started. It contains one or more commands that control VP-Info operation. Normal defaults, including function key values and SET functions, are controlled by this file. You can create this file using VP-Info's full-screen editor, a word processor that produces ASCII files, EDLIN, or the DOS COPY command. Notice the following VPI.CNF command lines. These serve as examples of what you can do with the CNF file.

```
FILES              ; Signals a FILES structure (Module 31).
TEMP*.*  = D:\     ; Sends all temporary files to a D drive (in this
*.DBF    = C:\     ; case, a RAMdisk).
*.NDX    = C:\     ; All datafiles and related files are on the C
```

File Type	Extension	Description

```
    *.FRM    = C:\                  ; fixed disk.
    *.PRG    = B:\                  ; All program files are on a B drive.
    *.CPL    = B:\
    *.TXT    = B:\
    ENDFILES                        ; Terminates structure.

    :F10 = 'RUN COMMAND /C '        ; Arms F10 with the RUN command.

    SET MEMORY TO 64                ; Sets aside room for the RUN command.

    SET SNOW OFF                    ; Toggles slower but less distracting CGA display screen.
```

System Config CONFIG.SYS This file is used by DOS when you turn on your computer. It lets you specify the number of files open at the same time. It also creates your selected number of buffers, which speeds up VP-Info operation by letting it work in memory buffers rather than having to read and write information to your disk during sorting and listing. This file should contain the following two lines (20 files and buffers yield optimum performance):

```
FILES=20
BUFFERS=20
```

You may wish to include other commands in your CONFIG.SYS file, such as a RAMdisk driver.

Compiled Commands .CPL For faster processing, you can create compiled versions of your program files. (VP-Info does this automatically when you call a program file, but it erases the CPL file when finished with it.) These files are covered in Module 14.

Database .DBF A standard database file is created and saved using the CREATE command. When the newly created database is saved, the extension DBF is added to the filename you specified.

Environment .ENV If you SET DO OFF, then VP-Info creates an environment file for each subroutine (DO file called by Do file), to keep track of any changes the subroutine might create.

Report form .FRM The WRITE *filename*.FRM command lets you create and save report format files that control the display and printing of data. The REPORT commands are described in Module 52.

Library .LIB The library file holds a collection of related text records in 256-byte blocks called volumes, keeping track of the records by their starting volume number. Their use is covered in Module 40.

Memory variable .MEM Memory files are created when memory variables are written to disk using the SAVE command with a filename which VP-Info assigns the default extension .MEM. This allows you to save memory variables to disk, and then clear memory to make room for more memory variables. See Module 63 for details.

Index .NDX An index file is created from information in an existing database file. The records within an index file are sorted (rearranged alphabetically or numerically) on one or more specified fields, which are referred to as "key" fields. Records retain their original record numbers, and the database file is unchanged.

Program .PRG A command (program) file is created and saved using the VP-Info full-screen editor or some other text editor. These are pure ASCII files and are transferrable (transportable) between different computer and operating systems. Command files are created and edited using the WRITE *filename* command.

Standard Data .TXT A standard data or text file is created by copying a database file with COPY TO *filename* SDF or DELIMITED. A .TXT file is also created when information is displayed while the SPOOL, SET ALTERNATE TO *filename* and SET ALTERNATE ON commands are in effect. The resulting file may be used by the TEXT command, added to a library file, or used by other programs, such as a word processor or spreadsheet.

Appendix C

VP-Info OPERATORS

INTRODUCTION

The term *operator* is just another name for an arithmetic expression, like plus, minus, divide by, equal to, and so on. Instead of spelling out these operators, symbols are used to represent them. There are four types of VP-Info operators: arithmetic, relational, logical, and string. Table C-1 contains a description and accompanying example of each operator.

Table C-1 VP-Info Operators

Operator Symbol	*Description*
Arithmetic Operators	Arithmetic operators are used to perform mathematical computations. They include addition, subtraction, multiplication, and division operators. **NOTE** In the following examples of operators, notice the `1>` prompt followed by a question mark. Typing a question mark and a space followed by the sample expressions lets you test operators.
`+`	The plus sign is the addition operator.
	`1>? 37+144`
`–`	The minus sign (hyphen) is the subtraction operator.
	`1>STORE 53 TO MNum` `1>? MNum-21`
`*`	The asterisk is the multiplication operator.
	`1>? 12*MNum`
`/`	The slash sign is the division operator.
	`1>? 208/52`
`( )`	Parentheses are used for grouping math operations.
	`1>? (27-(5+10)/3)*2`
Relational Operators	Relational operators are used to assign a relationship between two values. They include expressions like *greater than*, *less than*, *not equal*, and so on. There are many uses for relational operators, like finding all records in a database that contain a March transaction date or a dollar value relative to a specified value.
`<`	Less than operator.
	`1>LIST FOR ZIP_CODE < 78000`
`>`	Greater than operator.
	`1>SORT ON NAME TO NEWFILE FOR DATE > '01/01/83'`

Operator Symbol	*Description*
=	Equal to operator. `1>DELETE ALL FOR AMOUNT = 0`
< >	Not equal to operator. `1>DISPLAY ALL FOR STATE <> 'CA'`
< =	Less than or equal to operator. `1>REPLACE AMOUNT WITH AMOUNT*1.1 FOR QTY <= 10`
> =	Greater than or equal to operator. `1>LIST OFF FOR DATE >= '01/01/84'`
Logical Operators	Logical operators produce true or false results or establish logical "rules" in a mathematical expression. For example, logical operators can require that only those records greater than one date and less than another be listed (see the .AND. example), or only those outside of a certain range be listed (see .OR. example.).
.AND.	Joins two or more expressions to establish a value range. In the following example, the range is the full month of January. `1>LIST FOR $(DATE,4,4) >= '0101' .AND. $(DATE,4,4) <= '0131'`

.OR.	Joins two or more expressions to exclude a value range or to offer alternative selections. In the first example, the range excludes the month of March. In the second example, three dates are selected for display. In the third example, records meeting a match in either the NAME or COMPANY fields are located.
	`1>LIST FOR DATE < '860301' .OR. DATE > '860331'`
	`1>LIST FOR DATE = '870115' .OR. DATE = '870131' .OR. DATE = '870215'`
	`1>LOCATE FOR NAME = 'Johnson' .OR. COMPANY = 'Johnson'`

.NOT.	The "not true" operator is used to find conditions that are false. For example, if you have a customer list and want to list all customer's records with unpaid bills, which could be indicated by the presence of a F, N, or blank in the logical PAID field of each record, you could use the following command. `1>LIST FOR .NOT. PAID`
( )	As in arithmetic operators, parentheses may be used for grouping logical operators. The semicolon is used to continue a statement on the following line. `1>LIST FOR (AMT=12 .OR. AMT=52) .AND. .NOT. PAID`
String Operators	String operators are used to control the spacing between adjoining fields when information is listed on the screen or printer.
,	The comma is a union operator which joins database fields. It adds one space separating each pair of fields, and it allows you to mix field types (it is not, strictly speaking, a string operator). `1>LIST NAME,ADDRESS,CITY,STATE,ZIP`
+	The plus symbol is used to concatenate (connect) two database fields of character data when displayed or printed. It cannot be used with numeric or logical fields unless they have been converted to strings temporarily. `1>LIST NAME+ADDRESS+CITY`

Appendix D

VP-Info FUNCTIONS

INTRODUCTION

A function examines an expression and then returns a response to it. The expression may be a string, a number, a character, a filename, a combination of these types, or even a *null set* (in effect, no expression). The function response is some data of the string, numeric, or logical type. Functions allow you to manipulate data, controlling how it is stored or displayed. They let you examine or change certain characteristics of data. There are functions that let you convert numbers to characters, characters to numbers, or decimal numbers to whole numbers (or integers). The general form of a function is the function's identifying command or symbol followed by the expression in parentheses.

Function(expression)

The expression is usually the value of a field or memory variable, but it can be a numeric or character string that is directly entered from the keyboard. Table D-1 describes functions and provides examples.

Table D-1 VP-Info Functions

Function	*Description*
!(*string*)	Converts a string to uppercase.

Example:

```
1>? !('Andrew')
ANDREW
```

#	Returns the current record number.

Example:

```
1>USE ABC
1>? #
        1.00
```

# [TEXT Macro]	Used in a TEXT to indicate a SAY Variable for a fixed location in the TEXT. (Module 65)
$(*string,start,length*)	Extracts a portion of a string based on a starting position and length.

Example:

```
1>? $('Tom Jones',6,3)
one
```

% [TEXT Macro]	Used in TEXT to indicate a GET Variable for a floating position in a TEXT. A floating variable is placed in the next available cursor location on the screen.

Function	Description
& [Command Macro Substitution]	The macro substitution function makes use of the ampersand (&) symbol in front of a character-type memory variable name. When used, the contents of the memory variable are directly substituted for the &*memory variable* expression. A macro may not include the initial word in a command. (Module 63)

The form of the macro function is: &*memory variable*

Example:

```
                                           Remarks
1>STORE "NAME, EXTN, MAIL" TO MDISP     ; Stores text in quotes to MDISP.
1>DISP ALL &MDISP                       ; Makes command line.
```

& [TEXT macro] — Used in TEXT to indicate a SAY Variable for a floating position in a TEXT. A floating variable is placed in the next available cursor location on the screen.

* — Deleted function. Returns True if the indicated record is marked for deletion. May be used with most commands.

Example:

```
1>DELETE ALL FOR DATE<'870000'
1>GO 20
1>? *
T                        ; Record 20 is marked for deletion.
1>SKIP
1>? #,*
     21.00 F
```

@ [TEXT macro] — Used in TEXT to indicate a GET Variable for a fixed position in a TEXT. (Module 65)

@(*substring,string*) — Searches for a string in a larger string and returns the numeric value of the starting position of the string.

Example:

```
1>? @('one','Tom Jones')
      6.00
```

ABS(*number*) — Returns the absolute (positive) value of a number or expression. The example here stores 12 to a and 21 to b. Then use ABS( ) to determine the absolute value of the difference between a and b.

Example:

```
1>a=12
1>b=21
1>? ABS(a-b)
      9.00
```

ACOS(*number*) — Returns the arc cosine. The number may be an expression; the response is in radians.

Example:

```
1>ACOS(.05*2)
    1.47
```

Function	Description
ASIN(*number*)	Returns the arc sine of the number or expression.
ATAN(*number*)	Returns the arc tangent of the number or expression.

Example:

```
1>X = 12
1>ATAN(17*X)
    1.56
```

BIT(*string,position in byte*) — Returns logical (True or False) response to whether a given bit in the binary (8-bit) value of a string is 1 (True) or 0 (False). Each character in the string takes up 8 bits, so to check the second bit in the third character of the string 'that,' specify BIT('that',18), since 18 is ((3 – 1) * 8) + 2.

Example:

```
1>? BIT('a',3)
F
1>? BIT('A',3)
T
```

BLANK(*length*) — Creates a string of blank space of the given length.

Example:

```
1>? "Name ["+blank(20)+"]"
Name [                    ]
```

CEIL(*number*) — Returns the next integer value above the number.

Example:

```
1>? CEIL(3.14)
     4.00
```

CEN(*string,line length*) — Centers the string on a line of the given length (80 characters for the screen).

Example:

```
1>? CEN("The Middle of 40",40)
                The Middle of 40
```

CHR(*number*) — Produces the ASCII character that is equivalent to the number within parentheses.

Example:

```
1>CHR(65)
A
```

CLOSE(*file number*) — Closes the file that was assigned that number when it was opened with either ROPEN( ) or WOPEN( ). Returns logical True if CLOSE was successful. (Module 59)

Example:

```
1>ROPEN(RECORDS.TXT,1)
1>OK = CLOSE(1)
1>? OK
T
```

(i.e., the file was closed successfully).

Function	Description
COL( )	Returns the number of the current column (no expression in parentheses).

Example:

```
1>? COL()
       9.00
```

Function	Description
CONVERT(*selection,value*)	Converts string values to binary integers. Helpful for file header conversions and data coming into VP-Info from other languages, such as C. There are eight possible conversions to choose from:
CONVERT(1,*number*)	Synonym for CHR( ). ? CONVERT(1,65) returns 'A.'
CONVERT(2,*character*)	Synonym for RANK( ). ? CONVERT(2,'A') returns 65.00.
CONVERT(3,*number*)	Like CHR( ), but can handle two characters. ? CONVERT(3,16705) returns 'AA'; adding 1 changes it to 'BA,' and adding 256 changes it to 'AB.'
CONVERT(4,*characters*)	Like RANK( ), but it reads two characters. ? CONVERT(4,'BA') returns 16706, of which the 'B' is 66 and the 'A' is the rest.
CONVERT(5,*number*)	Handles up to 4 characters (However, a string of four characters becomes a 12 digit number, so you must filter this number through a PIC( ) function to get a printable result. ? CONVERT(5,1094795585) returns 'AAAA.' Adding 1 gives 'BAAA'; adding 256 gives 'ABAA'; and adding 65536 gives 'AABA.'
CONVERT(6,*characters*)	Reads up to four characters.
CONVERT(7,*number*)	Handles up to eight characters.
CONVERT(8,*characters*)	Reads up to eight characters. The eight-byte string is normally a floating point number.
COS(*number*)	Returns the cosine of the number or expression.

Example:

```
1>? COS(1.3)
       0.26
```

Function	Description
COSH(*number*)	Returns the hyperbolic cosine.
DATE(*number*)	Sets the system variable :DATE to the format type whose number is specified. There are nine formats:

ID number	Style	June 25,1976
1	yymmdd	760625
2	mm/dd/yy	06/25/76
3	Month dd, yyyy	June 25, 1976
4	Weekday, Month dd, yyyy	Friday, June 25, 1976 (weekdays are correct in format 4 only for dates between 1980 and 2079)
5	Month, ld, yyyy	June 30, 1976
6	dd-MMM-yyyy	25-JUN-1976
7	According to SET DATE TO command	
8	yyyymmdd	19760625
9	yymmld	760630

Example:

```
1>? DATE(2)
12/13/86
```

Function	Description
DATE(*number,string*)	When the format number is followed by a string, the string is read as a date and reformatted according to the table of formats. Dates prior to 1980 will default to twenty-first century values unless you specify all four year digits.

Example:

```
1>Ok=DATE(7)
1>? DATE(3,:DATE)
November 2, 1986
```

DAYS(*string,string*) — Compares two dates and returns the number of days separating them.

Example:

```
1>STORE '020287' to Birthday
1>? DAYS(:DATE,Birthday)
     92.00
```

DAYS(*string,number*) — Returns a date string the number of days after (positive number) or before (negative number) the given string.

Example:

```
1>? DAYS(:DATE,100)
870210
```

DBF(*choice*) — Returns information on file attributes, as follows:

DBF(1)	Returns type of data file (1, 2, or 3)
DBF(2)	Returns the file name, including path when appropriate.
DBF(3)	Returns the number of fields.

DBF(*choice,field*) — Returns information on specific existing fields in the data file, as follows:

DBF(4,1)	Returns name of field 1.
DBF(5,6)	Returns type of field 6.
DBF(6,2)	Returns length of field 2.
DBF(7,1)	Returns decimals in field 1.

DIR(*filespec*) — Returns the name of the first file name matching the specification, which may include wildcards. When the search is successful, the DIR function can be used without a *filespec*, and it will locate the next appropriate file.

Example:

```
1>? DIR('B:*.DBF')
DALYTRAN.DBF
1>? DIR()
EMPLOYEE.DBF
1>
```

DIR(*choice*) — Returns the following information about the last file found with DIR(*filespec*) or DIR( ):

DIR(1)	Returns the filename.
DIR(2)	Returns the file size.

Function	*Description*
DIR(3)	Returns the DOS file type as a value from 1 to 5. 1 = directory 2 = system 3 = hidden 4 = read only 5 = normal
DIR(4)	Returns time of last change to file (as shown in DOS directory).
DIR(5)	Returns date of last change.
ENV(*selection,task*)	Returns one of seven pieces of data about a given DBF file. The ENV( ) functions work with files whether ROPEN( ) or USE was employed to access them. When you have a file ROPEN and another in USE, the ENV( ) functions address the file in USE; if you have more than one file in USE, the ENV( ) functions address the SELECTed file. Here are the seven ENV( ) options:
ENV(1)	Returns the file type (1, 2, or 3).
ENV(2)	Returns the filename (only for files in USE).
ENV(3)	Returns the number of fields in the database.
ENV(4,*field#*)	Returns the name of the specified field.
ENV(5,*field#*)	Returns the field type.
ENV(6,*field#*)	Returns the field length.
ENV(7,*field#*)	Returns the field decimal allowance.

Example:

```
1>USE ABC
1>? ENV(4,1)
NAME
1>? ENV(6,1)
      20.00
```

EXP(*number*) — Returns e to the power of the given number.

Example:

```
1>? EXP(1)
      2.71
```

FIELD(*variable*) — Returns the field number of the specified variable. Can be used in error-checking to change the :FIELD value for data entry. (Module 34)

Partial Command File Example:

```
USE ABC
MName='                    '
MExtn='     '
@ 10,10 SAY "Name:  " GET MName
@ 11,10 SAY "Extn:  " GET MExtn
ON FIELDS
FIELD MExtn                  ; After reading MExtn
IF MExtn='     '             ; If MExtn is blank, check MName.
   LOCATE FOR NAME=MName     ; Check MName.
   IF EOF                    ; If no record for MName,
      @ 20,10 SAY "NOT FOUND"
```

Function	Description

```
        WAIT
        @ 20,10
        MName='                          '   ; Initialize MName.
        :FIELD=FIELD(MName)                  ; Return to MName field.
     ENDIF
  ELSE
     ? "ALT ROUTE"                  ; If MExtn is not blank, don't check MName.
  ENDIF
  ENDON
  READ
```

FILE(*filename*) — Returns logical True if the file exists.

Example:

```
1>? FILE("VPI.ERR")
T
```

FLOOR(*number*) — Returns the integer value immediately below a given number.

Example:

```
1>? FLOOR(3.77)
     3.00
```

GET(*variable name,length,file number*) — Reads from the file assigned the given number a string of the given length, beginning from the current position in the file, and assigns the string to the given variable name. (Module 59)

Example:

```
1>RFile="ABC.TXT"
1>ROPEN(RFile,4)
1>Ok=(Mname.20,4)
1>? Mname
Sergio, Vincent
```

IFF(*condition,iftrue,iffalse*) — Allows a variation of IF ... THEN logic in expressions. See Module 37.

Example:

```
1>B = 0
1>? IFF(B=0,"Yes","No")
Yes
1>
```

IN(*variable name,file number*) — Reads the next character in sequence from the given file into the given variable name.

Example (continuing from GET( ) example):

```
1>Ok=IN(Next,4)
1>? Next
3
```

INKEY( ) — Pauses operation to capture numeric value of next key pressed (0 to 255 for ASCII valued keys, 256 to 511 for function keys and ALT combinations).

Function	*Description*

Example:

```
                         Remarks
1>Ok=INKEY()          ; Cursor remains on line after <cr>. Press F7.
1>? Ok
    321.00            ; Numeric value of F7 key.
```

INSERT(*old string,new string,position*) Overwrites the old string, beginning at the specified position, with the new string. (The string stays the same length.)

Example:

```
1>Oldstring="XXXXXXXXXXXXXXX"
1>Newstring=" Pop! "
1>? INSERT(Oldstring,Newstring,4)
XXX Pop! XXXXX
```

INT(*number*) Converts a decimal number to a whole number; fractional parts are discarded.

Examples:

```
                             Remarks
1>STORE 123.456 TO MNum    ; Stores 123.456 to MNum.
1>? 144-INT(MNum)
     21.00                 ; The fractional portion is discarded.
1>STORE 0.06 TO MNum
1>? INT(MNum)
      0.00
```

LEFT(*string,number*) Returns a string containing the given number of the left-most characters in the given string.

Example:

```
1>? LEFT('Brigham',4)
Brig
```

LEN(*string*) Returns an integer value equal to the number of characters in the specified string.

Examples:

```
1>? LEN('Brigham')
      7.00
1>STORE 'Smith' TO X
1>? LEN(X)
      5.00
```

LOC(*file number*) Returns the current position in a file identified with the given number and opened with ROPEN or WOPEN. (Module 59)

Example:

```
1>? LOC(4)
     22.00
```

LOG(*number*) Returns the given number's natural logarithm.

LOG10(*number*) Returns the given number's base 10 logarithm.

Function	Description

Example:

```
1>? LOG10(100000)
     5.00
```

LOWER(*string*) — Converts all characters within a string to lowercase.

Example:

```
1>? LOWER('AbcdE')
abcde
```

LTRIM(*string*) — Trims any leading spaces from a string.

Examples:

```
1>? "XXX ["+LTRIM('     000] XXX')
XXX [000] XXX
1>? STR(123.456,8,2)
     123.46
1>? LTRIM(123.456,8,2)
123.46
```

MENU(*number of choices,width of lightbar*) — Creates a highlighted bar to move with the arrow keys to select a menu choice. (Module 18)

MOD(*number,remainder*) — Returns the remainder of dividing the first value by the second.

Examples:

```
1>? MOD(63,16)
    15.00
1>? MOD(217,8)
     1.00
```

MONTHS(*string1,string2*) — Compares two date strings based on the current input format, returns the difference between the first and second date. (Module 19)

Example:

```
1>? MONTHS('040166','070181')
   183.00
```

MONTHS(*string,number*) — Returns the date *number* months from the specified date *string*. If the date does not exist (February 30, for example), the function returns the last day of the month.

Example:

```
1>? :DATE
19880131
1>? MONTHS(:DATE,1)
19880229
1>
```

OUT(*string,file number*) — Writes a single character as specified in the string to the end of the specified file (or to File 1 if no number is specified), if the file was WOPENed and no read functions have been performed on it. (Module 59)

Function	Description

Example:

```
1>Term=CHR(26)
1>OK=OUT(Term)
```

PIC(*numeric expression,format*) — Displays the number in the specified format. Helpful for making temporary display format changes.

Examples:

```
1>? PIC(123.456,'999')
123
1>? PIC(1234/7,'$$$$999.99')
   $176.28
```

POW(*numeric expression,power*) — Returns the result of the first number to the power of the second.

Examples:

```
1>? POW(2,8)
    256.00
1>? POW(1+1,16/2)
    256.00
```

PRINTER( ) — Returns True if the parallel printer is ready to accept characters. Include in IF structure with SET PRINT ON commands to prevent lockups if the printer is not ready. Does not work with serial printers.

Partial Command File Example:

```
IF PRINTER()
  SET PRINT ON
ELSE
  ? "Check Printer"
ENDIF
```

PUT(*string,file number*) — Writes the specified string into the file, beginning at the current location in the file. The file must have been WOPENed and not subjected to any READ actions. (Module 59)

Example:

```
1>? PUT('Thomas, John          ',1)
```

RANK('*character*') — Returns ASCII value of specified character.

Examples:

```
1>? RANK('X')
     88.00
1>? RANK('x')-RANK('X')
     32.00
```

READ(*string,file number*) — Reads from the current position to the end of the line (to the next carriage return symbol [ASCII 13]) in an ROPENED file. (Module 59)

Function	Description

Example:

```
1>? READ(Current,1)
1>? Current
Harris, Robert        335322301985013138      1
```

REMLIB(*number*) Removes the specified volume from the current library. See Module 40 for more information on Library.

REPLACE(*oldstring,oldtext,newtext*) Searches the old string seeking the old text; when found, the old text is replaced by the next text. Equivalent to a word processor's Search and Replace function.

Example:

```
1>LineStr='This is the old string.'
1>? REPLACE(LineStr,'old','new')
This is the new string.
```

RESET(*string,bit*) Changes the bit in the designated position to zero. Each character in the string has eight bit positions. Since each position represents a power of 2, changing it to zero amounts to subtracting that power of two from it.

Example:

```
                                     Remarks
1>Name="van winkle"
1>NewName = RESET(Name,3)            ; Change Bit 3 of string.
1>? NewName                          ; Subtracting 32 from a letter
Van Winkle                           ; capitalizes the letter.
1>RealName = RESET(NewName,35)       ; Subtract 32 from fifth character.
1>? RealName
Van Winkle
```

RIGHT(*string,length*) The RIGHT function displays the right-most n characters of a string.

Examples:

```
1>? RIGHT(ABCDEFG,3)
EFG
1>? RIGHT(:DATE,2)
12
```

ROPEN(*filename,file number*) Opens a file for reading and assigns the file number to it. If the file number is not specified, the file is opened as number 1, automatically closing any file already opened as file number 1. (Module 59)

Example:

```
1>RFile="PICNIC.TXT"
1>? ROPEN(RFile)
T
```

ROW( ) Returns the current row number. Can be used in a command file to position the cursor relative to its current position.

Partial Command File Example:

```
CURSOR ROW()+5,COL()
? "Name not Found"
CURSOR ROW(),COL()
```

Function	Description
SEEK(*position number,file number*)	Moves the character pointer to the specified position in the file, counting from the first character, which is position 0. (Module 59)

Example:

```
1>Ok=ROPEN('PICNIC.TXT')
1>Ok=SEEK(22)
1>Ok=GET(Curr,5)
1>? Curr
Chips
```

SET(*string,bit*) — Changes the bit in the designated position to one. Each character in the string has eight bit positions. Since each position represents a power of 2, changing it to one amounts to adding that power of two to it.

Example:

```
1>String='WHILE'
1>? SET[String,35]          ; The third bit controls case.
WHILe
1>? SET[String,33]          ; Setting the first bit changes the word to WordStar format.
WHIL+
```

SIN(*number*) — Returns the sine of a numeric expression.

Example:

```
1>? SIN(1.3)
        0.96
```

SINH(*number*) — Returns the hyperbolic sine of the number.

SPACE( ) — Returns the data space currently available in the computer's memory area, in bytes.

Example:

```
1>? SPACE()
   24706.00
```

SQRT(*number*) — Returns the square root of the number.

Example:

```
1>? SQRT(2)
        1.41
```

SSEEK(*line number*) — Moves the pointer to the specified line number in a sequential file. Use SEEK( ) to move to a character position. (Module 59)

Example:

```
1>Ok=SSEEK(3)
1>Ok=READ(Curr)
1>? Curr
Miller, Gary                3Hot Dogs       6Packs
```

Function	*Description*
STR(*numeric expression,string length,decimals*)	Converts a number into a character string.

Example:

```
1>STORE 678.90123 TO X
1>? STR(X,3)
678
1>? STR(X,6,2)
678.90
```

TAN(*number*)	Returns the tangent of the given number or expression, expressed in radians.

Example:

```
1>? TAN(SIN(35))
          -0.45
```

TEST(*string*)	Returns True if the string is a valid expression. The test checks for existence of any variables named in the expression, whether all terms are of proper data types, and if they are combined correctly.

Example:

```
1>NStr='6'
1>NVal=5
1>? NStr+NVal
1. Invalid variable type found when executing an expression.
1>TEST('NStr+NVal')
F
```

TIME(*format number*) — Returns the time from the system clock as a string value and stores it as the system variable :TIME. There are three possible display formats:

ID number	Style	1:30 p.m.
1	hh:mm:ss	13:30:00
2	hh:mm am/pm	1:30 pm
3	sssss (Seconds since midnight)	48612

TRIM(*string*)	The TRIM function eliminates trailing blanks from the contents of a character type field. For example, if you have a field that can hold ten characters and it is holding a four-character expression, use the TRIM function to eliminate the extra six spaces. Exercise caution when using the TRIM function with an indexed file, as the index requires that all fields in a key have a uniform size in each record.

Example:

```
1>LN = 'Jones     '
1>? LEN(LN)
          10.00
1>X=TRIM(LN)
1>? LEN(X)
           5.00
```

TYPE(*string*)	The TYPE function is used to identify the string type of the following string or memory variable. Types are either character (C), numeric (N), or logical (L).

Function	Description

Examples:

```
1>? TYPE('123')
C
1>Lgc= T
1>? TYPE(Lgc)
L
1>Txt='123'
1>? TYPE(Txt)
C
1>Val=123
1>? TYPE(Val)
N
```

VAL(*string*) — The character to number function converts a series of numbers that have been stored as characters to a numeric value. The character string containing the numbers may have a sign and decimal point. If the string has any other characters in it, the value reading stops at the first non-numeric character.

Examples:

```
1>Num1='123.45'
1>Num2='-23.45'
1>Num3='12 oz.'
1>Num4='1 X 2 X 3'
1>Num5='1 2 3'
1>? VAL(Num1),VAL(Num2),VAL(Num3),VAL(Num4),VAL(Num5)
    123.45      -23.45        12.00         1.00         1.00
```

WOPEN(*filename,file number*) — Opens the specified file for writing data to it. (Module 59)

WRAP(*string,line length*) — Removes and displays as many words from the beginning of the string as can fit on the specified line. Note that the string is shorter by that many words after the function has performed.

Example:

```
1>TxtStr='The quick brown fox grabbed the fat, happy rooster and ran."
1>? WRAP(TxtStr,25)
The quick brown fox
1>? WRAP(TxtStr,25)
grabbed the fat, happy
1>? WRAP(TxtStr,25)
rooster and ran.
1>? LEN(TxtStr)
      1.00         ; The string is gone, except for one character.
1>? RANK(TxtStr)
     32.00         ; The character is a space (ASCII 32).
```

WRITE(*string,file number*) — Write the string to the end of the file as a new line. The file must have been WOPENed and not subjected to any READ functions. (Module 59)

Example:

```
1>Ok=WOPEN(WFile)
1>NewData="Anderson, Sherwood  2222912 1980122555    1"
1>Ok=WRITE(NewData)
```

Appendix E
NETWORKING WITH VP-Info

INTRODUCTION

VP-Info is designed to perform in a networked environment, and it provides a few commands which are intended exclusively for use in such an environment. Networking means running two or more computers while they are linked up to a shared piece of equipment and, often, using the same program and data. The simplest network merely involves attaching multiple computers to the same fixed disk and printers. A more elaborate network would allow three or four operators to all keypunch transactions into the same database at the same time. VP-Info can provide this elaborate network.

SYSTEM REQUIREMENTS A networked system requires, in addition to necessary hardware, a copy of VP-Info or the Runtime package for each workstation and DOS 3.1 or higher. If you are networked to a hard disk, you can operate with only one copy of all your PRG and data files, but the VPI program is needed in each computer on startup.

Your system requires a carefully constructed VPI.CNF file, preferably on each computer, containing the necessary FILES structure and other system information. The description of the FILES structure in Module 31 merely demonstrates a structure for a single computer with a single directory level. On a networked system, you must use well-designed subdirectory trees to keep the number of files from becoming unwieldy.

The CNF file should begin by informing VP-Info that you are in a network. To do this, begin the file with the command:

```
SET NETWORK TO 1
```

SHARING DATA IN A NETWORK The great benefit of networking carries with it some hazards. There must be mechanisms provided so that two people don't sell the same last pair of widgets to two different customers. VP-Info provides mechanisms for locking individual records or files while they are in use. Good programming techniques can create password mechanisms for locking out unauthorized users and error-checking mechanisms to simplify user training.

Networking Commands Here are the special settings, commands, and clauses for use in networking (the default settings are in boldface):

1. SET NETWORK TO **0**/1 The SET NETWORK command defaults to 0 (no network). If you set network to 1, whether on startup in the CNF file or through a command file, you enter the IBM 3.10 network interface compatible with many current networks. For current releases of

VP-Info, no numbers above 1 are implemented for alternative networks. With network set to 0 in a networked environment, any file you open is automatically locked against any other user, and networking commands are inoperative. You can share data files, but only by "taking turns."

2. USE. . .**LOCK**/READ/SHARE/WRITE Data and index files are locked unless you specify otherwise. If you attempt to open a file that is already open, you may open it for reading only or to read and write (share) it. If you try to open it while it is being used elsewhere, you will generate an error message. Good programming uses the ON ERROR mechanism (Module 44) to help the user past such a situation. Other files, namely TXT files, LIB files, and DOS files, are always locked and cannot be shared while in use.

When deciding how to open a file, keep the USE *filename* SHARE calls to the necessary minimum, as they slow down operation. Any operator who only needs READ access should not be provided more — not just to protect security and data integrity, but to optimize the operating environment.

To repeat: A file is either locked or unlocked. It can be simultaneously opened to READ and SHARE, with the reading user(s) able to look at data but not to change it, while the sharing user(s) can both read and write data in the file. However, once a file has been opened by one user, it is either locked or unlocked until closed again, and it cannot be opened by someone else as a locked file if it is open unlocked, nor vice versa. Both events generate the error message 63 stating that the file is locked (a little misleading if you encounter the message when trying to USE *filename* LOCK and the file is open unlocked).

3. SET LOCK ON/**OFF** A file is locked when you open it, unless you specify otherwise. If you have opened a file unlocked, with the USE *filename* SHARE command, you can set lock on before performing some data-changing activity with it, like EDIT or BROWSE. With LOCK set on, as you move the pointer, the current record is locked against changes by any other user. If any other user attempts to read or write your current record, that user receives error message 64: "Record locked . . . ." When writing your command files, use ON ERROR structures to handle such events.

4. **LOCK**/UNLOCK The most particular locking commands are used like a structure, surrounding an actual write operation and only locking the current record settings while a write operation is done to a file opened with the USE *filename* SHARE for the brief period when the actual write is occurring. For a fraction of a second, the current record of any data file the operator has in use, including those in use but not selected, is locked against others. If by some coincidence another user were to attempt to get at one of those current records, error message 64 would be generated. Provide ON ERROR structures for such contingencies.

LOCK INDEX/UNLOCK INDEX The LOCK command and the SET LOCK ON switch affect data files. The LOCK INDEX command locks the master index of a data file to prevent corruption of the index.

Locking a shared file must be done efficiently to keep the system running smoothly. Do not use more radical locking than the situation warrants.

System Variables for Networking The :RETRY and :USER system variables are for use in a network environment. The :RETRY variable telling VP-Info to try accessing a locked file 25 times before giving up and returning an error message. This variable can be set to any value up to 65000. The :USER variable identifies the workstation. In addition to the SET NETWORK TO 1 command, a VPI.CNF file for a network environment must also specify a unique user number, like this:

```
:USER = n
```

where *n* is an integer value not specified for any other user on the network.

Other Commands in a Networked Environment Common sense dictates some of the rules of working in a network. For example, any data-changing command that ranges over the entire database — DELETE ALL FOR *expression*, REPLACE ALL, or PACK, REINDEX, for example — should only be used while the file is locked and therefore not being used by someone else. Likewise, commands that read the entire database to calculate results — POST, UPDATE, COUNT, REPORT — should be used while the entire file is locked, or the results will be bizarre at best.

If you unlock a record between the time you retrieved it and the time you store the changes, include in your routine data-checking that confirms that no one else has made significant changes to the data in the interim. This may be done with an ON FIELDS structure (Module 34).

Error-handling If a user attempts to access a locked record, a "RECORD LOCKED" message appears on the screen, and pressing any key except Esc retries the access. If the lockup times are optimized, this mechanism should be adequate for most situations. Alternatively, you may want to provide an ON ERROR structure to cover more lengthy lockups and cases where the entire file is locked up.

Appendix F

VP-Info EXERCISES

1. About This Book
   a. What program is VP-Info similar to?
   b. What are two advantages of VP-Info over that program?
   c. How many disk drives are needed with VP-Info?
   d. How much memory is required to operate VP-Info?

2. VP-Info Overview
   a. Describe a database in your own words.
   b. Define *record* and *field*.
   c. Describe the field types used with VP-Info.
   d. List the following information:
      (1) Maximum characters within a VP-Info record ________
      (2) Maximum fields within a record ________
      (3) Maximum characters within a field ________
      (4) Maximum records within a database ________
   e. What is the CONFIG.SYS file?
   f. Write a step-by-step procedure for starting the VP-Info program.
   g. How are VP-Info commands entered?
   h. What is a *command file*?
   i. Prepare a list of the VP-Info keys.
   j. Describe two uses for the VP-Info full-screen editor.

3. Recommended Learning Sequence
   a. What is the advantage of following the *learning sequence*?
   b. How should the learning sequence be used?
   c. What is meant by an applications *model*?

4. ACCEPT, INPUT
   a. What type of memory variable is created with the ACCEPT command?
   b. What type of memory variable is created with the INPUT command?
   c. What is the difference between ACCEPT and ACCEPT TO?

5. APPEND
   a. Define the term *APPEND*.
   b. How is the APPEND function started?
   c. How is the APPEND function stopped?
   d. What is accomplished by APPEND BLANK?
   e. Describe two uses for the APPEND FROM command.

6. AT (@ row, col), BOX, ROW( ), COL( ) Positioning Text and Data
   a. Write a working example of the @ row,col SAY command.
   b. What is the difference between @ row,col SAY and @ row,col GET?
   c. How is @ row, col SAY different from the print (?) command?
   d. How can memory variables be used with the @ function?
   e. How are field and memory variable contents used with the @ row,col command?
   f. What does the SET UPPER command do?

7. AVERAGE
   a. What is the purpose of the AVERAGE command?
   b. Write the command to average all QTY fields within the active database.
   c. Write the command that stores the QTY field average to memory variable X.

8. BROWSE, BROWSE OFF
   a. Name three uses of the BROWSE command.
   b. How are new records added to a database when BROWSE is active?
   c. What key sequences are used to move up or down a line (record) at a time?
   d. Write the key sequence used to achieve the following:
      (1) Delete a character ________
      (2) Insert one or more characters ________
      (3) Mark a record for deletion ________
      (4) Write changes to disk ________
      (5) Abort changes and return to the VP prompt ________
   e. How can you limit the number of fields browsed?
   f. How can you display fields that extend beyond the 80-column limit?

9. CANCEL, RETURN
   a. Describe a common function of the CANCEL and RETURN commands.
   b. Describe the difference between CANCEL and RETURN.
   c. How might RETURN or CANCEL be used within an IF statement?

10. CHAIN, GLOBAL
    a. What are two differences between the CHAIN and DO commands?
    b. How does chaining back to a file differ from returning to it?
    c. When might you use the GLOBAL command?

11. CHR( ), RANK( )
    a. What is the meaning of "ASCII character?"
    b. What does the RANK('n') function return?
    c. How can the CHR( ) function be used to produce a "beep?"

12. CLEAR
    a. What is meant by *clear state*?
    b. Describe two situations where the CLEAR command might be used.
    c. What is cleared when CLEAR is typed from the dot prompt?

13. CLOSE
    a. When might you use CLOSE?
    b. How would you close a file in work area 1 without closing the file in work area 2?

14. COMPILE
    a. What are the advantages of a compiled program environment?
    b. How would you modify a program that has been compiled?
    c. What are the hazards of using compiled files? (Check Modules 10 and 25 for help.)

15. COPY
    a. Define the term *delimiter*.
    b. What does *SDF* mean and how is it used?
    c. Write three forms of the COPY command and explain each.
    d. What is a typical use for the SDF clause?
    e. What extension is assigned to a file copied with the DELIMITED clause, and how can you view such a file?

16. COUNT
   a. When COUNT is entered from the keyboard, what is displayed?
   b. Write three forms of the COUNT command and explain each.
   c. How might COUNT be used in a command file?

17. CREATE
   a. If you type CREATE newfile and press Return, what is displayed?
   b. Write the rules that apply to field names.
   c. Describe the three types of database fields.
   d. In numeric-type fields, how many places should you include for two decimal characters? Why?
   e. After the last field is entered, how do you stop the CREATE function? What are your options at this point?

18. CURSOR, MENU( )
   a. How do you create a menu lightbar that begins at Row 10, Column 20 and allows menu items 1 through 7?
   b. What is menu selection 0?

19. DATE( ), TIME( )
   a. Describe two uses for the DATE( ) function.
   b. What can you do with the TIME( ) function?
   c. How can you display the system date from the VP prompt?
   d. Write a command line that stores the system date to a memory variable.

20. DEBUGGING COMMAND FILES
   a. How does SET DEBUG ON change your operating environment?
   b. How does VP-Info perform while SET STEP is on?
   c. A program with three changing memory variables controlling a DO WHILE structure and a fourth controlling an IF structure goes into infinite loops and you must press Esc to stop. How might you debug the program?

21. DELETE, RECALL, PACK
   a. What does the DELETE command do when used with a database file?
   b. How can you verify which records are marked for deletion?
   c. Write four forms of the DELETE command and explain each.
   d. What does the PACK command do?
   e. Describe the use of the RECALL command.
   f. Write four forms of the RECALL command and explain each.
   g. Describe the purpose of the command LIST FOR *.
   h. You are positioned at Record 1 and you type
      DELE FOR AMOUNT< =0
      What is the maximum number of records that can be deleted from the file by this action?

22. DIM
   a. What is a matrix?
   b. What is the capacity of a matrix defined by the following command?
      DIM NUM Prices[10,4,25]

23. DIR
   a. Describe the purpose of the DIR command.
   b. Write the DIR command that displays all database files.
   c. Write the DIR command that displays all .PRG files.

24. DISPLAY, LIST, SYSTEM VARIABLES
   a. What is the difference between LIST and DISPLAY?
   b. Write six forms for the DISPLAY command and explain each.

c. How is the DISPLAY command used to show a list of disk files?
d. What does the command LIST STRUCTURE do?
e. Write a command line that makes use of :DATE.

25. DO
a. What is the purpose of the DO *filename* command?
b. Name two places from which the DO command is used.
c. How is a DO command issued from the VP prompt different from one issued by a command file?

26. DO CASE, CASE, OTHERWISE, ENDCASE
a. When might you use the DO CASE statement?
b. Draw a diagram of the DO CASE statement that uses OTHERWISE.
c. Describe two uses for the OTHERWISE command.

27. DO WHILE, BREAK, LOOP, ENDDO, EOF
a. What is the purpose of a DO WHILE loop?
b. Draw a diagram of the DO WHILE statement with an embedded IF statement.
c. Describe the purpose of the LOOP command.
d. What is broken by the BREAK command?
e. What is the consequence of a missing or misplaced ENDDO?
f. What does the editor provide to help you check structures?
g. How might EOF be used with DO WHILE?

28. EDIT
a. Describe the purpose of the EDIT command.
b. Write the command lines necessary to edit record numbers 12 through 15 of a database file named STOCK.
c. Write the EDIT command to restrict editing to the NAME and ADDRESS fields.
d. List the control keys used with the EDIT command.
e. How do you abort EDIT without recording changes?
f. How do you save changes and return to the VP prompt?

29. EJECT
a. What does the EJECT command do when executed in a command file?
b. How many line feeds are in an inch?
c. How many line feeds are in the standard 11-inch-long form?

30. ERASE, CLS
a. Write an ERASE command to erase the top half of the screen.
b. How does the CLS command effect open files and variables?

31. FILES, SET DEFAULT TO
a. In the environment of the recommended VPI.CNF file, you issue the command SET DEFAULT TO B:. Where does VP-Info look for PRG files?
b. Next, you execute a command file containing the following FILES structure:

```
FILES
  *.PRG,B:\PROGS\
ENDFILES
```

After you finish using the command file, where does VP-Info go to find DBF files? TXT files?

32. FIND
a. What must be done to a database before the FIND command is used?
b. What is meant by a *key field*?
c. Describe the purpose of SET EXACT ON.
d. Write a FIND command and explain what it does.

33. FLUSH
   a. Describe the difference between FLUSH and CLOSE.
   b. When might you want to use the FLUSH command?

34. GET, GET PICTURE, CLEAR GETS, READ, ON FIELD
   a. What other statements are frequently used with GET?
   b. Write a command line that displays the contents of the NAME field beginning at row 7, column 20.
   c. If the field contents are to remain unchanged, what statement must follow the above command line?
   d. If the field contents are to be changed, what statement is used on the following command line?

35. GO, GOTO, GO BOTTOM, GO TOP, SKIP
   a. Define the term *record pointer*.
   b. GO *n* and GOTO *n* both position the record pointer to record *n*. There is another alternative. Describe this third alternative and why one might prefer to use it.
   c. Write the command lines to move down one record, then back three.
   d. Write two command lines that position the record pointer to the last record in the open database and display the record number.
   e. Write three command forms that position the record pointer to the first record in a database.

36. HELP
   a. What is the purpose of the HELP command?
   b. What two ways can HELP information be displayed?
   c. What is the command form for displaying help information about the USE command?

37. IF, ELSE, ENDIF
   a. What is a command structure? Give three examples of such structures.
   b. Draw a diagram for the IF statement with an embedded ELSE.
   c. What is meant by nesting a statement within a statement? Write a command set with a nested structure.
   d. If the condition in the IF statement is false, what happens?
   e. Describe the purpose of the ENDIF statement.
   f. When might you use the ELSE statement?
   g. Describe two typical applications for the IF statement.

38. INDEX, REINDEX
   a. What filename extension is assigned to an index file?
   b. Write two forms of the INDEX command and explain each.
   c. Describe the purpose of the REINDEX command.
   d. Explain the difference between GO BOTTOM in a database file and in an indexed file.
   e. You have a database open with indexes A, B, and C. You create index D for the database. When the creation process is over, which files are open?

39. INTERACTIVE MODE (?), # (Record Number)
   a. What is another name for *interactive mode*?
   b. Write the command lines to create a memory variable and then display its contents in the interactive mode.
   c. Write a command line to add the following numbers:
      (1) 25.60
      (2) 34.56
      (3) − 11.73

40. LIBRARY, SET LIBRARY TO, REMLIB( )
   a. Describe the process for moving a TXT file into a library.
   b. What happens if you fail to close a library file when you are through with it?
   c. You have added a text to a library, assigning it the volume number in :AVAIL, which was 7. The text was 600 bytes long; what is the next volume number (the current value of :AVAIL)?

41. LOCATE, CONTINUE
    a. Contrast the LOCATE and FIND commands.
    b. What is the purpose of the CONTINUE command?
    c. Write a command line that locates a record containing Smith in the NAME field and Denver in the CITY field.
    d. Describe the use of NEXT with LOCATE.

42. MODIFY
    a. What is the purpose of the MODIFY command?
    b. What key sequence is used to insert a new field?
    c. What key sequence is used to delete a field?
    d. You decide to change the structure of a database which currently has full names in a NAME field to one with a LASTNAME and a FIRSTNAME field. How do you protect your current data from loss?

43. NOTE, *, ;
    a. Describe the purpose of NOTE or * as used in a command file.
    b. Describe three applications of NOTE or *.
    c. How is ; used on a command line?

44. ON ERROR, ON ESCAPE, INKEY( )
    a. Write a command to print 'Record Incomplete' when Esc is pressed.
    b. What is the purpose of the ON ERROR command?
    c. What is the purpose of the ON ESCAPE command?
    d. Describe the purpose of the INKEY( ) function.

45. PERFORM, PROCEDURE
    a. What is a PROCEDURE structure?
    b. What is in the last line of a PROCEDURE structure?
    c. How is a PROCEDURE called for use?

46. POST
    a. What is the difference between posting and updating?
    b. You are working with a SALES database and an ANNUAL database indexed on EMPLoyees to MEMP. You issue the command

       ```
       POST ON EMPL FROM SALES FIELD PAY WITH SALARY+COMM
       ```

       (1) What files are open?
       (2) If you have 20 employees and 360 sales of 32 products, how many records are in ANNUAL?
       (3) You hired a new employee this week. How does POST handle her?

47. Print Statement (?)
    a. What is meant by the term *print statement*?
    b. What characters must surround text for display?
    c. Write the command line that would display the following prompt.

       ```
       Don't press the "ESC" key.
       ```

    d. Write a hypothetical command line that displays text and the contents of the memory variable MX.

48. QUIT
    a. Describe the purpose of the QUIT command.
    b. Describe two ways in which the QUIT command is executed.

49. RENAME
    a. Describe the purpose of the RENAME command.
    b. Write a command line that renames STORE.DBF to WAREHOUS.DBF.
    c. Write the command line to list all files on the disk in drive B.

50. REPEAT
    a. What is a *delay loop*? When might you use one?
    b. Write a command file that creates a two-dimensional matrix variable capable of holding twenty variables, and initializes it with values from 1 to 40.

51. REPLACE
    a. Describe the purpose of the REPLACE command.
    b. Write three different forms of the REPLACE command and explain each.

52. REPORT, REPORT FORMS, SPOOL
    a. What is the purpose of the REPORT command?
    b. What is the extension of a report file?
    c. Which commands can redirect reports to a disk file?
    d. How is a report printed?
    e. Which keyword must always appear in a report form?
    f. Which keyword sends function or command codes to your printer?
    g. Write a REPORT command that writes a report with subtotals.
    h. What is the purpose of the NODETAIL clause?
    i. How are :COMPANY and :TITLE used in a report form?

53. RUN
    a. What is the purpose of the RUN command?
    b. What are two memory considerations effecting RUN?
    c. Write the command line that runs the DOS DIR command.

54. SAY, SAY GET, SAY USING, CLEAR GETS, READ
    a. What are the rules for using SAY with a printer?
    b. Write a command line that uses the SAY statement to display a prompt beginning at row 5, column 10.
    c. Describe the purpose of the USING clause.
    d. Write a command line that displays a seven-character, two-decimal place numeric field as dollars and cents.

55. SCOPE
    a. How does SCOPE interact with GO BOTTOM? With FIND?

56. SCREEN
    a. Why might you want to save a screen image?
    b. How many screens can you save?
    c. In interactive mode, if you redirect output to a background screen, what is the effect on the foreground screen's appearance?

57. SCROLL
    a. What is the effect of the command SCROLL 10,17 on a subsequent LIST command?
    b. Why might you use SCROLL inside a window?

58. SELECT, SET RELATION TO, SET LINK TO
    a. Describe the use of the SELECT command.
    b. How many work areas can be open at the same time?
    c. What is the purpose of the BUFFERS and FILES commands in the CONFIG.SYS file?
    d. When moving from one database to another, what happens to the position of the record pointers in the original database?
    e. How is a relation established between two databases?
    f. What is the difference between a RELATION and a LINK?
    g. Explain the function of LIST NAME, PAYCODE#2.

59. Sequential and Non-Sequential Files
   a. How is a sequential file different from a non-sequential one?
   b. What is the difference between these two commands:

```
? READ(Curr)
READ Curr
```

   c. You have WOPENed a file and located a record with SEEK(27). Now you are ready to add a new record. Write the necessary steps.

60. SET Functions
   a. In general, what do SET functions control?
   b. How can you determine the current status of SET functions?
   c. Describe the use of the following SET functions:
      (1) SET CONFIRM OFF/ON
      (2) SET INTENSITY ON/OFF
      (3) SET ALTERNATE TO *filename*, SET ALTERNATE ON
      (4) SET FUNCTION ON/OFF
   d. Under what circumstances might you want to SET STEP ON?

61. SORT
   a. Write the command line for sorting a database in numerical order on the ZIP_CODE field.
   b. Write the command line for sorting a database in alphabetical order on the NAME field.
   c. Write the command form for sorting two fields at the same time.
   d. Write the command form for sorting on a specific set of records.
   e. Describe two differences between sorting and indexing.

62. STATUS
   a. What are the three types of information available on the STATUS screen?

63. STORE, RELEASE, SAVE, RESTORE, VARIABLE
   a. What is a memory variable and why might you use one?
   b. How many memory variables can be active at one time?
   c. How many characters (or bytes) are available for memory variables?
   d. How many characters can a string memory variable contain?
   e. How many significant digits are in a numeric memory variable?
   f. Write the command line that displays all active memory variables.
   g. What is a macro?
   h. Write the command line that deletes the memory variable MNUM.
   i. How are memory variables saved to a disk file? Retrieved from it?
   j. What is the effect of the ADDITIVE clause?

64. SUM
   a. Describe the function of the SUM command.
   b. Write four forms of the SUM command.

65. TEXT, TEXT . . . ENDTEXT
   a. What is the purpose of the TEXT and ENDTEXT statements?
   b. Describe a common use of the TEXT and ENDTEXT statements.

66. TOTAL
   a. What does TOTAL do with the sum of matching fields?
   b. Write three forms of the TOTAL command.

67. UPDATE
   a. What is the purpose of the UPDATE command?
   b. What must be done before the UPDATE command can be used?

c. Write three forms of the UPDATE command and explain each.
d. How is UPDATE different from TOTAL?

68. USE
a. What is meant by opening and closing a database file?
b. What happens if you issue a database command with no database in use?
c. Write the command line for opening the MEMBERS database file.
d. Describe four ways in which a database file is closed.
e. Write a command line that opens the ADDRESS database in work area 2.
f. Write a command line that opens the ADDRESS database and its index file called CITIES.NDX.

69. WAIT, WAIT TO
a. What is the difference between WAIT and WAIT TO?
b. What is displayed when either of these commands are encountered in a command file?
c. Why might you want to pause command file operation?
d. What happens if you press the Esc key in response to the "WAITING" prompt?
e. Describe a typical application for the WAIT TO command.
f. Explain the difference between ACCEPT TO and WAIT TO.

70. WINDOW, COLOR
a. Write the command to create a window with ten working lines of fifty columns each, bordered by a double-lined box.
b. Write the command to turn that box white with red characters.
c. What will happen to this window when you use the CLS command?

71. WRITE
a. What other kinds of files are created with WRITE?
b. What is the assumed extension name if none is specified with the WRITE *filename* statement?
c. List ten control keys used in editing.
d. Describe what is meant by *database file structure*.
e. Explain the term *application structure*.
f. What is the purpose of "commenting" a command file?
g. When a command exceeds the 80-column screen limitation, what can you do to continue the command on the next line?
h. Describe a "short-cut" for creating a command file similar to one that already exists.
i. What are two commands used to test a newly developed command file?

72. ZAP
a. What is the purpose of the ZAP command?
b. What does VP-Info do to prevent you from accidentally zapping a database file?
c. When you ZAP a file, what is left?

Index